han a

Developments in ESP

CAMBRIDGE LANGUAGE TEACHING LIBRARY
A series covering central issues in language teaching and learning, by authors
who have expert knowledge in their field.

In this series:

Developments in ESP

A multi-disciplinary approach

Tony Dudley-Evans
Maggie Jo St John

CAMBRIDGE UNIVERSITY PRESS

PUBLISHED BY THE PRESS SYNDICATE OF THE UNIVERSITY OF CAMBRIDGE
The Pitt Building, Trumpington Street, Cambridge, United Kingdom

CAMBRIDGE UNIVERSITY PRESS
The Edinburgh Building, Cambridge CB2 2RU, UK
40 West 20th Street, New York, NY 10011–4211, USA
477 Williamstown Road, Port Melbourne, VIC 3207, Australia
Ruiz de Alarcón 13, 28014 Madrid, Spain
Dock House, The Waterfront, Cape Town 8001, South Africa

http://www.cambridge.org

First published 1998
Fifth printing 2003

Printed in the United Kingdom at the University Press, Cambridge

Typeset in 10.5/12pt Sabon   [CE]

A catalogue record for this book is available from the British Library

Library of Congress Cataloguing in Publication data applied for

ISBN 0 521 59329 8 Hardback
ISBN 0 521 59675 0 Paperback

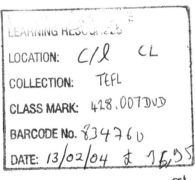

Contents

Contents

vi

Contents

Preface

In this book we attempt to pull together the theory and practice of English for Specific Purposes, drawing on our respective experience in English for Academic Purposes (EAP) and English for Occupational Purposes (EOP), and in different parts of the world. Between us we have lived and worked in a large number of countries in every continent of the world except – sadly – Australasia.

We have the particular aim of describing recent developments in English for Specific Purposes (ESP), especially in the areas of content/ language integration and the growth of Business English. ESP has continued to grow and expand into other areas – despite occasional rumours of its death – and now has a healthy body of research, publications and teaching materials. We have surveyed these areas in a way that we hope will be accessible to both graduate students embarking on a career in English Language Teaching (ELT) and teachers already working in ESP/ELT.

There are a number of features in the book that merit a brief introduction:

Activities

In each chapter, there are three categories of activity: orientation, task and reflection; the guidance notes provide responses to some of them; the symbol ➥ tells you when there are guidance notes at the end of the book.

Orientation tasks are to stimulate thought, and the ideas contained in them are developed in the text so we suggest you do them before reading further in the text. There is not usually a separate guidance note for orientation tasks as the text provides most of the ideas.

Tasks provide an opportunity to apply ideas within the framework of the book. There is a guidance note for each task.

Reflection tasks take you beyond the text to your own situation and ask you to think about and apply the ideas more specifically and more

viii

widely. There is not usually a guidance note for reflection tasks as these are open-ended and the responses depend on your situation.

Extracts

We have included a number of extracts from ESP textbooks and from academic and professional texts. Some of these provide examples for our discussion in the book, others are a source of activities in the tasks. These extracts come after the epilogue, before the guidance notes.

Recommended reading

At the end of each chapter we have noted some of the books, journals, articles and other sources of information we have found particularly useful. For reasons of space, we just give the name of the author and the date of publication there. Full details are in the bibliography.

Acknowledgements

As much of our ESP experience has been in different institutions, we begin by writing our own acknowledgements.

Maggie Jo

My greatest debt is to Tony who has stimulated, encouraged and supported me in the twenty years of my ESP career. He demonstrated to a then chemistry teacher the fascination and challenge of ESP; he has continued to be an inspiration; thank you, Tony.

John Swales was a powerful influence, first as a teacher and later as a colleague at the Language Studies Unit, Aston University, along with Ray Williams, Meriel Bloor, Sandy Urquhart and David Charles. In my freelance travels around the world, especially in Nigeria, Jordan, Brazil, the Philippines and Malaysia, I have met wonderful teachers and students who have inspired me and helped me formulate ideas. I owe special thanks to the Comskiptec team in Nigeria and the JUST team in Jordan, for all we shared.

Tony

I would like to acknowledge a particular debt to three people who have had a strong influence on my professional development and have remained good personal friends. Martin Bates first showed me in Tabriz in the 70s that ESP materials could be entertaining and inventive; Tim Johns has been a wonderful colleague to work with at Birmingham, especially in the early days of team-teaching; John Swales has been a close friend since the 60s and Libya, where I taught him to read Arabic newspapers, and an immense influence on my professional life, which has been constantly enriched by his ideas and enthusiasms.

I would also like to express particular thanks to all my colleagues in English Language Research at the University of Birmingham for providing a friendly and supportive environment to work in, and the many

x

students doing a PhD or following an MA course who have stimulated my thinking and kept me up to date on the reading. I would particularly like to mention Martin Hewings and Richard Cauldwell, who have helped me formulate many of my ideas, Malcolm Coulthard, who has provided much support and a benchmark of academic excellence, and Willie Henderson, of Continuing Studies at Birmingham, who was a stimulating colleague to work with on the discourse of economics. Outside Birmingham, Ann Johns, Liz Hamp-Lyons and Peter Master are/were great co-editors to work with on the journal *English for Specific Purposes*.

Maggie Jo has always been a wonderful and challenging person to work and live with.

Both of us

We owe a particular debt to Alison Sharpe, who showed great enthusiasm for our book and guided us through the publication process. We would also like to thank Mickey Bonin who took over from Alison and helped us through the final stages. We also wish to acknowledge the valuable contributions and comments of three anonymous reviewers and Catherine Kuebart, and our subeditor Sylvia Goulding.

Finally, working together on this book has been a great experience, extending and enriching an already full, exciting and unpredictable relationship.

The editors, authors and publishers are grateful to the authors, publishers and others who have given permission for the use of copyright material identified in the text. It has not been possible to identify, or trace, sources of all the materials used and in such cases the publishers would welcome information from copyright owners.

Brieger and Comfort. 1992. *Production and Operations, Business Management English*. Prentice Hall, on pp. 234–5; Herbert, A. J. 1965. *The Structure of Technical English*. Reprinted by permission of Addison Wesley Longman Ltd. on pp. 236–7; Bates, M. and A. Dudley-Evans. 1976. *Nucleus General Science*. Reprinted by permission of Addison Wesley Longman Ltd. on pp. 238–9; *Skills for Learning Foundation*, 1980. University of Malaya Press on p. 240; Hutchinson, T. and A. Waters. 1984. *Interface: English for Technical Communication*.

Acknowledgements

Reprinted by permission of Addison Wesley Longman Ltd. on pp. 241–3; Samuelson, P. 1955. *Economics*. McGraw Hill (New York) on pp. 244–5; Barclays Bank. 1983. *Economic Surveys: Current Accounts* on p. 245; Chrispeels, M. and D. Sadava. 1977. *Plants, Food and People*. W. H. Freeman and Co. (San Francisco) on p. 246; Steeds, W. 1957. *Engineering Materials, Machine Tools and Process*, Longmans Green and Co. Ltd. Reprinted by permission of Addison Wesley Longman Ltd. on p. 247; Lynch, A. 1983. *Study Listening*. Cambridge University Press on p. 248; Flower, L. *Problem Solving: Strategies for Writing*. Harcourt Brace and Company (Orlando, Florida) on p. 249; *The New York Times*, September 19 1979. Table on p. 249 by permission of *The New York Times*; Hamp-Lyons, L. and B. Healey. 1987. *Study Writing*. Cambridge University Press on p. 250; Swales, J. and C. Feak. 1994. *Academic Writing for Graduate Students: Essential Tasks and Skills*. The University of Michigan Press (Ann Arbor) on pp. 250–51; Robinson, P. 1991. The ESP family tree from *ESP Today* on pp. 250–51; Bates, M. and A. Dudley-Evans. 1976. *Nucleus: General Science*. Reprinted by permission of Addison Wesley Longman Ltd. on p. 12; Guy, V. and J. L. Mattock. 1993. *The New International Manager*. Kogan Page on p. 267; Weir, C. J. *Communicative Language Testing*. Prentice Hall, UCLES Business English Certificate 2, Sample Paper 1997. Reproduced by permission of the University of Cambridge Local Examinations Syndicate on pp. 252, 253, 260; UCLES CEIBT Certificate for International Business and Trade. Specifications and sample materials for the revised CEIBT June 1998. Reproduced by permission of the University of Cambridge Local Examinations Syndicate on pp. 254, 261; JMB UETESOL. June 1992. Hylo Parks. Reproduced by permission of the Northern Examinations and Assessment Board on pp. 255–7; Weir, C. J. 1993. *Understanding and Developing Language Tests*. Prentice Hall on p. 258; JMB UETESOL. June 1990. Reproduced by permission of the Northern Examinations and Assessment Board on pp. 259–60.

Acronyms and definitions

Acronyms

BALEAP	British Association of Lecturers in EAP
BE	Business English
EAP	English for Academic Purposes
EBP	English for Business Purposes
EEP	English for Educational Purposes
EGAP	English for General Academic Purposes
EGBP	English for General Business Purposes
ELP	English for Legal Purposes
ELT	English Language Teaching
EMP	English for Medical Purposes
EOP	English for Occupational Purposes
ESAP	English for Specific Academic Purposes
ESBP	English for Specific Business Purposes
ESOL	English for Speakers of Other Languages
ESP	English for Specific Purposes
EST	English for Science and Technology
EVP	English for Vocational Purposes
FCE	First Certificate in English
FUA	Federal University of Agriculture
FUT	Federal University of Technology
IELTS	International English Language Testing Service
JMB	Joint Matriculation Board
L1	First Language
L2	Second Language
LANA	Language Needs Analysis
LCCI	London Chamber of Commerce and Industry
LSA	Learning Situation Analysis
LSP	Language(s) for Specific Purpose(s)
MA	Master of Arts
MBA	Master of Business Administration
MSc	Master of Science
NEAB	Northern Examinations & Assessment Board

NNS	Non-Native Speaker
NRN	New Relationship Negotiation
NS	Native Speaker
ORN	Old Relationship Negotiation
OUP	Oxford University Press
PCA	Principal Component Analysis
PhD	Doctor of Philosophy
PR	Public Relations
PSA	Present Situation Analysis
PVE	Pre-Vocational English
TEEP	Test in English for Educational Purposes
TEFL	Teaching English as a Foreign Language
TESL	Teaching English as a Second Language
TESOL	Teaching English to Speakers of Other Languages
TOEFL	Test of English as a Foreign Language
TOEIC	Test of English for International Communication
TSA	Target Situation Analysis
UCLES	University of Cambridge Language Education Service
UETESOL	University Entrance Test in English for Speakers of Other Languages
VE	Vocational English

Definitions

Carrier content refers to the subject matter of an exercise; it is contrasted with the **real content**, which is the language or skill content of an exercise.

Collocation refers to the way words appear together with each other. For example we say: '*offer* an insight' rather than '*make* an insight'.

Concordance line refers to a line of text printed out from a computer corpus that shows the context in which the word being studied is used.

Discourse analysis refers to the study of how sentences in spoken and written language form larger units at a level above the sentence, for example in paragraphs, whole conversations or written texts.

Discourse community refers to a group who in professional contexts communicate with each other and have therefore developed mechanisms for doing so.

Gambits are lexical phrases used to show a speaker's purpose.

Genre refers to a text-type that has developed in response to a social or professional need. It generally has a predictable structure. Examples of genres include the academic article, the newspaper editorial, the business presentation, the sermon, the academic lecture.

Genre analysis refers to the study of the structural and linguistic regularities of particular genres or text-types and the role they play within a discourse community.

Kibbitzer is a short discussion on the Internet.

Logical connector refers to a word that links clauses or sentences, such as *moreover, however, therefore*. They are also referred to as **connectors, connectives, discourse markers** and **linkers**.

Macro-skills refer to the major skills (as outlined in chapter 5): reading, writing, speaking, listening and speaking, and listening to monologue. A macro-skill can be broken down into a number of micro-skills (see below).

Micro-skills refer to the lower-level skills that constitute a macro-skill. Listening to monologue, for example, can be broken down into micro-skills such as the ability to identify purpose and scope of lecture, the ability to deduce meaning of words from context.

Process approach generally refers to an approach to the teaching of writing that concentrates on the different stages of planning, organising and revising.

Product approach generally refers to an approach to the teaching of writing that concentrates on the features of the actual text – the end product.

Register analysis refers to the study of how frequently grammatical structures are used in texts.

Rhetoric refers to the study of how written or spoken texts are effective in persuading readers or listeners to accept their arguments.

1 Introduction

1.1 Aims

We begin by considering what English for Specific Purposes (ESP) is, how it developed, how it can be defined and classified, and what it can offer the learner and the teacher. We then consider the various roles of the ESP practitioner.

1.2 Overview

The teaching of English for Specific Purposes has generally been seen as a separate activity within English Language Teaching (ELT), and ESP research as an identifiable component of applied linguistic research. We believe that for some of its teaching ESP has developed its own methodology, and its research clearly draws on research from various disciplines in addition to applied linguistics. This openness to the insights of other disciplines is a key distinguishing feature of ESP which we see as underlying much of the practice and research we will describe.

If ESP has sometimes moved away from trends in general ELT, it has always retained its emphasis on practical outcomes. We will see that the main concerns of ESP have always been, and remain, with needs analysis, text analysis, and preparing learners to communicate effectively in the tasks prescribed by their study or work situation. It is often said that ESP lacks an underlying theory. We believe that a theory of ESP could be outlined based on either the specific nature of the texts that learners require knowledge of, or on the basis of the needs-related nature of the teaching. It is, however, interesting and significant that so much of the writing has concentrated on the procedures of ESP and on relating course design to learners' specific needs rather than on theoretical matters.

The study of languages for specific purposes has had a long and interesting history going back, some would say, as far as the Roman and Greek Empires. Since the 1960s, ESP has become a vital and innovative activity within the Teaching of English as a Foreign or Second Language movement (TEFL/TESL) (Howatt, 1984). For much of its early life ESP was dominated by the teaching of English for Academic Purposes (EAP); most of the materials produced, the course descriptions written and the research carried out were in the area of EAP. English for Occupational Purposes (EOP) played an important but nevertheless smaller role. In recent years, however, the massive expansion of international business has led to a huge growth in the area of English for Business Purposes (EBP). Within ESP the largest sector for published materials is now that of Business English, and there is burgeoning interest from teachers, publishers and companies in this area.

ESP activity used to be closely associated with projects led, and usually staffed, by expatriate British, North American or Australasian teachers, often in large numbers. Projects in the Middle East, in Iran (Bates, 1978), Kuwait and Saudi Arabia (Harper, 1986) for instance, are good examples (Mackay and Mountford, 1978). Local teachers seemed to play relatively small roles in such projects, and it was even occasionally argued by non-native speakers that ESP work was too difficult for them. We have always believed that local teachers' knowledge of their situations as well as their familiarity with their students' motivation and learning styles give them a potential advantage over native-speaker expatriate teachers.

ESP is part of a more general movement of teaching *Language* for Specific Purposes (LSP). LSP has focused on the teaching of languages such as French and German for specific purposes, as well as English. In many situations the approaches used are very similar to those used in ESP; some, however, place a much greater emphasis on the learning of vocabulary.

1.3 A definition of ESP

Orientation 1a

What is your definition of ESP? What aspects would you include?

We will begin by looking at three definitions of ESP found in the literature, and then give our own. The three definitions are all relatively late in time if we assume that ESP began in the 1960s, but they build on earlier definitions.

Hutchinson and Waters (1987) see ESP as an *approach* rather than a *product*, by which they mean that ESP does not involve a particular kind of language, teaching material or methodology. They suggest that 'the foundation of ESP is the simple question: Why does this learner need to learn a foreign language?' The answer to this question relates to the learners, the language required and the learning context, and thus establishes the primacy of need in ESP. Need is defined by the reasons for which the student is learning English, which will vary from study purposes such as following a postgraduate course in an English-speaking country to work purposes such as participating in business meetings or taking hotel bookings. These purposes are the starting points which determine the language to be taught.

Strevens' (1988) definition of ESP makes a distinction between four *absolute characteristics* and two *variable characteristics.* The absolute characteristics are that ESP consists of English Language Teaching which is:

- designed to meet specified needs of the learner;
- related in content (that is in its themes and topics) to particular disciplines, occupations and activities;
- centred on language appropriate to those activities in syntax, lexis, discourse, semantics and so on, and analysis of the discourse;
- in contrast with 'General English'.

The variable characteristics are that ESP

- may be restricted as to the learning skills to be learned (for example reading only);
- may not be taught according to any pre-ordained methodology.

Robinson (1991) also accepts the primacy of needs analysis in defining ESP. Her definition is based on two key defining criteria and a number of characteristics that are generally found to be true of ESP. Her key criteria are that ESP is *'normally goal-directed'*, and that ESP courses develop from a *needs analysis,* which 'aims to specify as closely as possible what exactly it is that students have to do through the medium of English' (Robinson, 1991: 3). Her characteristics are that ESP courses are generally constrained by a *limited time period*, in which their objectives have to be achieved, and are taught to *adults* in *homogeneous classes* in terms of the work or specialist studies that the students are involved in.

Each definition has validity but also weaknesses, either in the definition or in the features described. Strevens' definition is the most comprehensive of the three quoted, but can lead to a certain confusion. By referring to content in the second absolute characteristic it may confirm the false impression held by many teachers that ESP is always and necessarily related directly to subject content. Robinson's mention of 'homogeneous classes' as a characteristic of ESP may lead to the same conclusion. Much ESP work is, by contrast, based on the notion of a 'common-core' of language and skills that belong to all academic disciplines or cut across the whole activity of business. ESP teaching does not necessarily have to be related to content but it should always reflect the underlying concepts and activities of the broad discipline. Thus English for Academic Purposes (EAP), whether it is directly related to the specific disciplines that students are studying or not, should make use of the essentially problem-solving methodology of academic study (Widdowson, 1983). Similarly, Business English teaching should reflect the business context in which business meetings or negotiations take place (Charles, 1994 and 1996).

We believe that a definition of ESP should reflect the fact that much ESP teaching, especially where it is specifically linked to a particular profession or discipline, makes use of a methodology that differs from that used in General Purpose English teaching. By methodology here we are referring to the nature of the interaction between the ESP teacher and the learners. In more general ESP classes the interaction may be similar to that in a General Purpose English class; in the more specific ESP classes, however, the teacher sometimes becomes more like a language consultant, enjoying equal status with the learners who have their own expertise in the subject matter. We will look at these issues in more detail in chapters 3 and 10.

In our definition we stress two aspects of ESP methodology: all ESP teaching should reflect the methodology of the disciplines and professions it serves; and in more specific ESP teaching the nature of the interaction between the teacher and learner may be very different from that in a general English class. This is what we mean when we say that specific ESP teaching has its own methodology.

We also believe that language should be included as a defining feature of ESP. While the specified needs arising from needs analysis relate to activities that students need to carry out (rather than language), a key assumption of ESP is that these activities generate and depend on registers, genres and associated language that students need to be able to manipulate in order to carry out the activity.

In our definition we use absolute and variable characteristics. Our definition is:

1. **Absolute characteristics:**
   - ESP is designed to meet specific needs of the learner;
   - ESP makes use of the underlying methodology and activities of the disciplines it serves;

ESP is centred on the language (grammar, lexis, register), skills, discourse and genres appropriate to these activities.

2. Variable characteristics:
   - ESP may be related to or designed for specific disciplines;
   - ESP may use, in specific teaching situations, a different methodology from that of general English;
   - ESP is likely to be designed for adult learners, either at a tertiary level institution or in a professional work situation. It could, however, be used for learners at secondary school level;
   - ESP is generally designed for intermediate or advanced students. Most ESP courses assume basic knowledge of the language system, but it can be used with beginners.

Task 1b ●◆

Discuss whether, according to our definition, the following courses constitute ESP courses. Give reasons for your decision:

1. A course in remedial grammar for business people, with each unit based on a particular grammatical weakness identified by tests.
2. A course that teaches undergraduate engineering students from various branches (civil, electrical, mechanical etc.) to write reports on design projects.
3. A course that teaches reading skills to a group of postgraduate students from a range of disciplines, studying in a British university. The texts used are of a general academic nature, but are exploited to teach specific reading skills.
4. A course designed to prepare students for the Cambridge FCE examination. The course is based on a careful analysis of the contents of the test.
5. A course designed to teach social English to a group of business people. The level of the students' English is intermediate.
6. A course team-taught with a subject lecturer, that helps postgraduates of a particular discipline understand departmental lectures.

1.4   Classification of ESP

In this section we introduce and explain the many abbreviations that have been used in describing ESP, terms such as EAP, EOP, EST and EBP. ESP has traditionally been divided into two main areas: English for Academic Purposes (EAP) and English for Occupational Purposes

(EOP). The classification is generally presented in a tree diagram as in figure 1.1 (taken from Robinson, 1991: 3–4).

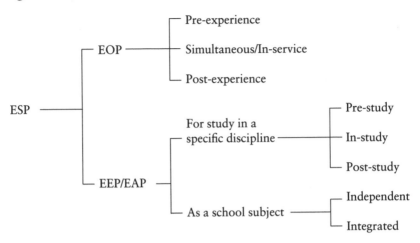

Figure 1.1   ESP classification by experience

The diagram has, as well as the division into EAP and EOP, a useful division of courses according to when they take place. These distinctions are very important as they will affect the degree of specificity that is appropriate to the course. A pre-experience or pre-study course will probably rule out any specific work related to the actual discipline or work as students will not yet have the required familiarity with the content, while courses that run parallel to or follow the course of study in the educational institution or workplace will provide the opportunity for specific or integrated work.

Another typical tree diagram for ESP, which divides EAP and EOP according to discipline or professional area, is shown in figure 1.2.

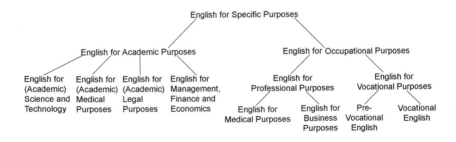

Figure 1.2   ESP classification by professional area

In EAP, English for Science and Technology (EST) has been the main area, but English for Medical Purposes (EMP) and English for Legal Purposes (ELP) have always had their place. Recently the academic study of business, finance, banking, economics and accounting has become increasingly important, especially on Masters in Business Administration (MBA) courses, but, as yet, no specific acronym has become established for such courses.

The term EOP refers to English that is not for academic purposes; it includes professional purposes in administration, medicine, law and business, and vocational purposes for non-professionals in work or pre-work situations. We may thus distinguish between studying the language and discourse of, for example, medicine for *academic* purposes, which is designed for medical students, and studying for *occupational (professional)* purposes, which is designed for practising doctors.

This classification places English for Business Purposes (EBP) as a category within EOP. EBP is sometimes seen as separate from EOP as it involves a lot of General English as well as Specific Purpose English, and also because it is such a large and important category. A business purpose is, however, an occupational purpose, so it is logical to see it as part of EOP.

Within English for Vocational Purposes (EVP) there are two sub-sections: *Vocational English,* which is concerned with the language of training for specific trades or occupations, and *Pre-Vocational English*, which is concerned with finding a job and interview skills. It also deals with succeeding in a job through an understanding of employer expectations and policies (Anne Lomperis, personal communication).

A distinction should also be made between common-core English for General Academic Purposes (EGAP) and English for Specific Academic Purposes (ESAP) (Blue, 1988a). The same distinction can be made between English for General Business Purposes (EGBP) and English for Specific Business Purposes (ESBP) (Dudley-Evans and St John, 1996). We discuss the differences in chapter 3 (EAP) and chapter 4 (EBP).

Reflection 1c

Into which categories of figures 1.1 and 1.2 would you place courses that you have taught?

The use of classification trees creates a number of problems by failing to capture the essentially fluid nature of the various types of ESP teaching and the degree of overlap between 'common-core' EAP or EBP and General English. The 'common-core' English and semi-technical vocabulary taught in many English for General Academic Purposes courses could well be extremely valuable in the teaching of what might be referred to in General English as 'factual description'. Similarly, the detailed focus on reading skills, such as 'establishing main points' or 'inferring meaning from context' that form a major part of EAP courses, can just as validly be taught as part of an intermediate to advanced General English course. Business English can also be seen as a 'mediating language between the technicalities of particular businesses . . . and the language of the general public' (Pickett, 1989), which puts it in a position between General English and specialist English.

We therefore suggest that an additional perspective can be gained through the presentation of the whole of English Language Teaching on a *continuum* that runs from clearly definable General English courses through to very specific ESP courses. Figure 1.3 illustrates this continuum. It seems that positions 2 and 3, which are towards the centre of the continuum, have much in common and it is only the overall context of the programme that decides whether a given course is classified as ESP or not. An advanced secondary school level course that includes a focus on, say, listening skills will be seen as General English as the course itself has the aim of teaching English as part of a broad educational process. However, a similar component taught as part of a pre-sessional course for international students about to embark on a postgraduate course taught in English in an English-speaking country will be seen as ESP because it is part of a focused course with a specific time period with clear and specific objectives. The teaching material might, in fact, be quite similar, but the teaching methodology is likely to be different.

The use of the continuum also clarifies the nature of more specific ESP work. At position 4, the work is very specific in terms of the skills taught, but the groups themselves are not homogeneous groups from one discipline or profession. When we talk of engineers, scientists or doctors, we are talking about broad groups: individual members may have quite different needs and backgrounds. So, on the one hand, detailed attention will be paid to a skill such as report writing, or particular features of language and/or discourse of, say, a business meeting, but, on the other hand, great care has to be taken in choosing the actual skill or skills to focus on and the contexts in which to do so. For example, some doctors will need to read and write medical journal articles, others will need oral skills for talking to patients. A group of

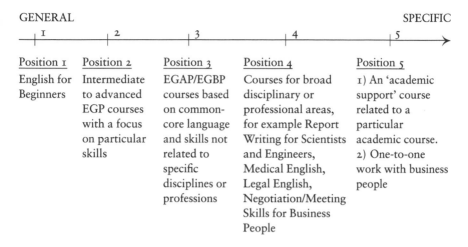

GENERAL   SPECIFIC

Position 1	Position 2	Position 3	Position 4	Position 5
English for Beginners	Intermediate to advanced EGP courses with a focus on particular skills	EGAP/EGBP courses based on common-core language and skills not related to specific disciplines or professions	Courses for broad disciplinary or professional areas, for example Report Writing for Scientists and Engineers, Medical English, Legal English, Negotiation/Meeting Skills for Business People	1) An 'academic support' course related to a particular academic course. 2) One-to-one work with business people

Figure 1.3   Continuum of ELT course types

engineers from a variety of branches such as civil, highways, electronic, chemical and mechanical will probably not take kindly to materials that use contexts from just one branch of engineering. Teaching material prepared for such groups needs contexts that are acceptable and under-standable to all branches.

It is only in position 5 that the course becomes really specific. The course can be geared to the specific needs of the target situation and of the individuals concerned, and can make extensive use of authentic material in their own subject area. It is a key feature of such courses that the teaching is flexible and tailored to individual or group needs as they arise.

This discussion leads to the inevitable question: does a precise classification really matter? Undoubtedly, any attempt at classification leads to overlap and potential confusion, but in our view it is important to make the attempt to define and classify what we mean by ESP.

1.4.1   Specificity and motivation

There are clear advantages in setting up an ESP course where students have specific needs. Strevens (1988) summarises the advantages of ESP with the following four points:

- being focused on the learner's need, it wastes no time;
- it is relevant to the learner;
- it is successful in imparting learning;
- it is more cost-effective than 'General English'.

9

The implication of these claims is that ESP teaching is more motivating for learners than General English. Generally speaking, this is true; the focused nature of the teaching, its relevance and cost-effectiveness ensure that its aims are widely accepted by learners. Opinions about specific work, however, vary. Many learners are hungry for material and advice that will help them with their specific course or with particular skills related to their course. Thus, for example, team-taught courses, where the language teacher works together with the subject lecturer to help international students understand actual lectures on postgraduate courses, appear to be highly motivating (Johns and Dudley-Evans, 1980). Similarly, academic writing courses that give specific guidance about the writing of essays and dissertations (Dudley-Evans, 1995) are extremely popular in British universities.

When the context is an English-as-a-Foreign-Language situation, motivation for more specific work may be much smaller. It is not uncommon to hear in such situations the cry that students are looking for a change in the English class from reading about the topics that make up their subject courses and are looking for a little variety. As Crofts (1977 cited in Swales, 1980: 67) argues 'when students are very familiar with a topic, they will be bored with any treatment of it as something not familiar . . . When they do not have the knowledge that is assumed to be known in a particular treatment of a topic given in the ESP materials, they will be unable to cope with the topic in the intended way without the help of the ESP teacher or some other source of information'. Crofts goes on to suggest that EAP material should concentrate on material that is parallel to the main subject course, but is not actually part of it; in other words, topics that could have been included in the main course, but were not.

The main conclusion here is that motivation in ESP has a profound effect on the question of how specific the course is. High motivation on the part of learners generally enables more subject specific work to be undertaken; low motivation, however, is likely to lead to a concentration on less specific work. Specialists in either academic or occupational contexts who need English for specific tasks will be impatient with an ESP course that does not address their difficulties with those tasks. Other students who are studying English because it is on the timetable of their institution or who have been sent on a course by their company and who do not have specific, immediate and clearly definable needs may be demotivated by more specific work and may be more motivated by ESP work that falls more towards the centre of the continuum outlined in figure 1.3 (p. 9).

Task 1d •◆

Look at the six courses described in Task 1b and decide where on the continuum (figure 1.3) they should be placed.

1.5 Carrier content and real content

While discussing the question of specificity in ESP, it is important that we clarify the role of the actual content. The notions of 'carrier content' and 'real content' are essential to the understanding of ESP work and to an understanding of motivation in ESP. In ESP, any teaching activity, whether its aim is to teach language or skills, is presented in a context. Thus in the following short extract (on p. 12) from *Nucleus: General Science* (Bates and Dudley-Evans, 1976) the aim of the exercise is to present and practise the expressions of time sequence used in the description of processes and cycles. It makes use of the context of the life cycle of a plant in order to present this language. It is not the aim of the exercise to teach students about the life cycle, although certain lexical items, such as *fertilised* or *decomposes* may be useful.

The life cycle of a plant is the *carrier content* used to teach the specific language that the unit in the book wishes to introduce at this stage. The unit itself is entitled *Actions in Sequence* and is concerned with the notion or scientific concept of *Process*. This exercise is just part of the unit and the writer made the decision that the life cycle is an appropriate topic which can be used to meet certain objectives of the unit. It is an authentic topic which can be used as a vehicle for the *real content* of the unit, the language of process. Students of any discipline can understand the life cycle and describe it without becoming entangled in difficult and technical content that will interfere with the main aim of the exercise, the language associated with process. Another example would be the use of a table of statistics to teach the language of comparison. The statistics constitute the carrier content, but the real content is the language used to make comparisons.

Task 1e •◆

Look at Extract E1.2 (pp. 234–235) and decide what the real content of the material is and what the carrier content is.

Extract E1.1

Bates, M. and A. Dudley-Evans. *Nucleus: General Science*. Longman, 1976, 1982.

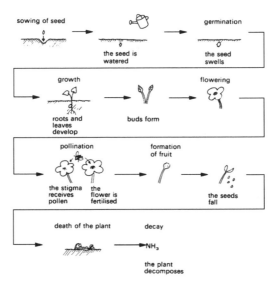

Stages in the life cycle of a plant

Look at these examples:

Preceding actions:
Before the plant *germinates*, it is watered.

$\left.\begin{array}{l}\textit{Before} \\ \textit{Prior to}\end{array}\right\}$ *germination*, the seed is watered.

Following actions:
After the plant *germinates*, the roots and leaves develop.
After germination, the roots and leaves develop.

Simultaneous actions:
As the plant *germinates*, the seed swells.
During germination, the seed swells.

And this example:

After the seed is watered, *germination* $\left\{\begin{array}{l}\textit{occurs.} \\ \textit{takes place.}\end{array}\right.$

Now answer these questions:
a) What happens prior to germination?
b) What occurs during growth?
c) What happens before flowering?
d) What takes place after pollination?
e) What happens after the seeds fall?
f) What occurs before the plant decomposes?
g) What occurs as the plant decomposes?

1.6 Roles of the ESP practitioner

Orientation 1f

ESP work extends beyond teaching. What other roles does an ESP teacher have?

It will already be clear that we regard ESP teaching as extremely varied, and for this reason we use the term 'practitioner' rather than 'teacher' to emphasise that ESP work involves much more than teaching. We see the ESP practitioner as having five key roles:

Teacher
Course designer and materials provider
Collaborator
Researcher
Evaluator

We will look briefly at each of these in turn in this chapter, but these roles underlie much of the discussion in this book.

1.6.1 The ESP practitioner as teacher

ESP is a practical discipline with the main focus on helping students to learn. With the 'common-core' EGAP or EGBP courses that we mentioned earlier (p. 7) the methodology of ESP teaching may not differ radically from that of General English. But there is one basic difference that affects the methodology and becomes more pronounced as the teaching becomes more specific: This is that the teacher is not in the position of being the 'primary knower' of the carrier content of the material. The students may in many cases, certainly where the course is specifically oriented towards the subject content or work that the students are engaged in, know more about the content than the teacher. It is often stated that this provides the ESP teacher with the opportunity to draw on students' knowledge of the content in order to generate genuine communication in the classroom. We do not disagree with this statement, but feel that the situation is much more complicated than the statement makes it appear.

In common-core situations using material such as the life-cycle of the plant, it can be assumed that the content is rather more 'general knowledge' than scientific knowledge, and that students do not need to be biologists to understand it. Teachers will need a reasonable understanding of the cycle before teaching the exercise, so that they can start and possibly lead an introductory discussion drawing on the students' understanding of the cycle before the actual exercise is tackled. Under these circumstances, we believe that teachers remain the classroom organisers; they have clear objectives for the class and a good understanding of the carrier content of the teaching material.

When, however, teaching a much more specific course on, say, how to write a business report, it is essential that the teacher adopts the stance of the consultant who has knowledge of communication practices, but needs to 'negotiate' with the students on how best to exploit these practices to meet the objectives they have. The relationship is much more one of partnership, and the Initiation–Response–Follow-Up moves characteristic of classroom discourse (Sinclair and Coulthard, 1975) are absent. In specific ESP teaching it may be the learner who asks the questions and the teacher who responds.

In some situations the role of the ESP teacher goes beyond that of the classroom teacher and extends to giving one-to-one advice to students. This is particularly common in EAP situations in Britain, USA and Australia where often the most effective means of improving students' ability to write essays, reports or dissertations is to give a tutorial or series of tutorials on the actual piece of writing that they are engaged with. A similar procedure is followed in non-English speaking countries where academics have to publish in international journals that use English and need advice on both language and discourse issues (Ventola and Mauranen, 1991). In EOP and especially BE situations, one-to-one work may focus on language features as well as particular skills. There is evidence that such individual attention often leads to dramatic improvements in both communicative skills and linguistic accuracy. We discuss one-to-one work in greater detail in chapter 10.

ESP teachers also need to have a great deal of flexibility, be willing to listen to learners, and to take an interest in the disciplines or professional activities the students are involved in. They must be ready to change tack in a lesson to take account of what comes up, and to think and respond rapidly to events. ESP teachers must also be happy to take some risks in their teaching. The willingness to be flexible and to take risks is one of the keys to success in ESP teaching.

1.6.2 The ESP practitioner as course designer and materials provider

ESP practitioners often have to plan the course they teach and provide the materials for it. It is rarely possible to use a particular textbook without the need for supplementary material, and sometimes no really suitable published material exists for certain of the identified needs. The role of ESP teachers as 'providers of material' thus involves *choosing* suitable published material, *adapting* material when published material is not suitable, or even *writing* material where nothing suitable exists (chapter 9).

ESP teachers also need to assess the effectiveness of the teaching material used on the course, whether that material is published or self-produced. The role of course designer and materials provider described here may seem a difficult and demanding role to someone new to ESP. It is, but we believe that such demands make ESP teaching interesting. There is, however, one danger. As Swales (1980) has commented, the role of materials *writer* has become such a desirable characteristic of the ESP teacher in the eyes of employers that there is a danger that the advantages of published material are ignored even when that material is suitable for a given situation. The point is often well made that there is a danger in ESP course and materials provision of constant 're-invention of the wheel'.

1.6.3   The ESP practitioner as researcher

Research has been particularly strong in the area of EAP, where there is a healthy and developing range of published research, especially in genre analysis (Swales, 1990; Bhatia, 1993). Research into English for Business Purposes is more patchy, but there is nonetheless a growing interest in investigating the genres, the language and the skills involved in business communication (see, for example, Dudley-Evans and St John, 1996, and the special issue (15: 1) of the journal *English for Specific Purposes* on Business English (St John and Johnson, 1996).

ESP teachers need to be aware of and in touch with this research. Those carrying out a needs analysis, designing a course, or writing teaching materials need to be able to incorporate the findings of the research, and those working in specific ESP situations need to be confident that they know what is involved in skills such as written communication. An ESP practitioner has to go beyond the first stage of Needs Analysis – Target Situation Analysis (TSA) which identifies key target events, skills and texts – to observe as far as possible the situations in which students use the identified skills, and analyse samples of the identified texts. As part of this process, ESP teachers generally need to be able to carry out research to understand the discourse of the texts that students use.

1.6.4   The ESP practitioner as collaborator

We have already argued for the importance of specific work as part of an ESP programme. We believe that subject-specific work is often best approached through collaboration with subject specialists (Johns and Dudley-Evans, 1980). This may involve simply *cooperation* in which the ESP teacher finds out about the subject syllabus in an academic context or the tasks the students have to carry out in a work or business situation. Alternatively, it may involve specific *collaboration* so that there is some integration between specialist studies or activities and the language. This might involve relating the reading component of an EAP course to the actual content of a subject course by exploiting texts in English that present additional relevant material, in other words, the subject teacher provides the 'carrier content' for the English course. Alternatively, it might involve the language teacher specifically preparing learners for the language of subject lectures or business presentations one or two days before the subject lecture or presentation (Henderson and Skehan, 1980). A third possibility is that a specialist checks and comments on the content of teaching materials that the ESP teacher has prepared. The fullest collaboration is where a subject expert and a language teacher *team-teach* classes; in EAP such lessons might help with the understanding of subject lectures or the writing of examination answers, essays or theses (Johns and Dudley-Evans, 1980), in EOP they might involve the language teacher and a business trainer working together to teach both the skills and the language related to business communication. We will look at these forms of collaboration in greater detail in chapters 3 and 4.

1.6.5 *The ESP practitioner as evaluator*

The ESP practitioner is often involved in various types of evaluation, including both the testing of students and the evaluation of courses and teaching materials. Tests are conducted to assess whether students have the requisite language and skills to undertake a particular academic course or career, and – usually but not necessarily at the end of the course – the level of their achievement. The first role is important in countries such as the UK, USA, Australia and New Zealand, where large numbers of international students do postgraduate courses or research. For the purpose of assessing whether these students will be able to cope from a language point of view, a number of internationally recognised and validated tests exist, notably the British and Australian International English Language Testing Service (IELTS) test, the NEAB's Test in ESOL and the American TOEFL test. All but the TOEFL test have an ESP orientation (chapter 11).

The ESP teacher also needs to be able to devise achievement tests to assess how much learners have gained from a course. Very few of these have been published, but the tests that were published with the Nucleus Series have some interesting ideas (Vance, 1981).

Evaluating course design and teaching materials should be done while the course is being taught, at the end of the course and after the course has finished. It is important to follow up with students some time after the course in order to assess whether the learners have been able to make use of what they learned and to find out what they were not prepared for. Evaluation through discussion and on-going needs analysis can thus be used to adapt the syllabus. In many situations the evaluation forms the basis of 'negotiation' with students about their feelings about the course, their needs and priorities, which are then fed into the next stage of the course. These steps are all part of 'formative' evaluation.

Reflection 1g

Which of the above roles do you already undertake? What would you need to feel confident in each role?

1.7 ESP as a multi-disciplinary activity

The title of this book refers to the multi-disciplinarity of ESP. We are interested in two aspects of multi-disciplinarity: the need and willingness to engage with other disciplines through teaching, and the need and willingness to draw on the insights of researchers in other disciplines. We have already indicated that we believe there is a need for some specificity in both EAP and EOP teaching, and we develop this further, especially in chapters 3 and 4. A glance at the bibliography will show that the journals and books cited come from wide-ranging disciplines.

A key feature of ESP work is research into how spoken and written texts work. In order to understand how these texts work, we need to understand how they are used within a particular discipline or profession, and how they attempt to persuade their audiences of the validity of their claims and arguments. Here the sociological studies of professions (for example Latour and Woolgar, 1979; Gilbert and Mulkay, 1984) and the rhetorical studies of how professions write (for example Bazerman and Paradis, 1991) are very helpful.

Similarly, if we are to understand how business is conducted, we find that texts from management training and human resource management tell something of how business people think and work (for example Fisher and Ury, 1981; Handy, 1992).

In all ESP work we now recognise that we have to be sensitive to cultural differences, both in the academic and professional worlds. In the academic world learners may not be used to having to participate fully in seminars; in the business world some negotiators may feel uncomfortable with a forceful result-oriented style of conducting a meeting. Work in the area of cultural difference (Hofstede, 1983) and cross-cultural communication (Trompenaar, 1993; Limaye and Victor, 1991) has had an impact on the teaching of Business English.

The influence is not all in one direction, however. ESP research is beginning to have its influence in other disciplines. Many of the findings of genre analysis have been taken on board by those working in L1 writing or composition research (for example Bazerman, 1988; Myers, 1989, both of whom have also had an influence on ESP), and the research into the rhetoric of different disciplines (for example McCloskey, 1994 on economics) has been strengthened through contact with applied linguists, especially those interested in genre.

1.8 Summary

We have in this introductory chapter presented a definition of ESP and discussed various classifications of the types of ESP teaching. We have also introduced the main themes that will be developed in this book: the differences between English for Academic Purposes and English for Occupational Purposes, especially in the area of Business English; the need for both common-core and specific work in ESP; the need to find out much more about the language, skills and genres used in these two broad areas; and the various roles of the ESP practitioner as teacher, course designer and materials provider, researcher, collaborator and evaluator.

1.9 Recommended reading

Pauline Robinson's (1991) book is a very comprehensive introduction to both the research and the materials developed in all branches of ESP, while Johns and Dudley-Evans (1993) presents a view of the state of ESP in the mid-1990s. Widdowson's (1983) book presents his most extensive statement about ESP. The journal *English for Specific Purposes* publishes a wide range of articles on ESP ranging from text analysis to classroom descriptions.

2 A historical perspective on ESP

2.1 Aims

In this chapter we wish to trace the development of ESP, from its origins in the 1960s to the situation today, at the turn of the millennium. This involves looking closely at the interaction between Applied Linguistics, ELT and ESP, the relationship between theory and practice in ESP, and the teaching materials that have been developed. We will also show how ESP has been influenced by developments in education, business and computer technology.

2.2 The balance between research and practice

ESP is essentially a materials- and teaching-led movement. It has been influenced by developments and changes in Applied Linguistics and ELT, but as a lively, 'feisty', ambitious, young movement within ELT it has also had considerable influence on ELT. ESP was, for example, very influential in showing how a communicative language curriculum could be turned into either a functional-notional syllabus or a task-based syllabus.

The original flowering of the ESP movement resulted from general developments in the world economy in the 1950s and 1960s: the growth of science and technology, the increased use of English as the international language of science, technology and business, the increased economic power of certain oil-rich countries and the increased numbers of international students studying in the UK, USA and Australia. The idea of language for specific purposes, however, has been around for a long time. Howatt (1984) argues that the need for commercial English for incoming Huguenot and other Protestant refugees to England in the 16th century led to a focus on Business English in early ELT and that actual textbooks on 'commercial English' and business letter writing were a feature of ELT from the 19th century.

It was undoubtedly in the mid- to late 1960s, however, that various influences came together to generate the need and enthusiasm for developing ESP as a discipline.

The relationship between theory and materials/teaching in ESP is fascinating to trace. ESP was given its initial impetus by work in the area of register analysis which looked at the grammar of scientific and technical writing, and pointed to certain areas of priority for teaching and materials production. Swales (1988), in his very influential *Episodes in ESP*, points to Barber's 1962 article on grammatical and lexical features of 'modern scientific prose' as the real beginning, and acknowledges its influence on his own work. This article built on the descriptive techniques of Linguistics, especially those that were eventually written up in Halliday, Strevens and McIntosh's 1964 book *The Linguistic Sciences and Language Teaching*.

Subsequently, much material was produced as a result of the practitioner engaging with the teaching situation, carrying out a limited text analysis and then writing a handout or series of handouts. This activity may then have been written up and published as an article, forming the basis of more extensive research.

This movement back and forth between theory and practice is reflected in Swales' choice of articles and materials for *Episodes in ESP*. The book traces the history of ESP up to 1981, and includes key published papers and teaching materials, each one constituting an episode. An analysis of the balance between theory and practice in the episodes shows that there are six that describe teaching situations and materials, five that discuss theory and linguistic analysis, and four presenting extracts from textbooks.

This indicates that ESP has at some points in its history drawn on more theoretical work in Applied Linguistics, at other times it has been ahead of Applied Linguistics, and ESP experience in needs analysis and materials production has fed into theoretical work.

2.3 Trends in English for Academic Purposes

We will look at the various trends in ESP under four headings – Register Analysis, Rhetorical and Discourse Analysis, Analysis of Study Skills, Analysis of Learning Needs – and illustrate through published teaching materials how these movements have influenced ESP.

Orientation 2a

What materials do you use with your ESP students? What view of language and language learning do they follow?

2.3.1   Register analysis

The work of Register Analysis (Barber, 1962; Ewer and Hughes-Davies, 1971 and 72, both reprinted in Swales, 1988) focused on the grammar and vocabulary of Scientific and Technical English using what Swales (1988: 1) refers to as an approach based on 'lexicostatistics'. The assumption was that, while the grammar of scientific and technical writing does not differ from that of General English, certain grammatical and lexical forms are used much more frequently. Thus the predominant tense is the present simple, and the passive voice is used much more frequently than in General English, but not more frequently than the active voice. This research also points to the importance of *semi-* or *sub-technical vocabulary*, such as 'consists of', 'contains', 'enables', 'acts as' that is more likely to occur in scientific, technical or academic writing than in general contexts.

The first significant ESP (EST) textbook, A. J. Herbert's *The Structure of Technical English*, was published in 1965. The book is designed for students who have studied some English but need training 'in the special structures and linguistic conventions of the English used in technical and scientific writing so that they may be able to follow the current literature in English in their particular subject' (the description on the back cover).

The Extract E2.1 (see pp. 236–7) is typical of the format of the book: it begins with a long specially constructed reading text on a technical topic, but one that appears to be based on a description from an encyclopedia rather than a textbook. This then leads into a number of exercises focusing on language, initially on semi-technical language and then on one of the key aspects of grammar identified by Barber, the passive form of the verb. Exercise 2 of this extract is interesting in that it takes the notion of quantity and presents a whole range of lexical items related to 'too much' and 'too little'. It is characteristic of the book that all the exercises – both in this extract and elsewhere in the book – focus on these lexical and grammatical points; there are no exercises checking comprehension of the reading passage or developing reading or other skills. In focusing on the 'notion' of quantity, however, it shows an early if limited awareness of the value of a functional/notional approach to the teaching of lexis.

As Swales (1988) remarks, *The Structure of Technical English* was driven by the linguistic analysis that underpinned it. The coverage of language, especially semi-technical vocabulary (for example word study in Extract E2.1 (pp. 237)), has been admired, but as a textbook for classroom use it left a lot to be desired. The passages were dense and lacked authenticity, the accompanying diagrams were not very supportive, and, worst of all, the exercises were repetitive and lacking in variety. All in all, most of those who taught with *The Structure of Technical English* found it a difficult book to use. There were also theoretical objections: these were that the concentration on a restricted range of grammar and vocabulary was an insufficient basis for a textbook on English for Science and Technology and that this concentration on *form* needed to be replaced by a concentration on language *use* and *communication*.

Most materials produced under the banner of Register Analysis followed a similar pattern, beginning each chapter with a long specialist reading passage. Beginning a unit with a reading passage, usually related to a specific discipline, seems to have been standard practice in EAP, probably arising from situations where General English materials were supplemented by subject-specific reading passages.

These perceived weaknesses of the Register Analysis approach and attempts to rectify them led to the second major movement in ESP, rhetorical or discourse analysis.

2.3.2 *Rhetorical and discourse analysis*

While the work of Barber and other 'lexicostatisticians' examined the language of specific registers, it offered very little explanation of why certain grammatical patterns are favoured by the English of Science and Technology, nor of how sentences are combined to form paragraphs and whole texts or 'discourses'. The pioneering work in this area was done by Lackstrom, Selinker and Trimble (1973) whose approach is perhaps best summarised by Trimble's later book *English for Science and Technology: A Discourse Approach* (1985). Trimble defines rhetoric as 'the process a writer uses to produce a desired piece of text' (p. 10) and an EST text as 'concerned only with the presentation of facts, hypotheses and similar types of information'. He suggests that a writer needs to organise a text at four rhetorical levels: level A – the objectives of the total discourse; level B – the general rhetorical functions that develop the level A objectives; level C – the specific rhetorical functions that develop the general ones; level D – the rhetorical techniques that provide relationships between the level C functions.

This work introduced the idea of relating language *form* to language *use*, making use the main criterion for the selection of ESP teaching materials. It was Widdowson, however, in his early writings with Allen who really made this approach the major movement in ESP in the 70s. Swales talks of the Barber article having 'a special importance for those few people involved in ESP in the mid-sixties' (Swales, 1988: 1, sentence reordered). For the relatively large numbers who began to work in ESP situations at the beginning of the 1970s, Widdowson's arguments for the primacy of language use over form (*usage* in Widdowson's terminology) and for an approach based on the communicative aspect of language were extremely influential.

The Focus Series was a series of textbooks that put Allen and Widdowson's ideas into practice; here the emphasis was on key functions in scientific and academic writing: *definition, classification, description* and *hypothesising*, all at level C in Trimble's chart, and on the linguistic forms of *cohesion*. *The Focus Series*, although influential from a theoretical point of view, was less successful as an actual textbook, as it seems not to have been based on any substantial trials in an actual teaching situation. More successful was *The Nucleus Series*, which originated from teaching material developed at the University of Tabriz in Iran. The series was strongly influenced by Widdowson's work, and also by work on semi-technical vocabulary. It concentrated on the rhetorical function of description, and introduced semi-technical vocabulary related to 11 key concepts or notions in science (Wilkins, 1976). It thus focuses on Trimble's Level D, as illustrated by Extract E2.2 (pp. 238–9) which is concerned with the description of structure.

The extract is taken from the *General Science* book, which acts as a core book for the series, and shows most of the features of the course (for a detailed description of how the course was written see Bates [1978]). The material is clearly derived from a teaching situation; it is entertaining and certainly avoids the laboriousness and predictability of *The Structure of Technical English*. There is also good visual support. The main drawback of the course is that it is still primarily concerned with teaching language. It does that effectively through the use of a functional-notional syllabus and a good range of exercise types, but neglects the development of specific study skills.

In the *General Science* book the real content, the semi-technical language of scientific description, is taught through a wide range of carrier content, from everyday to general science contexts. In the specific books, the carrier content is much more closely related to the discipline. There are exercises in reading and, in the specific courses, some attention is given to listening; moreover, the exercises in both the core course and the specific courses generate oral and written practice. None of the four skills, however, are given specific attention and there are few exercises that have the aim of developing particular study skills.

Specific work on study skills – missing from both *The Structure of Technical English* and *The Nucleus Series* – became the major focus in EAP work in the late 1970s.

2.3.3   *Analysis of study skills*

The interest in skills seemed to develop fairly naturally from the functional-notional materials we have discussed, and was consistent with the ideas of communicative language teaching. The growth of needs analysis, a trend that ran parallel with the rise of the skills approach, identified priorities amongst the four skills for a given situation. In many situations, especially when the medium of instruction was not English, for example in Latin America, this meant a focus on reading. In other situations it might involve a different skill, such as listening for international students embarking on academic courses in the UK, oral skills for business people conducting international negotiations, writing skills for engineers employed by an international company, or for international students writing a postgraduate thesis.

The main principle of these skills-based courses was that the teaching of language in itself is not sufficient for the development of the ability to perform the tasks required of a tertiary level student, a business person or a practising engineer. The basis of the approach is that, in addition to language work, there is a need to address the thought processes that underpin language use. These thought processes may either be fairly general, relating to all academic or professional activity, or specific to a particular discipline or profession. There is a clear overlap with related work in teaching study skills to native speakers (Williams *et al.*, 1984).

The skills were taught using general carrier content, and reading or listening passages were chosen on the basis of general academic interest and authenticity. It was assumed that the skills learnt through the exercises could be transferred to the students' own specific tasks.

We will exemplify this movement with an Extract (E2.3, p. 240) from the reading skills course *Skills for Learning*. This course was developed by the University of Malaya ESP Project (UMESPP). The University of Malaya, along with other Malaysian universities, had recently switched to a Malay medium policy but wished to retain the use of English as a 'library' language. The course focuses on certain specific skills associated with reading such as 'getting to know the main parts of a book', 'getting familiar with non-linear texts', 'learning to accept difficult words', 'reading for relevant information', 'using contextual clues', 'assessing how much to read'. The aim of each lesson is made explicit through the statement of why the skill is needed. We have chosen as an example parts of the first two pages from Lesson 20 *Using contextual clues*. The first exercise is a listening activity and a problem-solving task; thereafter the exercises focus on the main purpose, that of deducing meanings of difficult words from the context. This gradual 'atomistic' building up of a set of skills, either through individual, pair or group work, is characteristic of courses focusing on reading or listening skills.

The principles underlying the *Skills for Learning* course book are very similar to the *Reading and Thinking* series published by Oxford University Press in 1980. The main difference is that *Reading and Thinking* consists of four books which move from a focus on functions and notions to a concern with discourse matters, in particular with judging writers' stance towards the topics they are discussing.

2.3.4   Analysis of learning needs

In the late 1970s and early 1980s there was a period of consolidation in ESP. In the early 1970s it was important to establish the need and credentials for ESP work, and many articles, notably Strevens (1971) and Jordan and Mackay (1973) concentrated on this. The question was whether ESP courses were more successful than General English courses in preparing students either for working or studying in English. The answer generally came in the form of reports on the success of courses and materials and what Bowyers (1980) refers to as 'war stories and romances'. There are relatively few empirical studies on the effectiveness of ESP courses, although Foley's discussion of the ESP programme at the University of Petroleum and Minerals in Saudi Arabia (Foley, 1979) provides concrete evidence for the validity of the ESP approach.

Munby's (1978) model for Needs Analysis – initially a PhD thesis and later a book – was much discussed in the late 1970s and early 1980s. The rather cumbersome nature of the model has meant that it has had relatively little direct influence on the ESP profession, but at the time the publication of the model was an indication of the 'coming-of-age' of English for Specific Purposes.

Hutchinson and Waters' various papers (1979, 1980a, 1980b and 1981) indicate the consolidation of ESP work, but also, more significantly, a recognition that some of the accepted ideas of ESP needed rethinking. They have perhaps been particularly influential in their definition of what they consider ESP should *not* be. In their later book (1987, p. 18) they state that:

1. ESP is *not* a matter of teaching 'specialised varieties' of English. . . .
2. ESP is *not* just a matter of Science words and grammar for Scientists, Hotel words and grammar for Hotel staff and so on. . . .
3. ESP is *not* different in kind from any other form of language teaching in that it should be based in the first instance on principles of effective and efficient learning. . . .

While it is difficult to disagree with these actual statements, their position has been strongly associated with the argument against specific work in ESP, a rejection of the idea that ESP methodology differs from that of General English teaching, and even occasionally – although this is clearly not their view – with the idea that ESP is dead. While these negative associations are unfortunate, Hutchinson and Waters' ideas on a learning-centred approach to ESP are very interesting.

Hutchinson and Waters argued that ESP had concentrated too much on the end product as revealed by Target Situation Analysis (Chambers, 1980) and linguistic analyses of lectures, textbooks and articles, and, therefore, too little on the learning skills needed to enable students to reach the desired end behaviour. They argued that students (their ideas derived from a situation in which international students were being prepared for study at a British Technical College) need the 'target performance repertoire' – the end product – less than the 'underlying competence' that the lecturer assumes and which enables the student to reach the target performance repertoire. The underlying competence consists of familiarity with the 'standard visual modes of representation' (Hutchinson and Waters, 1980 reprinted in Swales, 1988: 180); semi-technical and colloquial language; 'familiarity with the world', that is with various metaphors frequently used in academic description, in this case the pump and the circulation system; and 'layman's technology' (*ibid.*, p. 181), that is the workings of a car, the circulation of water and electricity in the home, and domestic appliances.

These ideas are developed in their 1987 book and the concept of a learning-centred approach is outlined. This involves considering the process of learning and student motivation very fully and working out exactly what is needed to enable students to reach the end target. Thus, even though students may only need to *read* textbooks and articles in their field, it may be that oral practice will help them reach that end. Similarly, in reading a passage it may help students understand the text if the teacher reads it aloud to them while they follow. Listening to a text being read aloud is unlikely to be a skill that is required during their academic studies, but the process of following a text being read aloud clearly by a native speaker often helps students understand what are the main and what are the subsidiary ideas, and make the links between them (St John, 1989).

Another aspect of a learning-centred approach is that learners will have developed certain learning skills from their academic study, or experience at work, and these skills can be exploited in the ESP classroom. Johns and Davies (1983) take this idea a stage further: in arguing for an approach based on the text as 'a vehicle for information' rather than as 'a linguistic object', and on a topic-type analysis of text (for a fuller discussion of this approach, see chapter 6), they suggest a methodology that is based on group work in which learners 'puzzle out the meaning of the text' (Johns and Davies, 1983: 1). This problem-solving approach reflects the real situation where students will be reading on their own and trying to work out the meaning of a text; it is characteristic of 'real life'.

The learning-centred approach also takes into account the fact that different students learn in different ways. The emphasis on pair or group work and problem solving allows for these differences.

We will now look at part of a unit (E2.4 pp. 241–3) from the textbook *Interface* (Hutchinson and Waters, 1984) in which many of their ideas are put into practice. As the authors (1987: 112–3) explain in discussing another extract from the same textbook, the *starter* provides 'a context for the comprehension of the *input*', which enables students to feel their way into the topics or 'carrier content' of the unit and raises interest. In the rest of the extract, the comprehension questions encourage students to think for themselves and to draw on their knowledge of the subject and of the world in general. This section is concluded in step 4 by a task that pulls together topic and language, and involves the student in converting written information into a visual representation.

We have not included the whole section, but we will mention briefly the *Task* that rounds it off. Hutchinson and Waters (1987: 117) explain that the task 'provides a clear objective for the learners and so helps to break up the often bewildering mass of the syllabus *by establishing landmarks of achievement*' (emphasis added).

Reflection 2b

Look at extracts from published materials or your own in-house materials. Decide to which of the various trends or movements in ESP they belong. For courses taught in your organisation or your country, which trends currently have most impact?

2.4 Authenticity of text and authenticity of purpose

One issue that caused a good deal of controversy in the development of ESP was the question of whether texts used for reading, listening and writing exercises should be authentic or not. The exact meaning of authenticity has often been unclear. Many have used it with reference to unsimplified or 'genuine' texts that were used in ESP materials but were originally written for purposes other than language teaching. Others have recognised that genuineness of the text does not guarantee relevance and that a text is only truly authentic if it is exploited in ways that reflect real world use. In other words, authenticity of purpose is as important as genuineness of text.

In all the textbooks we have described, ideas for the texts were taken from academic contexts but the texts were either simplified or, as in the *Focus* or *Nucleus* series, specially written. Others (for example Phillips and Shettlesworth, 1978) argued that students need to be exposed to authentic texts and develop strategies for reading long, complex and unsimplified texts if they are to be able to develop independence in their study skills. They also suggested that texts simplified or specially written by ESP teachers may in fact be misleading models of text for students, as the ESP teacher may misconstrue the carrier content or write in unnatural and inappropriate language. In contrast, Hutchinson and Waters (1987) argued that it is more important to ensure that the activities based on the text reflect the learning process than to use genuine texts from the target situation.

A key aspect of authenticity is the level of the text exploited in the ESP class. An unsimplified text on a science topic designed for school pupils just beginning to study science is a genuine text, but is not an authentic text for university level students, as these students will not be able to use it to confirm or extend their knowledge of the topic they are studying on their course. A key question is whether the activities based on the text reflect the ways in which the text would actually be used by students in their course work. Exercises that ask students to answer comprehension questions by finding relevant sentences in the text are not authentic, but those that ask students to use information from the text in a task or problem-solving activity are.

Authenticity thus lies in the nature of the interaction between the reader (or hearer) and the text (Widdowson, 1978, 1983). Part of the process of needs analysis (see chapter 7) is finding out exactly how learners use different sources so that activities in the ESP class can reflect what happens in real life.

2.5 Trends in English for Occupational Purposes

The influences described under trends in EAP were also present in the EOP courses of the late 1960s and early 1970s. Courses were at that time largely concerned with written language.

The early commercial correspondence courses taught standard letter formats for business transactions ranging from *general complaints* and *requests for information* to specifics such as *import/export arrangements*. The underlying construct (the product approach) involved model letters to copy, specialised vocabulary and the standard, formal clichéd phrases of the time. The emphasis on specialised vocabulary was also seen in other materials where texts, including dialogues, were accompanied by glossaries of difficult terms and a few comprehension questions. The approach was definitely based on the linguistic system rather than the use of the language.

Rightly or wrongly, the assumption at this stage was that learners had a good grasp of language forms, after four or five years of school English classes, so that what was needed were words and expressions that occurred in work situations. An interesting point is that these texts were usually genuine. The debate as to whether materials should be simplified, simple versions or genuine seems to have been confined to EAP, EST and the academic world.

From the mid-1970s into the 1980s the focus switched more and more to spoken interactions based first on a grammatical, and then gradually a more functional, construct. Materials were based on functions such as Greetings, Making Introductions, Making Arrangements, Agreeing and Disagreeing. Formulaic language and gambits were taught and practised in dialogues and role plays.

Many of these materials were designed for use with commerce, secretarial and business students. One landmark in the development of Business English materials was *The Bellcrest File*, a video-based course book published in 1972. This marked the beginning of approaches which gave more attention to the four skills, albeit within the existing construct of grammatical syllabuses. The assumption was still that learners had a grounding in the grammar but there was writing and reading practice, together with plenty of drills and role simulations.

The first set of materials to adopt the business studies approach of case studies was published in this period. *Agenda* (Cotton and Owen, 1980) comprised cases for discussion with a separate workbook and cassette to provide language practice.

These materials assumed little knowledge and no practical experience. Gradually an understanding of the different needs of learners with job-experience led to new materials; from the mid-1980s there are materials based on business communication situations such as meetings and telephone conversations. A new video course, *Visitron: the Language of Presentations* (Howe, 1984) practised the language of presentations but did not exploit features such as body language (whereas a more recent publication, *Effective Presentations* [Comfort and Utley, 1995], has a unit called Body Language).

The most extensive coverage of business communication situations was through the *Longman Business English Skills Series* (Ellis, O'Driscoll and Pilbeam, Eds.). Beginning in 1987, books on socialising, telephoning, meetings and discussions, and presenting facts and figures were published, followed in the 1990s by others on topics such as exchanging information and negotiating. They follow a similar format, giving practice in listening to and completing exchanges, noting the kind of information given and matching it with language expressions; in the later books there is some treatment of formality and informality in these expressions. As students are asked to identify the purpose or type of contribution, they can begin to see recurrent patterns of information.

As the early books in this series illustrate, up to the mid-1980s attention was primarily on language and the teaching of language. Then the focus began to shift and the perspective broadened to adopt tenets of the business world, and this is still continuing. The interface between language and behavioural skills is being explored, with more courses paying attention to at least the basic skills, and management training approaches and methods are being integrated with language training techniques (see GEC Management College case study 1 in chapter 8).

There is a more general recognition that language teaching needs to take on board the business context within which communication takes place. In the more closely linked business world that has resulted from developments in technology such as telecommunications, computer networking, e-mail and video conferencing, it is vital for people to communicate effectively across borders and to bridge cultural gaps. Cross-cultural communication requires awareness and sensitivity to the diversity of values and customs around the world.

2.6 ESP now

Orientation 2c

What are the trends and developments in ESP nowadays?

There is currently no dominating movement in ESP as there was with Register Analysis, Discourse and Rhetorical Analysis, Skills-Based Approaches and the Learning-Centred Approach. As in other branches of ELT and many other human activities, there is now acceptance of many different approaches and a willingness to mix different types of material and methodologies. If there is less of the missionary zeal of the early practitioners, there is wide agreement that ESP has a role in ELT and that it is a movement which, while remaining firmly within the ELT/Applied Linguistics discipline, has its own particular characteristics. It is now also taught by many non-native speakers who are able to make use of their knowledge of the institution in which they are working and of students' learning styles and preferences.

Materials production and text analysis, of both written and spoken discourse, still predominate in ESP. Analysis of spoken and written texts, especially under the influence of Swales' *Genre Analysis* (1990), has assumed an important position in ESP. We will look at genre analysis in chapter 5; at this stage we will restrict ourselves to saying that it is an extremely useful tool of analysis that is of relevance to EAP, Business English and the other smaller branches of ESP such as Legal English. We believe, however, that it would be wrong to think of genre analysis as a *new movement* in ESP.

One area that has come back into something of a prominent position is Register Analysis, the analysis of grammatical features of specific texts in the way started by Barber. With the advent of computer-based corpora and the development of the ideas of genre analysis, it is possible to relate the quantitative data that emerge from computer analysis, especially from the use of concordancing programs (Johns, 1989; Flowerdew, 1995), to discoursal features of text. This renders the findings of Register Analysis much more meaningful. The work of Biber (1988) has been influential in this regard.

We show in this book that ESP is capable of drawing on disciplines outside Applied Linguistics; others, notably Swales in his final editorial as editor of the journal *English for Specific Purposes* (1994, 13:3) and Mauranen (1993), also suggest that ESP needs to be sensitive to movements in ELT and Applied Linguistics, such as the World Englishes movement and analysis of different national styles of rhetoric.

One major change has been the emergence of Business English as a major strand of ESP teaching. Early ESP work was dominated by English for Science and Technology and it has often been remarked that Swales' *Episodes in ESP* is essentially a history of EST. However, in the 1990s, as Dudley-Evans and St John (1996) note, the largest area of growth is Business English. And with the increasing numbers of international students taking Masters courses in Business, Finance, Accounting and Banking, the area of academic Business English is beginning to assume much greater importance in EAP.

ESP has tended to be associated with countries in the Middle East and Latin America; the growth of EBP has coincided with the growth in the economies of countries in South East Asia and the Pacific Rim. This geographical area, which has often been unjustly neglected in surveys of ESP (Tickoo, 1988, is a notable exception), is already becoming much more important in ESP work. Eastern Europe is also growing in importance, especially in the area of Business English.

There is thus growing diversity in ESP teaching with interesting variation between, on the one hand, the EAP situations in English-medium institutions and those institutions where English plays a subsidiary role to the national language, and, on the other, between approaches to EAP and to Business English. All seem happy to be considered as part of ESP, but the constraints of the very different situations lead inevitably to different types of material and methodologies.

Task 2d ●◆

We present below two controversial statements about ESP. What are the arguments in favour of and against these statements?

1. The increased specialism of ESP means that ESP teachers should also specialise. If they are teaching EAP, they should concentrate on one or two subject areas. If they are teaching Business English, they should concentrate on certain sectors, such as banking.

2. The increased specialism of ESP means that small EAP units should be attached to the individual academic departments that they serve. These small units would then replace the large ESP centres that serve a whole institution.

2.7 Summary

We have shown in this chapter that ESP has generally been concerned with procedures and practical outcomes. It has been in the vanguard of the developments in ELT, moving from grammatical, functional and notional syllabuses to a more eclectic and task-based approach. EST was the dominant movement for many years, but ESP today is a much broader activity in which English for Business Purposes (EBP) has become increasingly important. There is an impressive amount of research, particularly into the target events of the academic world, and this is becoming increasingly interdisciplinary.

2.8 Recommended reading

The following books are all relevant to the study of the development of ESP. Swales' (1988) book is designed as a history; Hutchinson and

Waters' (1987) has a good description of the various approaches to ESP; Mackay and Mountford (1978) contains descriptions of course development that expand points made in our chapter. The textbooks, Ewer and Latorre (1969), Allen and Widdowson Eds. (1974), Bates and Dudley-Evans Eds. (1976) are examples of earlier approaches to ESP.

3 English for Academic Purposes

3.1 Aims

English for Academic Purposes (EAP) refers to any English teaching that relates to a study purpose. Students whose first language is not English may need help with both the language of academic disciplines and the specific 'study skills' required of them during their academic course. The study skills may involve any of the main skills (see chapter 6) depending on the context. It is very important to be aware of how, as the study situation changes, the emphasis on different skills also needs to change. The key aspect here is the extent to which either English or the national language is used as the medium of instruction for subject courses.

EAP has sometimes been seen as one movement within ESP; we shall suggest that there are four different types of situation and that teachers need to look very carefully at accounts of courses and materials before deciding whether they are relevant to their own situation. We will also look in detail at ways in which the language teacher can take the initiative in developing cooperation with departments.

3.2 Four types of EAP situation

The key determinant of what an EAP course should contain is whether or not the subject course is taught in English. In this regard there are four types of situation, exemplified here using tertiary level institutions. Some features may also apply to the teaching of English at secondary school level, where, particularly in the senior, immediately pre-university classes, English courses will have EAP components. We will, however, focus here on the tertiary level. Teachers need to think carefully about whether the success claimed for one kind of situation will transfer to another. For example, materials teaching note-taking from lectures on a pre-sessional course in a British university are unlikely to be relevant to teaching note-making for reading in an English as a Foreign Language (EFL) situation.

As illustrated in table 3.1, the four types of situation are:

1. An English-speaking country, such as UK or USA.
2. An English-as-a-Second-Language (ESL) situation where English is the official language of education and is widely spoken, as in former British colonies in Africa or South East Asia. (We are using ESL in the specific British sense referring to this kind of situation, as opposed to the more general American use of the term, which applies to all EFL/ESL teaching.)
3. A situation in which certain subjects, such as medicine, engineering or science, are officially taught in English, while for other subjects and at other levels of education the national language is used.
4. A situation where all subject courses are taught in the national language, but English may be important for ancillary reasons.

We will look at each of these in turn.

Table 3.1 *Situations in which ESP is taught*

Situation 1 e.g. UK, USA, Australia	Students come from another country to study in a foreign system; for them both general and academic culture may be different; everything around them operates in English.
Situation 2 e.g. Zimbabwe	Education at all levels has been mainly in English; the Civil Service uses English, but people mostly use their first language (L1) in everyday life.
Situation 3 e.g. Jordan	In tertiary education some subjects are taught in L1, but others, such as medicine, engineering and science, are taught in English.
Situation 4 e.g. Brazil	All tertiary education is taught in the L1; English is an auxiliary language.

Orientation 3a

Look at table 3.1 and consider how the needs of students, on entry to tertiary education in the four situations, differ. Take into account the students' likely level of English, the different skills they need in English and the communicative events they need English for.

3.2.1 EAP in an English-speaking country

It has long been a tradition that universities in English-speaking countries accept large numbers of international students, and they have generally set up English Language Units charged with the responsibility of helping such students reach their full academic potential. Teaching is done both on pre-sessional and in-sessional courses. The pre-sessional courses generally run for between 4 and 12 weeks prior to the beginning of the academic year and focus on both academic language and the 'study skills' related to all the main skills. The courses aim to prepare students for the studies they are about to embark upon. The focus is therefore on common-core academic language and skills; some more specific work is usually included, but cannot be very extensive as the pre-sessional is a pre-study course. In-sessional work, however, runs in parallel with the subject courses and therefore provides the opportunity for integrated subject-language teaching and more specific work on the key skills of academic listening, writing and reading, as well as more 'common-core' EAP courses.

As this work emanates from university settings, it has been widely written about and has generated much interesting applied research. In Britain, for example, the work of such units has become widely known and influential through a number of publications under the auspices of the British Association of Lecturers in EAP (BALEAP) describing the needs of international students and courses designed to meet those needs (for example Robinson, 1988; Brookes and Grundy, 1988; Adams *et al.*, 1991; Blue, 1993; Hewings and Dudley-Evans, 1996).

Task 3b ●◆

Imagine two students, one doing a Masters course in Business Administration (MBA), the other doing a PhD research degree in a science subject. Both students are from a non-English medium country in South East Asia, such as Taiwan or Thailand. What do you predict to be the main components each one needs on a four week pre-sessional course? Draw up two lists.

3.2.2 EAP in ESL situations

An increasing amount of EAP work is being done in Anglophone countries in Africa such as Zimbabwe, Nigeria and the new South Africa (not strictly Anglophone but using English for much tertiary education), and in South-East Asian countries, such as Singapore, Philippines and, to some extent, Malaysia. In these countries (with the exception of Malaysia) English is used throughout the education system, in most cases from the primary school level, in others from the secondary level. The language level may, in fact, be quite high, but it has been found that many students in these situations need help with adjusting to the demands made of them when they begin an undergraduate course. This is particularly the case with students from rural areas who may well have had rather less exposure to English and may have been less well taught at school level.

Students' needs are in the area of study skills and in adjusting to the abstract nature of the language of theory or model building (Bazerman, 1988; Mason, 1990; Henderson and Hewings, 1990) which they may be encountering on a large scale for the first time at the beginning of an academic course. Their English tuition up to tertiary level will generally have been in the area of General English, and is unlikely to have included specific preparation for study at university level, or for the specific tasks carried out in English in a work or business context. In many of these countries there has also been a tradition of study of literary aspects of English, which is unlikely to prepare learners effectively for studying a non-literary subject in English at tertiary level.

It has often been remarked that the needs of such students span the needs of non-native speakers following an English-medium course and those of native speakers in need of developing communication skills. The most successful communication skills courses in ESL countries make use of a combination of ideas from the EAP tradition and the communication skills for native speakers tradition (see for example Williams *et al.*, 1984).

There have, nonetheless, been different focuses in such courses. Some, as for example in Nigeria or Kenya, have concentrated on developing 'common-core' study skills courses for students from a mixture of disciplines, focusing particularly on reading and writing skills (Chukwuma *et al.*, 1991; Monsi *et al.*, 1995; Obah, 1993). It is often difficult to find material and activities of a common-core nature that are sufficiently challenging and motivating for students with the relatively high language level that we have already noted. The work reported from the University of Zimbabwe (Mparutsa *et al.*, 1991) and the University of Witwatersrand in South Africa (Starfield, 1994) would suggest that more specific and subject-related courses have been more successful in motivating students and really meeting their needs. Love's work on geology (1991 and 1993) and Mparutsa's work on economics (Mparutsa *et al.*, 1991) are particularly interesting in this regard; they show that introducing first year students to the basic underlying content schemata of the subjects and the formal schemata (Carrell, 1983) of the writing tasks expected of students is effective in both motivating these students and bringing about improvement in their performance in subject courses.

In other situations, notably in South East Asia, the focus of EAP/ Communication Skills courses has been much more on preparing students for the communication tasks that they will have to carry out in work situations once they have finished their academic course. A course at Nanyang Technological Institute, Singapore, identifies the following three key objectives, which are based on the recommendations and advice of professional bodies and consultants (Cheung and Wong, 1988: 93):

1. to communicate technical and business information effectively in the work and academic setting in several modes: written, oral, audio-visual and graphic;
2. to adapt material prepared in one form for presentation in another, for example to adapt a written business proposal for a boardroom presentation;
3. to communicate effectively with specialist and non-specialist audiences in job-related tasks, for example writing memos and letters, chairing meetings, and interviewing or being interviewed.

The classes designed for such situations will largely be in-sessional and included as part of the general timetable. Various reports (for example Johns, 1981; Makina-Kaunda, 1995) point to the danger of the English class being allocated the worst timetable slots, such as Friday afternoon or its equivalent. In courses built on a credit system it is essential that the English course carries credit. If it does not, or if the English class always takes place at a bad time of the day, it will not have status in the eyes of students and motivation will fall.

3.2.3 EAP situations in which certain subjects are taught in English

In many countries, notably in the Middle East, English is used as the medium of instruction for certain subjects, particularly medicine, engineering and some science subjects. What distinguishes these situations from those in the African and South-East Asian countries described above is that there is no particular or general tradition of English-medium education in the country, and the school system mostly uses the national language to teach all subjects. Thus students have to make the adjustment from studying all subjects in their national language at school level to studying subjects such as science, medicine and engineering in English at tertiary level. This has led some countries to include some EAP work in the English curriculum at upper secondary school level (see for example a description of the use of an ESP textbook in Egyptian secondary schools [Dudley-Evans, 1987a]).

Students begin the courses with a much lower level of English than in the ESL situations described in the previous section. This lower level often leads to a situation where subject lecturers, most of whom are themselves non-native speakers of English, may deliver lectures in a mixture of English and the national language. This may involve delivering the lecture in, say, Arabic, but dictating notes in English. Examinations and assignments will be written in English, but are sometimes designed so that they do not make large linguistic demands on students. Full essays or technical reports may not be required, and students will be tested through multiple choice questions, calculations, diagrams and short-note answers (Douglas, 1977; Swales, 1980). In other situations, for example the Jordanian University of Science and Technology (JUST), students are required to write term papers in English, but lecturers may not pay very much attention to linguistic errors and weaknesses of presentation (Mustafa, 1995).

The crucial thing then is to find out how English is really used. This may, of course, be quite difficult as the question of whether the course is truly English medium may be an extremely sensitive one. Graves (1975) talked of a difference between the *formal* and *informal* orders. The formal order is the official view of how the course runs and how students succeed or fail within the system. The informal order is 'the same institution as perceived and operated by its members' (Graves, 1975).

Swales (1980) describes how the formal order of a particular course stipulated that 50 per cent of the mark was assigned to a written report and 50 per cent to a map. After three years of poor attendance at the English class, Swales found out that the informal order was to allocate 90 per cent of the marks to the map. He discussed the issue with the department and a new 'practicable formal order' was set up where the amount of writing was increased and the language teacher became involved in overseeing drafts of the report.

3.2.4 EAP situations where subject courses are taught in the national language

Our final situation is where the subject courses are taught in the national language but English is included on the timetable. In many situations, for example in Latin America, countries in South East Asia such as Thailand and Indonesia, in mainland Western Europe, Eastern Europe and Scandinavia, the medium of instruction is normally the national language.

In South America, EAP has often been referred to as Technical English (Ingles Instrumental), and the courses have focused almost exclusively on reading. In Chile and Colombia, university-specific projects led to the writing of materials that were published and became available internationally (Ewer and Latorre, 1969; *Reading and Thinking in English*, 1980); in Brazil the focus is much more on developing a framework for materials and on teacher training, but allowing individual institutions to write their materials within the overall framework (Alderson and Scott, 1992; Celani *et al.*, 1988). The materials focus on key micro-skills related to the overall macro-skill of reading, but also teach certain lexical and grammatical items relevant to the comprehension of undergraduate academic reading texts.

The actual methodology used to teach this material is also fascinating: the classes are taught in Portuguese and this enables the teacher to lead some very detailed discussions about the linguistic features of the text and the techniques of deducing meaning from a text in a foreign language. In some respects, the classes resemble a problem-solving class in applied discourse analysis with teacher and students analysing in great detail the workings of an English text (Alderson and Scott, 1992; Scott, 1981a and 1981b).

The commitment of the teachers and their involvement in the writing of materials lead to high motivation on the part of both teachers and students. There are, however, many reports in the literature (Hutchinson and Waters, 1987; Bates, 1978) which suggest that such mono-skill courses are often rather less motivating, and in Brazil, too, there are moves to introduce more variety.

The motivation problem is in a sense similar to that in the third type of situation – it can be very difficult to decide what students' real needs are. In theory, students need to focus on the reading skill; in practice, the reading of English textbooks or articles may be little more than an optional extra and students may be more motivated by materials that focus on other skills, or on *delayed* needs rather than supposed *immediate* needs. By delayed needs we are referring to needs that arise either in the final year (for example project work) or to communication needs in future work.

The classes are again generally in-sessional, and the same issues of status and motivation highlighted in the descriptions of the two previous situations – ESL and English-medium situations – apply. A further particular problem of all these situations is that English is often taught only in the first year of the academic course. We have found that there is a case for delayed or additional teaching of English in the final years. While teachers on training courses readily accept this idea, very few (if any) reports exist in the EAP literature of experiments on the timing of the English course. This mismatch between the institutions' perception of students' need and their true needs and 'wants' (Hutchinson and Waters, 1987) often results in a lack of student motivation and the consequent disillusionment of teachers, as well as being a waste of resources. Swales (1984) points to a loss of confidence in English Language Centres that concentrate exclusively on first year support work and suggests the expansion of their role to the teaching of 'research English' to postgraduates and young academic staff.

Reflection 3c

We began this section by warning that what works in one situation may not work in another. Which of the four situations do you have experience of? What examples of this 'non-transferability' have you come across?

3.3 English for General Academic Purposes (EGAP) and English for Specific Academic Purposes (ESAP)

An awareness of the distinction between English for General Academic Purposes (EGAP) and English for Specific Academic Purposes (ESAP) is crucial to a full understanding of EAP (Blue, 1988a). EGAP refers to the teaching of the skills and language that are common to all disciplines; ESAP refers to the teaching of the features that distinguish one discipline from others.

English for General Academic Purposes isolates the skills associated with study activities such as listening to lectures; participating in supervisions, seminars and tutorials; carrying out practicals (largely in science or engineering courses); reading textbooks, articles and other reading material; and writing essays, examination answers, dissertations and reports (Blue, 1993). There are particular skills associated with each of these, so that, to take one example, reading almost any textbook involves understanding the main ideas, distinguishing the main ideas and the supporting detail, making notes on the main ideas, evaluating the writer's point of view, and, where necessary, skimming to understand the gist of the argument or scanning to find specific information. Another example is writing essays, reports and dissertations, which will involve the forming of accurate sentences, the coherent structuring of the ideas and adopting the appropriate stance for citing previous work on the topic.

English for Specific Academic Purposes integrates the skills work of EGAP with help for students in their actual subject tasks. It adopts a developmental role (Turner, 1996) by showing how students can transfer the skills they have learnt in the EGAP classes to the understanding of their actual lectures or reading texts, or in writing the essays and reports required of them by the department. This kind of work generally involves some cooperation with the actual subject department. Such contacts with the department and the possibilities for research into disciplinary communication often raise the status of the EAP lecturers in the eyes of subject departments.

Widdowson (1983) relates the specificity of an ESP class to a dichotomy he sets up between *training* and *education*. Training involves the development of certain skills and familiarity with specific schemata while education aims to develop a general capacity or set of procedures to cope with a wide range of needs. Widdowson sees ESAP courses as more concerned with training and EGAP courses with education. We disagree with Widdowson on this point: while we accept that certain narrow-angle EAP courses focus on specific skills and schemata, and are logically classified as training, most ESAP courses are as much concerned with education and developing learners' capacity as EGAP courses. The difference is that ESAP courses focus on the actual tasks that students have to carry out while EGAP courses select more general contexts.

Some writers on EAP, for example Hutchinson and Waters (1987), have argued against subject-specific work. Blue (1988a) argued that EAP teachers should concentrate on EGAP and that students will learn ESAP through individualised project work. While this may be true on a pre-sessional course, in all the other situations we feel that students need and welcome a two-pronged attack on their needs and difficulties. This benefits both motivation and the transfer of skills and language learnt in the EGAP courses. The common-core EAP work makes more sense and is more relevant if it is supplemented by specific work. In Colombia, in the mid-1980s, staff teaching the *Reading and Thinking* series had to respond to student wants by supplementing the common-core course with specific work.

3.4 Engaging with the disciplines

For subject-specific work we suggest there are three levels of cooperation: *Cooperation, Collaboration* and *Team-Teaching*.

3.4.1 Cooperation

Cooperation is the first stage and involves the language teacher taking the initiative in asking questions and gathering information about the students' subject course, how English fits into their course and what the department and students see as priorities. This is part of the Target Situation Analysis required for needs analysis (see chapter 7). Some of this can be related to the investigation of what Hutchinson and Waters (1987) refer to as students' wants; it also relates to establishing what the expectations of the department are and, as far as possible, balancing these expectations with students' wants. This process is very important as there are clear dangers in ESP teachers operating without much consultation with the departments that students are studying in.

Yet cooperation is much more than this; it means finding out about the conceptual and discoursal framework of the subjects students are studying and occasionally introducing material that provides a slightly different perspective on that content (see discussion of Crofts' work p. 10). Cooperation is encouraged by the language teacher taking an interest in other aspects of the courses that students are following. We are not suggesting that the ESP/EAP teacher *has* to do this, rather that the dangers of ESP/EAP teaching becoming a 'dry affair' are reduced when the teacher has an interest in and enthusiasm for the discipline that students are following.

This interest and enthusiasm may also lead to a more systematic attempt to find out about how a discipline works through analysis of key texts in the discipline. An example is provided by research carried out by Love (1991 and 1993). As a result of extensive discussion with colleagues in the Geology department and research into the discourse of the main first year textbook used in the department (Read and Watson's *Introduction to Geology* [1968]), she found that there is a 'discourse cycle' which encapsulates the basic underlying principle of the discipline as taught in the first year of the undergraduate programme, that principle being the key relationship in geology between geological product (present features) and geological process (past processes). The discourse cycle is (Love, 1991: 92):

$$\begin{array}{ccc} & \text{are evidence for} & \\ \text{present geological features} & & \text{past geological processes} \\ & \text{are produced by} & \end{array}$$

This research has arisen from a healthy curiosity about the discipline, fuelled by discussions with lecturers in the Geology department at the University of Zimbabwe, which in turn have set the agenda for a small-scale research project. ESP/EAP needs a lot more research of this nature.

3.4.2 Collaboration

If cooperation largely involves the language teacher taking the initiative and finding out what happens in the subject department, collaboration involves the more direct working together of the two sides, language and subject, to prepare students for particular tasks or courses. In collaboration the language and subject teacher work together outside the classroom. The collaboration has clear goals but also defined limits. There are three options for collaborative work:

1. The planning of a series of classes where the language class prepares the students for a subsequent subject class taught in English.

2. The running of a class on a specific skill or related to a specific task where the subject department has a specific input to the materials or the language teacher uses material produced by the department.

3. The North American 'adjunct' model, in which the adjunct acts as a back-up class to the subject, helping students with difficulties with that class.

A good example of the first option was the collaborative economics-and-language course run for Iranian students of Finance at the University of Birmingham in the 1970s (Henderson and Skehan, 1980). The language level of the students was low and a major aim of the course was to move students from a dependence on rote learning towards developing critical thinking and a more questioning approach to learning. The economics lectures were based on a 20-minute tape accompanied by a set of 15 to 18 slides. Although the content and organisation of the course were appropriate for the students, the language was too difficult. A simplified version of the script was therefore written by the language teacher working with the subject teacher and recorded for use in the economics class.

All the language material was designed to prepare for the tape/slide presentation run by the economics teacher and its aims were thus subordinate to the aims of the economics class. Other English classes running in parallel with this course presented a more systematic approach to the teaching of relevant skills and language. Henderson and Skehan (1980) conclude that the course was successful because the collaboration resulted in a set of materials that were at the right linguistic level for the students, but also had validity from the subject point of view. They also recommend what they refer to as a 'phased approach to team-teaching', a point that we will take up later in this section (pp. 47–48).

An example of the second option is a reading programme run for first-year Biology students in Colombia in the 1980s. The subject courses were taught in Spanish, but an English reading course was a compulsory part of the overall course. The material for the reading course was selected by a biology teacher who was collaborating with the language teacher. The material was carefully selected to run parallel with the subject course; it revised the content but also introduced ideas or examples that were not taught in the subject course. A key aspect of the integration was that students would be rewarded in the subject examinations (written in Spanish) for any points or examples taken from the English reading material.

If, in the first option, the objectives of the English class are subordinated to those of the subject course, in this example of option two there is a complementarity between the objectives of the English course and those of the subject course. There is a true integration between the EAP class and the subject class which has a positive effect on student motivation.

The third option is a rather different model for subject-language integration which has been developed in North America (Snow and Brinton, 1988; Shih, 1986). The adjunct classes run parallel with the subject course and students register for the adjunct class at the same time as they register for the subject course. The adjunct classes focus on the difficulties that students are facing in following the lectures, reading the prescribed texts or writing the assignments set. The courses tend to be attended by non-native speakers, but can be attended by native speakers. Subject teachers do not attend the adjunct class and merely have to agree that students can register for the adjunct class related to their subject course; naturally many contribute rather more than this.

3.4.3 Team-teaching

The final level of subject-language integration is the actual working together in the classroom of the subject and language specialists, usually referred to as team-teaching. Much has been written about this aspect of EAP teaching, particularly the work at Birmingham University (Johns and Dudley-Evans, 1980; Dudley-Evans and Johns, 1981). The Birmingham work has been in two main departments, Highway Engineering (originally Transportation) and Plant Biology, and has focused on two main skills: listening comprehension and academic writing; the format of the team-taught sessions is similar.

The work on listening comprehension involves the recording of a subject lecture and the setting up of a follow-up tutorial run by both the language and the subject lecturer who actually gave the lecture. The procedure is as follows:

Stage 1: The language lecturer records the subject lecture.
At the beginning of term a timetable for recording is worked out so that most lecturers teaching on the course are included and know when they are due to be recorded.

Stage 2: The language lecturer listens to the recording and prepares a handout with comprehension questions on key points of the lecture and a check on understanding of the language used in it.
The focus is on checking that students are taking effective notes on the content and can understand the technical and semi-technical vocabulary used in the lecture.

Stage 3: The language lecturer checks the questions with the subject lecturer.
In the early stages of the team-teaching project it was vital to establish good relations between the two teachers through this stage.

Stage 4: The session itself.
The session generally caters for 8 to 12 students considered to need special help with English. The handout prepared in stage 2 forms the basis of the session and the language teacher takes the lead in asking the questions, with the subject lecturer commenting on the answers and generally acting as an adviser. Students bring their lecture notes and use these to answer the questions; a main aim is to show students whether their notes have been effective in capturing the main points of the lecture. Clearly the session provides a detailed follow-up to the lecture that has been recorded, but the objective is to 'empower' students to understand and take notes on *all* lectures. By seeing where their notes have been inadequate and becoming aware of which points the lecturer was expecting them to have grasped, students are able to adjust their listening and note-taking practices. There is also an element of learning to listen to *lecturers* as opposed to *lectures*; the student indirectly learns something of the expectations of each lecturer and something of the individual style that each lecturer adopts. The session is run by the language teacher with the subject lecturer acting as an adviser, but gradually, as the focus of the session moves away from the actual questions on the handout to more general queries and questions, the subject lecturer may play a more prominent role.

The team-taught sessions on writing have generally focused on the writing of examination answers. The subject lecturer chooses a relevant question, and the language teacher manages the discussion about the meaning of the question and the planning of the answer. The subject lecturer again acts as a kind of adviser commenting on the students' suggestions about the meaning of the question and the plan. The session often ends with students writing part of the answer and both lecturers providing feedback.

The early team-teaching work described in Johns and Dudley-Evans (1980) concentrated almost entirely on lectures and examination answers. Subsequently, the work diversified to include work on research project outlines, the writing of titles (Dudley-Evans, 1984), dissertations and essays (Dudley-Evans, 1995). We believe that there are three reasons why this work has been successful and lasted for more than ten years:

1. As far as possible the roles of the two teachers have been clearly defined.
2. The programme makes relatively few demands on the time of an individual subject lecturer.
3. There is a mutual respect between the two teachers and an acceptance of the other's professionalism in his or her area of specialisation.

It is not uncommon for language and subject teachers to be rather suspicious of each other, sometimes even highly critical. Clearly where there is suspicion or hostility, collaboration or team-teaching is unlikely to be successful. For example, if the language teacher feels, as some do, that the main difficulty for non-native speakers in tackling a discipline is that subject lecturers cannot write well or communicate effectively, that language teacher will almost certainly have difficulty in establishing the necessary rapport with the subject teacher. Similarly, if the subject teacher secretly feels that the language teacher should not 'meddle' in subject matters or does not really know much about the way that communication takes place in disciplines, he or she is unlikely to have the openness and flexibility required for collaboration.

3.4.4 *From cooperation and collaboration to team-teaching*

1. Begin with *cooperation*. Get in touch with the department. Get hold of the syllabus for the different courses. Find subject teachers who are interested in language and the discourse of their discipline; those who have studied in an English-medium country often have this interest. Take into account Selinker's (1979) suggestions about the qualities of a good specialist informant. The key qualities are an interest in and a sensitivity to language issues.
2. Discuss with these subject teachers points about their courses and the way they use language. Ask for advice on texts which could be used to supplement texts in the discipline. Move on to ask specific questions about texts and seek comments on your analysis of these texts.
3. Where this cooperation is working well, extend to *collaboration* and then to *team-teaching*. Seek to obtain the support of the Head of

Department for this work; if s/he is supportive, it is more likely that individual members will be cooperative.

Task 3d ●◆

a) Consider the applicability of the three types of cooperation to each of the four EAP situations described in the first part of this chapter. How feasible is each type in each situation? Complete the following table by inserting *very feasible, possible* and *unsuitable.*

b) For a course you teach (have taught), consider the feasibility of some type of cooperation: Who would you talk to? What would students' attitudes be?

	Situation 1	Situation 2	Situation 3	Situation 4
Cooperation				
Collaboration				
Team-teaching				

3.5 Professional disciplines: EAP or EOP?

As we noted in chapter 1, EAP has often been divided into different specialisms. The most important of these has been English for Science and Technology (EST), but English for Medical Purposes (EMP), English for Legal Purposes (ELP) and English for Economics are all course types which teaching materials have been prepared for. The rapid growth in tertiary level courses on Business Management, Finance and Accounting, and Administration means that courses have been set up for these disciplines.

What is problematic about these categories is that they seem to fall between two points: on the one hand, the focus on 'common-core' EAP and, on the other, the concentration on the particular features of a specific discipline that we have emphasised in the previous section on cooperation. Do the very disparate disciplines in Science and Technology such as Geology, Biology, Mechanical Engineering, Highway Engineering have features in common that distinguish them *as a set of disciplines* from courses in the Social Sciences and Humanities? Do even the various branches of Engineering – Civil, Chemical, Mechanical, Electrical and Electronic – have that much in common with each other? When we discuss a more specialist branch of ESP, such as Medical

English, it is not always clear whether we are talking about the needs of medical students (EAP), or practising doctors, or consultants in hospitals (EOP); each one of these groups needs awareness of and an ability to use different genres.

Medical students, for example, have to read textbooks and articles, and write essays and short clinical reports. These are EAP needs. Practising doctors have different needs; as well as reading specialist articles, they may prepare papers and slide presentations for conferences and, if working in an English speaking-country, interact with patients in English. These are EOP needs. Similarly, nurses have EAP needs while following the academic part of their course and EOP needs when on the ward.

So the terms English for Science and Technology (EST), English for Medical Purposes (EMP), English for Legal Purposes (ELP) and all the others may be little more than useful umbrella terms derived from teaching situations and the writing of teaching materials. There is, though, some valuable research related to how professionals in these areas communicate:

Medical English for *academic* purposes is often conflated with English for Science and Technology. Malcolm (1987), for example, in discussing tense usage in EST uses 20 experimental reports from the *Journal of Paediatrics* and makes the (unstated) assumption that the findings apply to the whole of EST. Pettinari (1982) refers to Medical English as one type of EST, but suggests that the influence on the discourse of social structure and cultural tradition is greater than in other types of EST.

In *medical English* for *occupational* purposes, there are three main areas of research: the use of English in written medical communication, the delivery of papers and slide presentations in English at international medical conferences, and the role of English in doctor/patient interaction. The importance of English in the dissemination of medical research has grown dramatically since the 1960s; Maher (1986) shows that by 1980, 72 per cent of the articles listed in the *Index Medicus* (the index of articles published in medical journals all over the world) were published in English. He also shows that to obtain a wider readership *domestic* medical journals may be written in English; for example, 33 per cent of medical journals published in Japan were written in English.

Research also shows that in academic medical journals there are four main genres: the research paper, the review article, the clinical case notes and editorials. Pettinari (1982, 1985) looked at another genre, the surgical report, and noted differences between those written by native speakers and those written by non-native speakers. Salager-Meyer (1994) and Adams-Smith (1984) investigate hedging and author comment in medical journals and show that there is variation between genres.

Dubois (1980, 1981 and 1987) looked at short biomedical slide presentations and found that presenters discuss aspects of the research that go wrong more openly than in an article. There is also a considerable stylistic shift in the presentations: the introductions and conclusions are scripted while the commentary on the slides is more informal.

Similarly, spoken interaction between doctors and patients, and dentists and patients (Candlin *et al.*, 1976 and 1981; Coulthard and Ashby, 1976) has been a very fruitful area of research, and one where ESP has had an influence on the subject discipline. Insights from such research have fed into courses on communication with patients, run for native-speaker medical students (Skelton, 1994).

The language and discourse of *economics* have been the subject of considerable analysis, although it is not clear whether it is the specific discipline or the broad disciplinary area that is under discussion. Much of the research has been concerned with the textbook and with the abstract language and metaphors used to set up the models essential to economic description (Henderson, 1982; Henderson and Hewings, 1987 and 1990; Hewings, 1990). More recently researchers (Dudley-Evans, 1993; Bloor and Bloor, 1993) have shown that there are differences between academic articles in economics and those in EST in terms of how authors present criticism of other authors and make knowledge claims. This research has been taken up by economists themselves, particularly those interested in questioning the rhetoric used in economics (McCloskey, 1994; Backhouse, 1993; Brown, 1993). This again shows how ESP has a role in influencing debate within disciplines and demystifying the processes of communication.

English for Legal Purposes (ELP) is an important but 'relatively uncultivated corner of the ESP field' (Swales and Bhatia, 1982, special edition of *English for Specific Purposes* newsletter). Bhatia (1983: 2) divides legal writing into three main areas: *academic legal writing*, which consists of legal textbooks and research journals; *juridicial writing*, consisting of court judgements, case-books and law reports, the purpose of which is to report the proceedings of the court and the decision of the judge; and *legislative writing*, which consists of Acts of Parliament, statutory instruments, contracts, agreements, treaties, all of which serve to legislate.

He argues that two main genres, legal cases and legislative writing, should be the focus of attention and that the intertextuality between the two genres should be brought out (Bhatia, 1987). He suggests that the key moves in a legal case are (1) the *Facts*; (2) the *Argument* of the judge including discussion of earlier cases; (3) the *Principle of law* deducible from the case; (4) the *Decision* of the judge. In analysing legislative writing, Bhatia (1982 and 1983) is essentially concerned to show how the variety of ways in which statements can be qualified contributes to the complexity of the language. He also points to the dangers of the EAP teacher treating a legal case as an example of the narrative genre rather than a specific genre. Howe (1990, 1993) draws on this research and her own research to develop courses in ELP for international students following undergraduate Law courses in Britain. She argues that an understanding of the structure of problem questions and law reports is of great help to such students.

We feel that text analysis has shown that all academic disciplines share a common-core of language and discoursal features, and that the most significant differences lie at the genre level. Each broad disciplinary area, such as Engineering, Medicine or Law, makes use of a number of genres. The set of genres varies from one disciplinary area to another and the actual features of given genres may well also vary. Various researchers (notably Swales, 1990; Hopkins and Dudley-Evans, 1988; Thompson, 1993) have shown very convincingly that there is a general pattern of organisation that predominates in the different sections of an article or thesis from any discipline, but there is also variation between different disciplines. Writing in the areas of science and technology has, however, remained more strongly constrained by academic discourse conventions and expectations of the relevant discourse communities. Furthermore, it seems that EST discourse is the proto-typical academic discourse that has acted as the model for the development of distinctive discourse styles in other disciplinary areas (Crookes, 1986).

We are *not* arguing, as does Spack (1988), that the lack of clear differences between the broad disciplinary areas and the confusion between academic and professional contexts mean that we should only concentrate on the common-core. Rather the opposite: we believe and argue consistently in this book that if we are to meet students' needs we must deal with subject-specific matters. Our case is that subject-specific work needs to be into specific disciplines rather than into broad disciplinary areas.

Task 3e ➥

The two texts E3.1 and E3.2 (pp. 244–5) are both from the field of economics. E3.1 is a section from a textbook; E3.2 is a forecast published in a Barclays Bank survey. For each text consider: the tenses used, the amount of abstract language and the different audiences. What do your conclusions imply for the teaching of English for Economics?

3.6 Summary

We have covered a lot of ground in this chapter, from a classification of four general types of EAP situations to a detailed discussion of the value of specific work in EAP and a description of various broad disciplinary areas in EAP. Our purpose in this chapter has been to draw out the differences between the four different types of EAP situation and emphasise that what works well in one situation may not work equally well in another. We have described various approaches to English for Specific Academic Purposes and stated our position that, where the EAP course runs in parallel with the subject course, the EAP course will benefit from some engagement with the actual subject course. EAP needs both its general component and its specific component.

3.7 Recommended reading

Jordan (1997) provides an overview of EAP with an emphasis on British EAP. A good mix of theory and practice in British EAP comes in edited collections from BALEAP conferences: Robinson (1988), Adams *et al.* (1991), Blue (1993) and Hewings and Dudley-Evans (1996). Tickoo Ed. (1988) is not exclusively about EAP, but contains a useful overview of EAP and EOP work in South East Asia. British Council *ELT Document* 106 (1980) contains papers on cooperative work in ESP, while Brinton *et al.* (1989) presents an American perspective on cooperation and Selinker's (1979) article describes identifying and working with a subject specialist. Bhatia (1993) covers aspects of Legal English; the *EMP Newsletter* (discontinued, copies in the Language Studies Unit, Aston University) had a wide range of articles on English for Medical Purposes; Dudley-Evans and Henderson (1990) look at the language of economics.

4 English for Business Purposes

4.1 Aims

In this chapter, we illustrate how the principles of ESP are applied in English for Occupational Purposes (EOP) with a detailed look at English for Business Purposes/Business English (EBP/BE), which is currently the area of greatest activity and growth in ESP. Like English for Science and Technology (EST), EBP is an umbrella term. Our discussion here is concerned mainly with adult learners, working or preparing to work in a business context, and deals with Business English in an occupational, not an academic context. The academic Business English required by students on courses in disciplines such as business, finance, accounting and banking has more in common with the study of other EAP disciplines.

We will consider general and specific purpose business courses, identifying who the learners are, and the implications for teachers and courses. We shall also discuss ways in which interdisciplinary issues and research are altering perspectives. Aspects of the language of Business English and the role of the skills are covered in chapters 5 and 6. We begin here by considering who is using what as Business English.

4.2 Characteristics of Business English

4.2.1 Users of Business English

English has become the international language of business. A Finn conducting business in South Korea uses English; a Brazilian doing business with the Dutch uses English; the French in China often use English; and an American and a German probably also employ English. Thus most English-medium communications in business are non-native speaker to non-native speaker (NNS-NNS), and the English they use is International English, not that of native speakers (NS) of English-medium countries such as the UK and Australia. This is a point made in management books as well as language books, for instance Guy and Mattock (1993) use the term 'offshore English' for the English spoken between Europeans who do not share first languages and have learned English for practical rather than academic purposes.

One of the consequences of the role of English as the international language is that 'non-British managers may be able to understand each other more easily when speaking English together than they can understand a native speaker' (Barham and Oates, 1991, who by 'non-British' presumably mean non-native speakers); and the non-native speakers (NNSs) may understand each other more easily than the native speaker (NS) understands them. People who share a first language (L1), may share a common use of English which is not the NS use. The NS may have to learn to move from a literal understanding to a contextually based one. For example, the NNS may immediately understand the meaning behind 'I insist on the importance of this' and 'to resume our ideas'. A NS may have to shake off the emotional impact of 'I insist' and then recognise that the intended meaning is 'I emphasise the importance of this'; and how easily a native speaker understands that 'to resume' is not 'to pick up again on earlier ideas' but 'to summarise our ideas' could depend on the context and their experience.

International English is about effective communication and, as one of our course participants put it, 'I'm not a native speaker. I don't want people to forget that. We come from different cultures and ways of thinking; if my language sounds too good, people won't remember that.' NNSs want to communicate effectively, but not necessarily like NSs; and NSs of standard English also need to learn to use International English. There are aspects of NS language which are unhelpful to NNSs. For instance, phrasal verbs are generally less transparent than alternative phrases. How many NNS learners would understand that 'Business should take off next year' means that the business should really start to do well next year?

4.2.2   A definition of Business English

Business English is difficult to define and limit in linguistic terms. Pickett highlighted the fact that there is more than one face to business communication with some of it being 'a lot nearer the everyday language spoken by the general public than many other segments of ESP' (1986: 16). The diagrammatic representation he used suggests two particular aspects to business communication: communication with the public and communication within (intra) a company or between (inter) companies:

general English

↕

communication with public

⇕

Business English

⇕

communication among businesses

↕

specialised language of particular businesses
(such as insurance, pharmaceuticals)

For many businesses, communication with the public is most likely to be in the L1. The Business English that NNSs require is mainly for inter-company and, in international conglomerates, intra-company dealings (Nickerson, 1998).

The distinction Pickett makes is useful but probably not fine enough for today's wide-ranging business activities. Even within a particular business, the language requirements of the team negotiating, say, a £2m contract to build a generating station and of the team in charge of on-site installation may be very different. The purposes of the interactions, the topics covered and the professional relationships will all affect the choice of language.

4.3 English for General Business Purposes (EGBP) and English for Specific Business Purposes (ESBP)

In the same way as EAP can be divided into English for General Academic Purposes (EGAP) and English for Specific Academic Purposes (ESAP), so we can talk of English for General Business Purposes (EGBP) and English for Specific Business Purposes (ESBP)

English for General Business Purposes (EGBP) courses are usually for pre-experience learners or those at the very early stages of their career. They are similar to general EFL courses with the materials set in business contexts. Many learners attend these courses at a language school and groups will usually be formed on the basis of language level rather than job. There is a range of good published material for students and teachers to choose from, with input in text, audio and video format plus CD-ROM. The published course books are mainly designed for use on the extensive courses that have one or two sessions a week, over several months or years. Most units contain work on the traditional four skills plus specific grammar and vocabulary development.

The underlying construct of the course is often grammatical, as in the *Macmillan Business English Programme* (Badger and Menzies, 1993) and *Business Objectives* (Hollett, 1991). These courses are designed to cover the grammar of English systematically with particular attention given to verbs – tenses, conditionals and modals – which constitute 50 per cent of the grammar units in *The Language of Business English* (Brieger and Sweeney, 1994) and two-thirds of those in *Grammar and Practice* (Duckworth, 1995).

The focus is presentation, through listening and/or reading, followed by exercises to practise grammar and vocabulary. These focus on accuracy and have correct answers. Finally, there are activities which are more open-ended and develop fluency in one or more of the four skills. The settings include 'meeting people', 'making arrangements', 'talking about yourself and your company', and 'travelling'. Typical business carrier content topics include organisational charts, marketing, branding, advertisements and product development.

Such courses teach a broad range of English through business settings rather than English for specific business purposes. The vocabulary range of EGBP books clearly differs substantially from that of EGP but the language activities are core EFL ones and the answers are often predictable with more closed, right/wrong responses than unpredictable, open responses.

In contrast, *English for Specific Business Purposes (ESBP)* courses are run for job-experienced learners who bring business knowledge and skills to the language-learning situation. These courses are carefully tailored and likely to focus on one or two language skills and specific business communicative events. The materials often include selections from a range of published books, framework materials (chapter 9) and specially written activities, probably stemming from the learner's own business context. Courses are frequently intensive; groups are small, a maximum of 6–8, and senior staff may opt for one-to-one tuition. Company courses may have groups with widely differing language levels. They may be run in-company by company staff, in-company by external trainers or off-site on the trainers' premises (in-company courses are known as workplace English in the United States of America).

In these courses, a focus on presentation and practice in accuracy and fluency is uncommon. Instead, a more deep-end (chapter 10) approach is followed, starting from a fluency activity, progressing to language and skills work based on outcome, and leading to further fluency practice. Settings and carrier content are mainly taken from the learners' own business contexts.

We saw that for EAP courses important variables were the language of the surrounding environment and the medium of academic study. Table 4.1 shows important variables on Business English courses.

Table 4.1 *Key variables in Business English courses*

Variables	Factors to be considered
course duration	Is it intensive or extensive?
participants	Are they all from the same company or is it an open registration course?
group size	Is it one-to-one or a small group?
location	Is it in-house, in country or overseas; residential or non-residential?
mode of learning	Is it class teaching, telephone teaching, self-study?
trainers	Are they company employees or outsiders?

The answer to these questions can, to a degree, be predicted from the position of learners in their company. Senior and middle management are more likely to attend residential intensive courses in English-speaking countries with one-to-one teaching while secretarial and junior staff might be offered in-country, extensive, open registration courses (Ellis and Johnson, 1994: chapter 7).

Reflection 4a ●◇

a) For a teacher, what would be some of the differences in teaching EGBP courses or ESBP courses?

b) For a language school manager, what would be some of the differences in providing EGBP or ESBP courses?

4.4 The role of needs analysis in Business English

Needs analysis may be even more fundamental in Business English than in, say, English for Science and Technology as learners' needs can be much more varied and the spectrum of language and skills less predictable. The approach to needs analysis depends on the situation and context. Pilbeam (1979) suggests that needs analysis should be concerned with establishing both a target profile of language skills which sets down the actual activities that the participants have to carry out (*Target Situation Analysis*) and a profile of personal ability in which the participants' proficiency in these activities is evaluated (*Present Situation Analysis*). Such a *language audit* is particularly relevant to in-company work and helps to decide how many hours of language tuition are needed to bridge the gap, or what should be prioritised where time is limited.

Brieger (1997) suggests needs analysis for Business English will set out to identify the range of general and specialist language knowledge required, together with general and professional communication skills (pp. 88–9).

A language audit may involve any of the techniques of needs analysis that are discussed in chapter 7 plus a number of stages. Holden (1993) uses a three stage analysis: the first stage tabulates information through which target language needs are identified; the second stage is an interview (or questionnaire) to establish learners' perceptions of communication within their corporate culture; and the final stage is a questionnaire to establish preferred learning styles. Another multi-stage approach is the LANA system which uses inter-views and communication modelling at corporate and departmental levels and a computer questionnaire with individuals (Reeves and Wright, 1996). Cost-effectiveness is an important reason for carrying out a thorough needs analysis in the development of a company-wide training programme which may cover hundreds of employees over a number of years.

For short intensive courses, less time and fewer resources will be available but the EBP teacher can usually obtain some pre-course information: participants may be willing to complete a short form and supply examples of commonly used documents. This information means that the EBP teacher can design the framework of the course before participants arrive and determine specific needs when the learners are on-site. In a one-to-one situation this can be achieved through quite extensive interviewing and discussion as the learner is fully involved in using the language during this process. In group situations, learners may not want to spend much time sharing needs; however, the early activities can be designed to combine this and language practice. In twos or threes learners can interview each other about their company, their job, their use of English and then report back individually or summarise similarities and differences. The on-going evaluation we discuss and recommend in chapter 7 is also effective for needs analysis.

Task 4b ●◆

A short questionnaire has produced the following profiles of two learners. Each will attend a separate four-and-a-half day residential course with four tutor-contact sessions a day. (a) What would be the main features you would include in their courses? (b) What would you aim to find out when they arrive?

Learner M is Brazilian. Company produces and distributes veterinary products. Major client is a Dutch company. Communicates by fax. Occasionally meets Dutch colleagues in Brazil, less often in Holland.

Learner P is French. Works in ship building. Joint French-British projects. Major contracts for Asian customers. Needs English for meetings with British and Chinese.

On extensive EGBP courses less effort may be put into establishing individual learners' needs. There are reports of attitudes such as 'We don't have time to do a thorough needs analysis', 'We just use a quick chat before the course starts', 'Our students are happy with a set course book' (Nelson, 1995). Nelson suggested that 'these kinds of attitudes to needs analysis were still quite widespread in the industry'. To combat this he has created a computer-integrated system which combines questionnaire responses with placement test results. These can be administered at the start of the course and quickly provide details for the selection of suitable material.

4.5 Teachers of Business English

Orientation 4c

What do you feel are some of the characteristics that an EBP teacher needs? In which ways might teaching EBP be different to teaching EFL/EAP? Three factors to consider are: a) behaviour, b) knowledge required, c) skills required.

Personality, knowledge and experience are important to a Business English teacher. In the larger EAP classes there may be few opportunities for personal contact; on a one-to-one or small intensive course, personal contact is a key factor and trainers need to be outgoing, tactful and genuinely interested in business issues (Ellis and Johnson, 1994: 27). Successful Business English teachers will have the flexibility and adaptability of any ESP teacher; they will like people and be good at handling them.

Most ESP teachers have a language teaching background and do not have first-hand experience of the content and context of other disciplines or business. There can be a good deal to learn and, for an EBP teacher, more in one respect than for an EAP teacher: EAP teachers have all been students themselves and been through the academic environment. The study skills that are integrally linked on many courses with language development are familiar. A teacher can say of examinations, listening to lectures, note-taking, 'I've been there, I've done that' – although their environment may have differed from that of some of their learners in various ways including subject culture and genres.

Most EBP teachers have not worked in business; they cannot say of budget-setting meetings or sales negotiations, 'been there, done that'. In non-EAP situations fewer teachers have experience of or actually work within their students' context. Acquiring such knowledge and skill takes time and comes from reading, from talking to people – perhaps shadowing them at work – from attending courses and conferences, and through experience. Howe (1993) describes how, after some criticism of her well-intentioned efforts, she set out to 'find out about the law' because 'I had to know a great deal about the law and its language before I could tangle with the Law School again' (p. 148). On-going professional development of this kind is essential for ESP practitioners. The interdisciplinary nature of ESP is both a stimulus and a challenging demand!

Being an effective business communicator depends not only on verbal language proficiency but also on personal and interpersonal skills. Increasingly ESP practitioners who work in-company or on company-specific courses are delivering both language and skills. The trend is towards 'shorter, highly job-specific courses and an increasing emphasis on skills courses' (Pilbeam, 1992, 13.1: 3). In addition, intercultural issues are increasingly a component of such courses. The complexities of effective international communication place increasing demands on us as English for Business Purposes practitioners.

Particularly for those involved with company language training, acquiring knowledge and understanding in five areas seems necessary:

- a knowledge of the communicative functioning of English in business contexts;
- an understanding of the business people's expectations and learning strategies;

- an understanding of the psychology of personal and interpersonal interactions in cross-cultural settings;
- some knowledge of management theories and practice;
- first-class training skills.

We shall consider some of the research and experience available to Business English teachers in each of these five areas in the next section.

4.6 Key issues for Business English

4.6.1 The communicative functioning of English in business contexts

We shall look at some of the research findings into language and communication in Business English under four categories, moving from the macro-level of discourse communities and genre to key communicative events and the micro-level of grammar and lexis.

a) discourse communities

In the area of ESBP the trend towards finding out how discourse communities operate, noted in ESAP, is increasingly important. A concern for Business English research is to discover how the language and discourse used in business communication relate to the context – the business relationship – in which it takes place. Charles (1994: 4) put it very effectively in her research question: 'How is the nature of the business relationship within which *a(n)* . . . *event* is carried out reflected in the interaction of the event?' (. . . We have omitted the word 'negotiation'). The discourse and thus the language stem from the relationship. The concern is to go beyond textual studies (such as those discussed in the next section – Bhatia on promotional letters) to investigate in detail how the discourse is affected by the relationship. Three factors seem particularly significant: whether the relationship is new or old; where the balance of power lies; and cultural values and attitudes.

Charles (1996) shows that a key factor in the analysis of negotiation discourse is whether the business relationship is a new one (new relationship negotiation, NRN) or an old, established one (old relationship negotiation, ORN). If it is new, then it is likely that the Buyers and Sellers will follow the roles expected of them by the business community: established business patterns and, during the negotiation, various politeness strategies are used to save the *professional face* of the other side. If the relationship is established, then the roles expected by the business community may well be relaxed and the established business

Developments in ESP

patterns set aside so that the politeness strategies used serve to save the *personal face* of the other side. ('Face' is the negotiated public image, mutually granted to each other by participants in a communication event. For a full discussion of face and politeness strategies see chapter 3 of Scollon and Scollon, 1995.)

The 'rules of the game', or atmosphere, that apply in an interaction are partly a product of the history and mythology of the past – and each party has their own version of these; they are also affected by personalities, the immediacy of pressures, the legal framework and the power of each party.

The relative power of each party is related to who needs who most or who can hurt the other most. Where each side has relatively equal power, there is likely to be give and take. Where power is unequal, the party with most power will generally dictate the outcome. Yli-Jokipii (1994) investigated power relationships as demonstrated through the written documentation of the transactional stages of the buying and selling process, noting that power almost invariably lay with the buyer. However, power is present in all relationships and not merely in the buying/selling process.

A third factor affecting the business relationship concerns cultural values and attitudes. The assumption has been that it is possible to talk about the business community as one international discourse community – the shared philosophy of that community resting on the Western market system, however new that is to some countries. This, however, seems a false position. Research suggests that Western models of communication do not represent the complexity of cross-cultural communication (Limaye and Victor, 1991).

b) business genres

Swales (1990: 54) notes that 'a discourse community's nomenclature for genres is an important source of insight'. In the academic community the use of terms such as 'academic article', 'review article', 'letter' and 'essay' are significant and an indication that there will be important generic differences between them. The names used by business communities to describe their activities are rather less useful than the names used by the academic community. Barbara *et al.* (1996) discovered from a preliminary needs analysis among Brazilian businesses that there was a 'clear mismatch between what the researchers meant by labels . . . namely project, report, prospectus, memo, presentation and meeting, and the respondents' perception of the meaning of these terms. It also became apparent that the terminology mismatch was not only between researcher and organisation, but also between organisations.'

It is important that analysis of Business English is carried out on texts – both written and spoken – to determine which genres exist, that is to understand significant differences and specific communicative purposes. For example, there may be certain discourse features common to all business letters, for example the opening and the closing moves, but they do not share one communicative purpose, and may even serve several purposes. Letter writing in business and commercial English courses used to be taught through the product-modelling approach (see chapter 6). Given the changes to international business communication, the validity of categories of business letter such as the 'transmittal letter', the 'request letter', the 'response letter', the 'confirmation letter', the 'complaint letter' needs verifying to establish whether they really are separate genres. For instance, Bhatia (1993) analysed sales promotion letters and job application letters and found the pattern of moves so similar that they can be categorised together as a *promotional genre* (see chapter 5).

Meetings and negotiations are also difficult to separate. It would appear that a meeting within a company may serve various purposes such as exchange of information, decision making, or a presentation from an individual or a group. When, however, a meeting takes place between representatives of two different companies the meeting will almost certainly be a negotiation, however little actual bargaining takes place during the actual meeting. The meeting may act as a forum for sensing the position of the other side and checking up on developments that are important to the business relationship between the two sides. Charles (1996) has shown that negotiations are more likely to involve the cooperative exchange of information than the 'cut-and-thrust' competitive bargaining that many older training manuals describe. This perhaps reflects the influence that the Harvard model of negotiating has had on businesses (see Fisher and Ury, 1981) and the achievement of win/win scenarios.

Thus, as Firth (1995: 6) points out, negotiation activity takes place in many contexts, such as 'offices, committee rooms, marketplaces, consultancy rooms, shops, used car lots'. The actual bargaining may be done by telephone, fax or e-mail after the meeting. Nonetheless, in business the sales negotiation does have clear purposes and may be considered a genre.

c) key communicative events

There is more of a consensus on the key communicative events of business. Some of the results of needs analysis (Holden, 1993; Yin and Wong, 1990; Khoo, 1994) and current prublished materials (*Longman*

Business English Series) identify seven core events. The five events requiring primarily oral language are referred to as: telephoning, socialising, making presentations, taking part in meetings and negotiating; those that require the written form are: corresponding and reporting.

'Socialising' is probably a misleading term: it suggests that the focus of interaction is social when, in fact, it remains business. The 'social' aspect of interactions is primarily aimed at establishing a good relationship in order to enhance the conduct of business.

Modern technology is changing the format of written correspondence, and this is a category that can be broken down in a number of ways. We have standard letters, individualised letters, faxed memo letters and e-mail; we also have standard order forms and invoices. What constitutes an acceptable e-mail or faxed message is still evolving. What is certain is that they have accelerated the move away from formal, impersonal written communication; such messages still need the hallmarks of good written communication, such as a clear purpose and organised ideas, but format and language can be more informal and personal – especially as they are more likely to be transmitted directly and not passed through the hands of a bilingual secretary. However, where there is a probability of e-mail messages becoming hard or shared copy, they will be less casual than some of the e-mail messages in, say, academic circles.

d)   functions, grammar and lexis

Until recently, Business English has been an experience-, intuition- and materials-led movement, and reported research findings have been slow to emerge and feed into practice. Thus earlier textbooks taught quite elaborate gambits for functions such as taking turns, expressing opinions and disagreeing. For example: *With the Chair's permission I would like to take up the point that . . .; It's my considered opinion that . . .; on the whole I agree with you, but it could be said that . . .* With more real data to hand, practitioners are realising that in many situations much shorter and more informal phrases are used, and that gambits can be both verbal and non-verbal: topic closure markers can be verbal as in 'OK OK', 'Well well', 'Good for you', or non-verbal as in shifting papers or taking out car keys. Topic introduction and topic shift can be signalled by 'What next?', 'So anything else?', 'On to X' or by opening a new file (Linde, 1991).

Much of the language-based research has been on written documents, yet spoken transactions are fundamental to business. In addition, little of the research has considered interaction between two non-native speakers, although this is the communication that predominates internationally. Thus there is, as yet, no identifiable core grammar and lexis for Business English, but some broad areas to focus on are discussed in chapter 5.

4.6.2   Learners' expectations and strategies

The expectations of business people can differ substantially from those of secondary and tertiary level students and place very different demands on providers of ESP courses. There may be expectations concerning the physical resources, the management of the course and the learning strategies.

Task 4d ●◆

For university students and business people in your country, consider what they would expect or accept on an English course. Complete the table below.

Course variables	Students	Business people
* group size * hours/day * materials / handouts * pace of classes * course length * learners' age * physical facilities * assessment procedures * pre-course information * quality and style of presentations * appearance/dress of tutors		

Business managers attending ESP courses may expect small groups of no more than 6–8 people, or to have one-to-one tuition. Time is a valuable commodity and they expect to maximise its use; so many courses are short – a few days – and intensive. Participants may expect up to eight hours a day contact time plus some language preparation or practice in the evenings. Each session needs to be well paced, with continuous momentum and clear objectives. As professionals, paying directly for the course, they will look for high standards, quality and value for money. In many countries, the average academic classroom would be considered unsuitable; carpets, whiteboards, overhead projectors, small tables and comfortable chairs are minimum requirements and handouts need to be more up-market than the ubiquitous wads of blurred photocopies. Learning strategies need to be adapted to the group's needs; for professionals a task-based, problem-solving, deep-end approach is often appropriate as it mirrors their work style and they learn experientially through involvement.

Most working people cannot afford to take much time for language learning and look for practical ways to build language development into their working pattern. Some build language learning into their work programme through telephone classes and tutored self-study. Telephone classes provide individual tuition with no time loss for getting to a class; arrangements between learner and tutor can be flexible but regular. The tutor and learner work through specially designed materials, either as a supplement to a class or as a sole activity (Mascull Ed., 1993). Listening to cassettes while travelling to work is practical and there may be a role for taped material that extends beyond listening activities. Tutored distance-learning on the Internet is starting to develop and CD-Roms are also viable for individual learning, although at the moment the material is limited in interactivity and does not cover much more than basic language (chapter 10).

Many jobs involve constant switches of attention and activity so sitting in a classroom for several hours can feel uncomfortable. Learners will benefit from varied activities that place them in different roles and interactions. Problem-solving can tap into their existing skills and ways of working.

4.6.3 The role of cross-cultural communication

One description of culture is 'the way we do things round here'; another is 'the way in which a group of people solves problems' (Schein, 1985 cited in Trompenaar, 1993: 6). Culture is complex and comprises different aspects such as national, professional, organisational and personal cultures. The essence of culture is not in fact what we can easily see (the tip of the iceberg) but what lies underneath.

A sensitivity to cultural issues and an understanding of our own and others' values and behaviours is important in ESP. Language reflects culture and culture can shape language. When we and our learners are aware of the issues we may avoid misunderstandings and conflict which can unintentionally arise from an inappropriate use of language.

Task 4e ●◆

WARNING: In dealing with cultural differences we have to beware of stereotyping. Activities such as this one raise issues for discussion and may not match the habits of the individuals you meet and work with.

How would you rank the following items in importance (1 = most important, 10 = least important) for a foreign business person visiting your country? Can you rank them for other countries you are familiar with? (The key contains information on Britain, France, Italy, Germany, Switzerland, Sweden, Japan, Spain and Hungary.)

Be patient
Smile
Accept invitations to go drinking
Understand local politics
Dress carefully for meetings
Arrive exactly on time for meetings
Have good local introductions
Be prepared to work late
Learn the local language
Say what you think directly

The 'Golden Rules' of International Business (from *The New International Manager* by Vincent Guy and John Mattock, Kogan Press, 1993).

Trompenaar (1993), in his book on cultural diversity in business, discusses seven dimensions of culture which he has found to be significant. Five concern relationships with other people, one concerns the passage of time and one the environment. While all seven dimensions are important, the four that seem most significant for Business English teaching are the relationship dimensions of neutral:emotional; individualism:collectivism; specific:diffuse; and universalism:particularism.

How much eye contact is appropriate? What is the size of private body space? How transparent are feelings in tone or body? These questions are all related to the neutral:emotional dimension of culture. A preference for working alone, competing with others or collaborating can depend on the individualistic:collective dimension. In specific or segregating cultures, different aspects of life are kept separate, while in diffuse cultures they spill over into each other. In diffuse cultures, such as China and Indonesia, the boss is the boss at all times, whether at work or social events. In specific cultures, such as Australia and the Netherlands, the boss is only the boss in the work context. Where an individual stands in this dimension affects how they do business and whether getting to know people first is important (diffuse) or comes later (separate).

The universalist approach is based on the concept of 'one good way' whereas particularism pays attention to the obligations of relationships and circumstances. So universalists apply the same rules and procedures across the board, while particularists encourage flexibility. For instance, self-access centres can be quite well used in the UK tertiary system where students have relatively few contact hours and live on or near campus. Where they have been introduced elsewhere by UK specialists however, they have often been less successful. Those specialists were operating as universalists, thinking that what would work in one country would work in another. Given the different circumstances such as fuller timetables and long travelling times, particularists might have recognised that the system would have to be substantially altered to be successful.

Trompenaar refers to each dimension as a dichotomy, as in universalism:collectivism. Other writers discuss where, along a spectrum of values and beliefs a culture lies. Thus, Hofstede (1991) refers to a *high* and *low* tendency, for example *high* power distance, *low* masculinity. Hofstede's (1980, 1991) dimensions include power distance, uncertainty avoidance, individualism and masculinity.

In high power distance cultures, decisions are accepted from those with power and status (usually derived from position and connections) – as in most South American countries and Japan. In low power distance cultures, people prefer to participate in decision making and status is based on achievement and professional know-how – for example in Scandinavian countries and Belgium. How people will behave in meetings is affected by this dimension as it affects the style of chairing, the degree of participation and the roles played.

In high uncertainty avoidance cultures, rules, plans and timetables are important, and uncertainty is avoided by making it clear what will happen and when – for example in Greece, Belgium, France, Japan, Korea. In low uncertainty avoidance cultures, people are more relaxed about rules and procedures – as in Great Britain and Malaysia; uncertainty is acceptable so there is more flexibility about what happens and when.

Highly individualistic cultures are 'I' cultures and include the USA, Canada, Australia, and Great Britain. Low individualistic, highly collective cultures are 'we' cultures such as Central American, South American and Asian countries; the group (for example the family) is more important than the individual. High masculinity is associated with competitiveness – as in Japan, Austria, Switzerland; while in low masculinity cultures, relationships, welfare and social justice are valued – as in Scandinavian countries and Canada.

Within the interplay between language and culture, a crucial question is 'What does this event or statement mean to the other person?' We need to recognise when statements have a cultural bias. A comment that letters written within the USA by NNS (Sims and Guice, 1992) are 'too personal . . . contain too much', reflects the culture of individuals from a neutral culture; such personal statements may be appropriate for members of emotional cultures.

How are cross-cultural issues dealt with in EBP?

Business English has been much more open than EAP to the idea that there is variation between different cultures but it is only recently that this factor has really begun to affect teaching materials and course content. A sensitivity to differences between cultures is necessary for successful business communications in matters such as the purpose of meetings, the use of direct or indirect negotiation tactics, the structuring of information or the use of politeness strategies in letters or meetings.

All communication is cross-cultural in that each individual is unique. At the moment most cross-cultural work in BE consists of discussing issues, as in Task 4e, with attention focused on national characteristics. However, we need to extend this to how different professional cultures and gender affect language use. One vital question for BE teachers is the extent to which the language taught is appropriate for an English-speaking culture, the learners' culture or the cultures within which the business transactions will take place. EGBP textbooks teach expressions such as 'Could you possibly . . .?', 'Do you mind my asking if . . .?', 'If it's alright with you . . .?' These represent the indirectness of British culture. The first question that needs to be asked is: To what extent do British business people actually use these? How authentic are they? The second question is, even if British business people do use them, does a speaker from another, more direct culture want to? If 'Will you . . .?' fits the culture better than 'Could you possibly . . .?' then that may be the appropriate language. Likewise 'I can't agree' may be uncomfortable where face saving is important.

It is not just verbal language but also body language that differs between cultures. Even silence plays a role. In a simulation or case study, a learner may be silent because of language lacks or because his/her culture says that silence is appropriate. Silence is in fact a useful negotiating tactic – one that Europeans and Americans may be uncom-fortable with but which suits Asian cultures.

Stress and frustration can be lowered and success raised through an awareness of the impact of all these issues in cross-cultural communication. One of the first decisions is how to address the other person: whether first names or family names are used can depend on status, role, company culture and national culture. Another example is how the process and language of an interaction are affected by the degree of formality; Charles (1994) showed that a Finnish old relationship negotiation (ORN) resembled the interaction in a British new relationship negotiation (NRN).

Deciding what is a suitable strategy in a given situation, for example how to break a deadlock in a negotiation, is not the job of the BE teacher. It is his or her job, however, to understand that such a strategy has to be chosen and how it will affect the language used. Class activities need to raise these issues in the preparation phase so that learners can decide on their approach and assess their communication accordingly. The language that would be appropriate for each group will differ with their strategy.

4.6.4 Management theory and practice

An EBP teacher is not a business person and does not need to be one. What EBP teachers need, just like any ESP teacher, is to understand the interface between business principles and language. What do learners do in their jobs? What are the fundamental concepts and attitudes? What do people communicate about and how do they go about it? 'Shadowing' business people (that is, following them around, listening and observing) can be a fascinating learning experience.

There are also plenty of materials to read or listen to: course books for Business Studies/ MBA courses; popular 'business made easy' books (Drucker, 1993; Belbin, 1996; Kennedy *et al.*, 1987); magazines and journals; business pages of newspapers; company literature, both public and internal – just glancing at the contents pages of course books for Business Studies and MBA courses provides a feel of what the key areas are. Skimming through the business pages of newspapers and magazines, particularly the feature articles rather than news stories, provides a picture of current concerns, as do radio and TV programmes. Management training videos are useful for illustrating the interactions that are promoted as desirable.

This reading and listening may be in English or other languages. The advantage of access to English-medium sources is that at the same time as acquiring a feel for the business concepts the BE teacher can also acquire the lexis and typical phrases. Business is good at inventing new terms for its activities, and keeping abreast of these and their acronyms is hard. Ask many a non-business native English speaker what JIT,

TQM, the 4Ps and SWOT stand for (just-in-time; total quality management; price, product, position and promotion; strengths, weaknesses, opportunities and threats), or the difference between downsizing and retrenching, and they may not know (cutting the workforce; cutting expenditure).

4.6.5 Communication skills training

There is also an interface between language and communication skills; in some areas language and skills cannot be separated. A spoken message comprises the words themselves and the way in which they are spoken; a face-to-face spoken message also contains body language. The impact of each of these components depends on the context. What is significant is that the words can play a very small role in the impact of the message. Mehrabian (1971) researched this interplay and found that only 8 per cent of listeners' belief in a message came through the words, 37 per cent came through how they were said and 55 per cent through the body language. If people 'hear' one thing in the body language and another in the words, it is the body language they believe.

While the main focus of BE courses for effective spoken language may be language, pronunciation and intonation, body language and basic communication skills cannot be ignored; the language may be fine but how effective will a presentation be if the presenter faces the overhead projector screen and the audience just sees a back? Similarly, a course which develops effective written language will need to take account of audience, purpose, planning, information structuring and layout of text, because choices at the macro-level affect the language.

There are many First Language management training courses covering appropriate skills for meetings, negotiations and business correspondence; attending these is an invaluable learning experience for Business English teachers. The BE teacher's role may not include teaching these skills but we need to 'walk the talk': that is to have a strong beginning and end to our presentations; to use visual aids appropriately – not to read overhead transparancies aloud, to remember that OHTs are *visual* aids and want very few words; to take turns as appropriate; to chair adequately – to agree a process, to control, to gain commitment; to write persuasively; to structure and lay out information effectively. An important technique for Business English teachers is that of handling video feedback effectively, because of its impact on confidence and motivation. A positive approach which looks first at strengths and then at improvement points, and where the speaker/writer can comment before peers or the teacher, is adopted in management training.

Management training principles sit comfortably with ESP since the learning process is primarily experiential. Where participants have experience and want their skills honed, combined language development and skills development courses can bring benefits. How effectively and appropriately this can be achieved by language trainers alone must depend on the background and experience of tutors. As in EAP work, one option in such a situation is to team-teach (see case study 1, chapter 8). For busy people a combined approach is very powerful, giving delegates the language, the skill and the confidence to take action. The BE teacher's own training skills develop through team-teaching and there can also be valuable insights into language and its use in business settings. The work described in chapter 6 on active listening and questioning is derived directly from our team-teaching.

4.7 English for Business Purposes versus English for Academic Purposes

While the principles and approaches of ESP are as relevant to EBP/BE as EAP, this chapter has shown some significant differences between the two fields. For instance, there is a conceptual difference that affects how those principles are practised: EAP operates within a world where the fundamental concern is the acquisition of knowledge by individuals, while in EBP the purpose is not centred on the learner as an individual but as a member of a transactional world where the fundamental concern is the exchange of goods or services. Every successful business transaction will impact on other people – from the provider of raw materials, to production staff, to policy makers. Thus there are different priorities: 'knowledge for its own sake' and 'knowledge for a profit margin'.

Another difference between the two fields is the language background of users. In most EAP situations there is an interaction between native and non-native speaker, whether through the NNS reading an English-medium textbook, listening to a lecture given by a NS or writing an assignment or dissertation which will be read by a NS. There is an inbuilt imbalance between the interactants at the level of English language competence. In addition, there is a further imbalance of power and authority, since the NNS often has a dependency on the NS's academic position and role. In EBP, most interactions are between non-native speakers, and the balance of power depends on their business relationship. It is not possible to predict on the basis of language where power lies.

Associated with this is the issue of culture. Language and culture cannot be separated. In English L1 EAP situations, the NNS generally has to adapt to both language and culture. In EBP situations, the NNS may use the language but not adopt the culture: it is unlikely to be appropriate for a Finn negotiating with a Vietnamese to adopt an English-speaking cultural attitude.

We also mentioned that EBP teachers do not generally have any direct experience of their learners' context whereas all EAP teachers have studied in an academic environment.

4.8 Summary

Business English is the current growth area in ESP and covers both courses for pre-experience learners (EGBP) and courses for job-experienced learners (ESBP). The primary concern is to communicate effectively, not necessarily totally accurately. As professionals, business people have very clear purposes and expect high quality, value for money and professionally delivered courses. More courses now combine language and skills development and more account is taken of the business context and business relationships. It is being recognised that the language depends on variables such as status, power and how well established the relationship is. Although many of the short, intensive courses are for spoken interaction, writing is important. With more personal computers and e-mail and less secretarial support, more business people have to compose their own correspondence. With the growth of transnational corporations, NNSs may have to write in English because documents will be read or copied to a NS Head Office or to NS staff. The professional demands placed on Business English teachers may well be higher than on those in other fields.

4.9 Recommended reading

Dudley-Evans and St John (1996) and the special edition of *English for Specific Purposes* (vol. 15.1) provide an overview of both research and materials in the 1990s in BE. Ellis and Johnson (1994) provide an introduction to the teaching of BE. The books by Scollon and Scollon (1995) and Mead (1990) provide useful introductions to intercultural issues. The books by Trompenaar (1993) and Handy (1992) will interest those who want to find out more about business ideas and philosophy. The BESIG Newsletter and *Language and Intercultural Training* publish practical articles related to BE and training issues.

5 Language issues in ESP

5.1 Aims

In this chapter we will look at various language issues in ESP, focusing on both EAP and EBP and considering in detail the questions of grammar, vocabulary and discourse. This will also involve some discussion of recent developments in 'genre analysis' and its relevance to the teaching of writing in particular, as well as to the teaching of reading and speaking. We will begin by looking at the tricky question of grammar and vocabulary in ESP.

Orientation 5a

How much of the ESP teaching in your situation is concerned with grammar and vocabulary? Which actual features of grammar should we teach?
What is your students' attitude to grammar and vocabulary teaching? How far should we attempt to meet their wishes in this respect?

5.2 Grammar in ESP

There are many misconceptions about the role of grammar in ESP teaching and, indeed, it is often said that ESP teaching is not concerned with grammar. While much of the skills-oriented work in EAP or EBP does not concentrate on grammar in itself, it is incorrect to consider grammar teaching as outside the remit of ESP. Where students have grammatical difficulties that interfere with the essentially productive skills of speaking and writing, or the essentially receptive skills of listening and reading, it is necessary to pay some attention to those difficulties. How much priority is paid to grammatical weakness depends on the learners' level in English and whether priority needs to be given to grammatical accuracy or to fluency in using the language. If priority is given to accuracy, then direct teaching of grammatical forms to express particular meanings will be required.

For reading, where the learners' grammatical weaknesses interfere with comprehension of meaning, the relationship between meaning and form can be taught or revised in context through analysis and explanation. This often includes the verb form, notably tense and voice; modals, particularly in relation to the expression of certainty and uncertainty; logical connectors such as 'however', 'therefore' and 'moreover'; noun compounds; and various expressions related to the notion of 'cause and effect' (this list arises from discussions with Brazilian teachers working on the ESP reading project there). Where English is used as the medium of communication and students are expected to present written work and make oral presentations in accurate English, serious weaknesses in grammar require more specific help. This may mean allocating time to concentrate on the given difficulty, teaching both the form and its use in contexts relevant to learners' needs.

5.2.1 Key grammatical forms

Verbs and tense

Which tenses should be taught? As we noted in chapter 2, in the early days of ESP, register analysis led to conclusions about which verb forms and tenses predominated in scientific and technical English. The main conclusion drawn by Barber (reported in Swales, 1988) was that any grammatical work done on the verb in EAP should concentrate on the present simple, active and passive voice and the modal verbs.

More recent research (for example Swales, 1988, in his introduction to Barber's article) has, however, suggested that frequency counts carried out on a corpus containing a number of genres without distinguishing between the genres may produce results of limited value. For example, the use of the present perfect may be very important in the academic article, where the pattern of tenses is as shown in table 5.1.

Table 5.1 *Tenses in academic articles*

Section	Tense Predominantly Used
Introduction	Present simple (active and passive), present perfect
Method	Past passive
Discussion/Conclusion	Results: past Comments: present

75

Voice

The idea that scientific or academic writing uses the passive voice more frequently than the active is a myth; what is true is that such writing uses the passive voice more frequently than some other types of writing. Wingard (1981) found that in his corpus of medical writing approximately 60 per cent of the verbs were in the active voice and 40 per cent in the passive. The choice of active or passive is constrained by functional considerations; writers tend to use the we-form active when they describe their own procedural choices (for example *we selected certain patients for detailed study*) but the passive when standard procedures are being described. Similarly, where writers contrast their own work with previous work in the field, they tend to use the we-form active for their own research, but the passive for the previous research (Tarone *et al.*, 1981, 1998).

Modals

Modals, especially *may, might, could, would,* are one way of indicating the degree of certainty of a writer's commitment to a statement or claim. If a writer states that 'the discrepancy in the results *may* be due to incorrect calibration of the instruments', s/he is making a cautious statement. If, however, s/he states that 'the discrepancy in the results *could* be due to incorrect calibration of the instruments', the statement is even more cautious. The writer is distancing him/herself from the statement rather more with *could* than with *may.*

This phenomenon is generally referred to as *hedging.* There are many other means of expressing hedging, for example the use of a reporting verb such as *suggest, appear to, seem to, tend to* in order to distance the writer from the statement that s/he is reporting. Compare:

• The data quoted in the Financial Times *show* that the value of the dollar is rising.
• The data quoted in the Financial Times *suggest* that the value of the dollar is rising.

In the first sentence the writer is aligning him/herself with the claim through the use of the reporting verb *show*, while in the second the use of *suggest* distances the writer from the claim and shows a neutral position. On the other hand, it may be because the writer wishes to soften a statement, for example to mitigate a criticism of another member of the research or professional community. For example, if a writer criticises another by saying: 'Jones *appears not have understood* the point I was making', the use of *appears* mitigates the criticism and is a politeness device rather than a distancing device. The writer is committed to the criticism, but follows the convention that criticisms are made politely.

Learners need to be able to appreciate the role of hedging in academic, professional and business genres and to manipulate its actual linguistic devices. They also need to understand why a writer of an article or a report is using a hedging device.

We believe that the aspects of the verb form we have described in this section, while not actually different from general English grammar, have their own specific characteristics worthy of particular attention in ESP grammar teaching. Other grammatical areas that are of particular relevance to ESP follow exactly the same rules as in general English grammar. These are the articles, nominalisation and logical connectors.

Articles

Certain uses of the articles are of particular importance in ESP. These are the absence of an article (o article) in general statements with an uncountable noun, as in:

> Copper is a reddish metal.
> Downsizing is a business phenomenon of the 80s and 90s.

Another area that seems to cause particular difficulties is the use of 'the' with named methods, procedures, formulae, graphs, cycles and other concepts as in:

> the Smith hypothesis, the water cycle, the Fry model

These two aspects of article usage seem to cause problems for non-native speakers, yet can be taught by making the rules of usage specific. We have found that concentrating on these two aspects can make a significant difference to the writing of students, while a detailed analysis of all uses of the articles as in Huckin and Olsen (1991) can be very confusing for students. Concentration on a limited number of uses that can be easily explained is usually more effective.

Nominalisation

Nominalisation, that is the use of verbal nouns usually ending in suffixes such as *-ation*, *-ition*, *-ity*, *-ment* or *-ness*, is a major feature of the abstract language favoured by academic writers (Mason, 1990). The use of nominalisation (or grammatical metaphor in Halliday's [1985] phrase) enables complex information to be packaged into a phrase that is simple from a grammatical point of view and that can be picked up in the theme (first constituent) of the following sentence. Consider the short text below:

> A high primary *productivity* is almost invariably related to a high crop yield. High *productivity* can be achieved by ensuring that all the light which falls on the field is intercepted by the leaves, and that photosynthesis itself is as efficient as possible. Greater *efficiency* in photosynthesis could perhaps be achieved by selecting against photorespiration. (Chrispeels and Sadava, 1977: 198–9).

The nominalised phrase which acts as the grammatical subject in sentence 1 is also the grammatical subject of the second sentence. A key part of the meaning is packaged in this nominal phrase; contrast what we might say in informal language where we might transfer the main meaning to the verb phrase, for example 'the crop *produces* a large amount'. In the quotation above the meaning in the first sentence is carried by the initial nominalised phrase and the final phrase 'a high crop yield', another nominalised phrase. They are linked by 'related to'. The meaning of the rest of the second sentence is carried by the verb phrase 'is intercepted by the leaves' and the adjectival phrase that follows the copula 'as efficient as possible'. In the third sentence the adjective 'efficient' is nominalised to 'efficiency' to carry the discourse forward. Notice that we have in this short passage two examples of the verb 'achieved', a verb without a great deal of meaning that carries the noun phrases 'high productivity' and 'greater efficiency in photosynthesis'.

Abstract language is a feature of any language used in academic contexts and students who have had considerable experience of reading and writing in their native language will be familiar with the use of abstract language in their L1. They will only need to adjust to the way abstract language is used in English; on the other hand, students with little or no experience of abstract language in their L1 will have to get used to the whole concept and the way that meaning is packaged and carried forward with such language.

Logical connectors

Logical connectors, such as *moreover, however, therefore*, have always had a high profile in EAP teaching. They are generally seen as a key to understanding the logical relationships in texts and therefore relevant to the teaching of reading, listening and writing in EAP. Useful sources for lists of logical connectors and their meanings are Swales and Feak's *Academic Writing for Graduate Students* (1994: 22) and Jordan's *Academic Writing* (1990).

While not in any way denying their importance, we have sometimes felt that they have been over-emphasised in ESP materials and text-books. We have noticed a tendency on the part of some students to use these connectors to an excessive degree which may in fact interfere with communication rather than help with it.

5.2.2 Grammar in Business English

As noted by Robinson (1991) and Dudley-Evans and St John (1996), much less research has been published in the area of BE. The amount of research is growing and will undoubtedly increase dramatically in the next ten years or so. Nevertheless there is not as yet an established 'common-core' of business language in the way that there is in EAP.

We can draw up a list of grammar areas that business grammar reference books single out. All place emphasis on the verb form, especially tense and voice; then on modals and verbs of *saying*, *reporting* and the difference between *make* and *do*, *have*, *have got* and *got*. Wilberg and Lewis (1990: 104–107) select 24 'business verbs' and practise their forms: *accept, advise, agree, confirm, consider, explain, invite, object, offer, order, point out, propose, query, recommend, refuse, reject, remind, reply, respond, say, speak, talk, tell* and *wonder*. And they give a longer list for reference (pp. 144–6).

Brieger and Sweeney (1994) also list some key functions of Business English and give a number of grammatical realisations for each one. The list contains a number of familiar functions that we would expect to see such as *ability and inability, agreeing and disagreeing*; these are relevant to a general English course as well as a Business English course. There are also interesting additions to the standard list of functions that are clearly very relevant to a BE course, *assertion and downtoning* and *checking and confirming* (see also Duckworth, 1995).

The features of nominalisation noted as a feature of academic English are also characteristic of certain more formal genres in Business English, such as reports, contracts and some letters, yet there is much greater variability as we will see in the discussion of genre below.

5.2.3 The teaching of grammar in ESP

Reference books outlining the meaning and form of grammatical points can be particularly useful for the ESP teacher, and we list some in our recommended reading.

How do we actually use such supplementary material? We see no problem in dealing directly and specifically with grammatical points within the context of a class or programme that, in other components, follows a more communicative or functional approach. In some situations the work on grammar will be integrated into the teaching of language use, such as how to express basic concepts like 'cause and effect', 'model building' and 'quantity' or generic features of text like 'the review of the literature', 'hedging' and 'making recommendations'. In other cases it will be integrated with comprehension work, and in yet others it may involve the availability of self-study material and Computer Assisted Language Learning (CALL) programs which allow students to home in on their own particular difficulties (see chapter 10).

Much of the grammar work we have discussed here goes beyond traditional sentence-level grammar practice to encompass awareness of the use of grammatical form in specific contexts. The context determines what aspect of grammar is appropriate. Certain very specific contexts will involve very particular uses of grammar, and the ESP teacher needs to be sensitive to these contexts.

Task 5b ●◆

Look at the two texts E5.1 and E5.2 (pp. 246–7); one is taken from a biology textbook, the other is a business memo. Consider the grammatical features of the texts.

a) Do they have the features of nominalisation and hedging described above?
b) How many logical connectors are there?

5.3 Vocabulary in ESP

The importance of the teaching of vocabulary in ESP is now widely accepted (Swales, 1983). Our major concern will be with what is referred to in EAP as *semi-technical vocabulary* (or occasionally *sub-technical vocabulary*) and in EBP as *core business vocabulary*.

In discussing the teaching of ESP it has often been said (for example Hutchinson and Waters, 1987; Higgins, 1966) that the teaching of technical vocabulary is not the responsibility of the EAP teacher and that priority should be given to the teaching of 'semi-technical' or 'core vocabulary'. We believe that this idea oversimplifies the true situation and we will therefore begin by discussing the teaching of technical vocabulary briefly before moving on to discuss the definition and teaching of semi-technical and core business vocabulary in some detail.

5.3.1 Technical vocabulary

We believe that the situation with regard to the teaching of technical vocabulary is rather more complicated than the simple notion that 'the ESP teacher should not touch it'. While in general we agree that it should not be the *responsibility* of the ESP teacher to teach technical vocabulary, in certain specific contexts it may be the *duty* of the ESP teacher to check that learners have understood technical vocabulary appearing as carrier content for an exercise. It may also be necessary to ensure that learners have understood technical language presented by a subject specialist or *assumed to be known* by a subject specialist (note emphasis). In any ESP exercise which exploits a particular context, that context will use certain technical vocabulary. It is important that both the teacher and the learners appreciate that this vocabulary is acting as *carrier* content for an exercise, and is not the *real* content of the exercise. However, students usually need to be able to understand the technical vocabulary in order to do the exercise.

How do we deal with this technical vocabulary? In some circumstances a term will be cognate with the equivalent term in the students' first language and will not therefore cause difficulty. Let us assume that the carbon cycle in biology is being used as carrier content. Both *carbon* and *cycle* and something similar to the noun compound *carbon cycle* may exist in the students' L1 although it may reverse the order (for example *ciclo de carbono* in Spanish). The only difficulty may be with pronunciation, as, for example, with the pronunciation of *cycle* in English (saikl) compared with that in most other languages (siːkl).

If the term is not cognate and is unfamiliar, then it may need to be introduced and explained before the exercise is tackled. In many cases there is a one-to-one relationship between the terms in English and the learners' L1, and so it will be enough to translate the term into the L1 after a brief explanation.

In ESAP and ESBP situations where the subject specialist is not present, for example a one-to-one consultation, the language teacher will need to adopt a questioning role about technical vocabulary. Has the learner fully understood the term? If not, how can s/he check the meaning? This will involve the use of technical dictionaries or other such sources. An example is the use in medical writing of the expression 'the patient presented with the symptoms of . . .'; this may sound unnatural and ungrammatical to the non-expert, but is in fact normal in Medical English.

In some situations learners starting a new academic course or professional training programme will need help with technical vocabulary that is completely new for them. One way to prepare learners for such a situation is for the language teacher and the subject expert to prepare a glossary of new terms with straightforward explanations of the terms. Houghton (1980) reports how she collaborated with the teacher of accounting to produce a specialist in-house dictionary designed for students new to accounting (which was then published – Houghton and Wallace [1980]).

5.3.2 Semi-technical and core business vocabulary

Our main concern in this chapter is with semi-technical vocabulary and core business vocabulary. While most ESP literature agrees on the need for teaching such vocabulary, there is not yet a satisfactory definition of the concept.

Baker (1988: 92) lists six categories of vocabulary, all of which relate to EAP. They are:

1. items which express notions general to all specialised disciplines;
2. general language items that have a specialised meaning in one or more disciplines;
3. specialised items that have different meanings in different disciplines;
4. general language items that have restricted meanings in different disciplines;
5. general language items that are used to describe or comment on technical processes or functions in preference to other items with the same meaning, for example *occur* rather than *happen*;
6. items used to signal the writer's intentions or evaluation of material presented.

Task 5c ●◆

Read text E5.3 (p. 247). Consider the following vocabulary items or phrases. Which of Baker's six categories do they fit into? *readings, load, extension, plot, worked, elastic, rapidly, proportionality, mild (steel).*

We would suggest that the six categories overlap very considerably and that there seem to be two broad areas: vocabulary that is used in general language but has a higher frequency of occurrence in scientific and technical description and discussion (essentially categories 1, 5 and 6 in Baker's list); and vocabulary that has specialised and restricted meanings in certain disciplines and which may vary in meaning across disciplines (Baker's categories 2, 3 and 4). See the examples given in table 5.2.

Table 5.2 *Vocabulary*

Type of Vocabulary	Examples
General vocabulary that has a higher frequency in a specific field	academic: *factor, method, function, occur, cycle*; evaluative adjectives such as *relevant, important, interesting*; tourism: verbs such as *accept, advise, agree, confirm*; collocations, such as *make a booking, launch a campaign*
General English words that have a specific meaning in certain disciplines	*bug* in computer science; *force, acceleration* and *energy* in physics; *stress* and *strain* in mechanics and engineering

In terms of teaching ESP, it is the first category that should be given priority, and this is the area that we shall refer to as semi-technical or core business vocabulary. The specialised uses of general vocabulary in specific disciplines we would regard as an aspect of technical vocabulary.

Semi-technical vocabulary can also be defined through the use of computer-based corpora. Yang (1986) came up with the most comprehensive definitions of general, semi-technical and technical vocabulary which are useful for those wishing to go into these concepts in more detail. There are several useful word count lists: Xue and Nation (1984); Lyne (1983); Ghadessy (1979); West (1953); Hindmarsh (1980); and McArthur (1981).

5.3.3 The teaching of vocabulary in ESP

The teaching of vocabulary in ESP follows similar general principles to those in EGP. It is important to distinguish between vocabulary needed for comprehension and that needed for production. In comprehension, deducing the meaning of vocabulary from the context and from the structure of the actual word is the most important method of learning new vocabulary. For production purposes, storage and retrieval are significant. Various techniques have been suggested for storing vocabulary: the use of word association, mnemonic devices and *loci*, that is the use of visual images to help remember a word (Nattinger, 1988).

Different learners favour different techniques, and it is important that teachers encourage learners to find out what works best for them. Each of these techniques involves cognitive processing rather than mechanical learning of lists. There are three ways in which vocabulary may be gathered to facilitate cognitive processing.

1. Situational, semantic and metaphor sets

Nattinger (1988) suggests that the use of word meaning is the key to successful retrieval and that meanings can be presented in the form of semantic, situational and metaphor sets. The retrieval of a vocabulary item from memory is aided by the grouping of words according to their meaning. This may be according to topic (situational sets), so that the words associated with a *library* such as *book, shelf, borrow, loan period, fine* and so on can be taught together. Or it may be according to chains of association (semantic sets) so that synonyms (for example *dear, expensive*), antonyms (high quality, low quality) superordinates and subordinate terms (vehicle, car) are taught. Alternatively, retrieval may be aided by metaphor. Henderson (1982), for example, has shown how the metaphor of the 'wild horse' has been used to describe inflation in economics writing (such as out of control, run-away inflation, galloping inflation, inflation – the riderless horse).

These examples have clear implications for the teaching of vocabulary and argue for materials that encourage learners to build their own sets. They also justify the syllabuses that are built on notions; one of the perhaps understated strengths of using notions such as *cause and effect, measurement, quantity* and *structure* is that each one brings together vocabulary items that naturally belong in sets.

Reflection 5d

Take (i) the *situational* set of a 'restaurant' (waiter, menu), (ii) the *semantic* set of 'cause and effect' (result in, lead to) and (iii) the *metaphorical* set that 'argument is war' (he defended his claims, he attacked the idea that . . .) and think of other vocabulary items that fit into each set.

---

2. Collocation and the use of corpora

The development of corpora of specific texts has provided an invaluable research and teaching tool for vocabulary. The corpora provide the opportunity to draw up lists of key lexical items in general EAP or EOP texts, or in specific disciplines. Of particular value is the opportunity to examine the context in which a lexical item occurs, its collocation (Scott and Johns, 1993).

Collocation describes the company that a word keeps; from this we can examine *lexical sets*, a family of words the members of which collocate with each other, for example *strong* and *powerful* which both collocate with *argument*. This leads to the notion of *lexical phrases*, certain phrases that always appear in the same form, such as *by pure coincidence* (Carter and McCarthy, 1988). Lexical phrases are discussed in the next section.

The following 'kibbitzer' taken from Tim Johns' web-page (see chapter 10, p. 209) shows how an unnatural collocation can be explained and corrected using examples taken from an appropriate corpus. An international student had written in a draft chapter of his dissertation the following sentence:

> The variation of these ratios *presents some insight* about the financial intermediary role of banks.

As Johns explains, the unnaturalness of the collocation of *present* and *insight* led him to examine the collocations of both words. He looked at concordance lines in a computer database and the examples he found included:

Insight

1. inquiry is a mouthwatering one, *offering an insight into* the detail
2. own accord'. Mr. Aleksashenko's analysis *offers an insight into* the mess
3. its yolk and white, the rotation of nuclei *offers insights into* their fluid

Present

1. record findings, interpret data and *present findings* for different audiences
2. the method used by the Guardian to *present findings*, but doubted whether
3. immunity certificates. This inquiry will *present its findings* later this

As a result of this search the students' sentence was revised to:

> The variation of these ratios *offers* some insight into the role of banks as financial intermediaries.

The main advantage of such an approach is that it takes vocabulary teaching away from looking just at the word to looking at the word in context.

As will be discussed in chapter 10, the big question with the use of corpora and concordance lines is whether they should be used as research tools for the ESP teacher/materials writer, or as teaching material from which learners deduce rules about grammar or lexis. Johns (1991) has argued persuasively for the latter; our own experience is that some students are not very curious about the printouts from the corpus, and prefer to have the teacher summarise findings.

3. Lexical phrases

Research into vocabulary learning (for example Nattinger and De-Carrico, 1992; Peters, 1983) has also suggested that learners do not store vocabulary as individual words, but as chunks of language. We will refer to these chunks as *lexical phrases*, short set phrases that are frequently used in certain situations. In ESP, phrases such as *'the table suggests that . . ., as shown in the diagram, sales fell sharply'* are examples.

Task 5e ●◆

Look again at the texts E5.1 and E5.2 (pp. 246–7).

a) Underline all the words that you consider to be semi-technical in the biology text and those that you consider to be core business vocabulary in the memorandum. Can you think of any situational, semantic or metaphor sets that they belong to?
b) List any collocations that you think worth pointing out to learners;
c) List any useful lexical phrases.

We believe that these lexical phrases tie in very well with the ideas about the predictability of genres as outlined in the next section. To express certain moves, a number of lexical phrases can be identified and taught. For example, expressions such as *sales fell sharply*, are very useful in the description of data in a discussion section of an academic article, or thesis, or in a business presentation.

We do not advocate the unthinking learning of set phrases to express the moves in genres, but there is no reason why we cannot introduce a range of lexical phrases to provide learners with a number of options for expressing moves when teaching speaking or writing. Indeed, when learners have a limited need for English in certain predictable situations, the learning of key lexical phrases may provide a very quick road to the proficiency required of that situation (see Henry, 1996 for a description of the use of an approach of this type with bank cashiers in Saudi Arabia).

5.4 Discourse and genre analysis

Orientation 5f

The term *genre* is widely used in film, music, literature as well as in language teaching. What is your understanding of a genre in these fields, as well as in ESP teaching?

In this section we will look at the burgeoning influence of discourse studies in general, and genre studies in particular on the development of research in all areas of ESP. First, however, we should be clear about how we will use the two overlapping terms of *discourse analysis* and *genre analysis*. Any study of language or, more specifically, text at a level above that of the sentence is a discourse study. This may involve the study of cohesive links between sentences, of paragraph structure, or the structure of the whole text. The results of this type of analysis make statements about how texts – any text – work. This is 'applied' discourse analysis. Where, however, the focus of the text analysis is on the regularities of structure that distinguish one type of text from another type, this is genre analysis and the results focus on the differences between text types, or genres.

We thus see genre analysis as part of discourse analysis. Discourse analysis is both the global (umbrella) term for text analysis and, at the applied level, an actual and specific method of analysis. The methods of applied discourse analysis are valuable in looking at spoken text, especially turn-taking and topic shift in spoken business discourse, and certain general patterns in written text. On the other hand, genre analysis with its particular focus on the distinguishing features of different texts is especially useful in looking at both written and spoken texts in all areas of ESP.

5.4.1 The findings of discourse analysis

We have selected two areas of particular interest to ESP in discourse analysis: firstly certain text patterns that may be used at any time and in any text; secondly turn-taking and topic change within dialogue. We will begin with one particular text pattern found in all text types, the problem-solution pattern. This pattern was first extensively researched by Hoey (1983) and Jordan (1984). The basic pattern consists of four parts:

Situation
Problem with that situation
Response to that problem
Evaluation of that response

If the *evaluation* of the response is negative, this starts another problem sequence. Although the problem-solution pattern is a universal discourse pattern available to any speaker or writer in any kind of situation and which can be pinned down linguistically, it is also a strategy that is widely used to present ideas in both academic and business contexts (Ann Johns, personal communication). Indeed there is evidence that the presentation of a report making recommendations is more effective from a rhetorical point of view if it makes its case using problem-solution patterns.

We have emphasised the problem-solution pattern, but mention should also be made of three other discourse patterns that we have found to occur frequently in both spoken and written text. These are the *hypothetical-real, claim-justification* and the *general-particular* patterns, all types of matching relations (Winter, 1982, 1986; Hoey, 1983). The *hypothetical-real* pattern is widely used, particularly in academic lectures, to contrast what the *theory* predicts (*the hypothetical*) and what happens in *practice* (*the real*). Similarly, the hypothetical-real pattern may be used to evaluate previous work in the field: the previous work is set up as the 'hypothetical', whereas the writer's own results are the 'real'. The *claim-justification* pattern is used where a *claim* needs to be supported by *evidence*. The *general-particular* pattern is widely used to provide detail after a generalisation. An audience needs the writer or speaker to provide a framework or situation statement before specific points.

In spoken text the issues of turn-taking, and opening and closing moves in conversation have been the focus of analysis in both discourse analysis and the ethno-methodological conversation analysis (CA). Discourse analysis has been particularly interested in the role of *discourse markers* such as 'well', 'so', 'right', 'oh' and 'I mean' that show the speaker's intentions. Micheau and Billmyer (1987) conducted research into the strategies used by both native and non-native speakers in a discussion of a case study in an academic context in the USA. They found that non-native speakers had a number of inappropriate strategies for the situation they were participating in at an American university. In particular, they failed to take advantage of the turn-taking possibilities open to them and tended to violate the turn-taking principles by interrupting at unsuitable points. They also used turns that were over-long and often attempted to enter the discussion through the use of over-elaborate phrases.

The implications of these findings for teaching students to participate in meetings or academic seminars are clear, and this study makes good use of the essentially text-bound findings of discourse analysis to investigate a situation in which cross-cultural differences led to difficulties of communication. In general, however, there is a danger that the findings of discourse analysis, which are concerned with texts and how they work as pieces of discourse, fail to take sufficient account of the academic or business context in which communication takes place.

5.4.2 The findings of genre analysis

We will conclude this chapter by picking up the various strands of discussion of genre analysis that have already occurred in earlier chapters and by giving a full account of this developing area of research. Genre analysis in ESP began with Swales' pioneering work (Swales, 1981 and 1990) on the introduction to an academic article. Swales notes that there is a regular pattern of 'moves' and 'steps' that appear in a certain order in the majority of introductions investigated. A 'move' is a unit that relates both to the writer's purpose and to the content that s/he wishes to communicate. A 'step' is a lower level text unit than the move that provides a detailed perspective on the options open to the writer in setting out the moves in the introduction.

Swales' model (Swales, 1990: 141) for the article introduction is shown below:

Move 1	**Establishing a Territory**
Step 1	Claiming centrality
	and/or
Step 2	Making topic generalisations
	and/or
Step 3	Reviewing items of previous research
Move 2	**Establishing a Niche**
Step 1A	Counter-claiming
	or
Step 1B	Indicating a gap
	or
Step 1C	Question-raising
	or
Step 1D	Continuing a tradition

Move 3	Occupying the Niche
Step 1A	Outlining purposes
	or
Step 1B	Announcing present research
Step 2	Announcing principal findings
Step 3	Indicating research article structure

This model and its earlier version (Swales, 1981) have had a major influence on research and the teaching of writing in EAP. The advantage is that the moves and steps seem to reflect a reality in text and in the way in which writers approach the task of writing up their research. From a pedagogic point of view it is possible to convert the analysis very readily into teaching material that provides a way into both the organisation of writing and the relevant language forms (see, for example, Weissberg and Buker, 1990; Swales and Feak, 1994).

Swales' work led to parallel research into other sections of the research article such as the Results, Discussion of Results and Abstract. Dudley-Evans (1994) then suggested an extension of the model to account for the greater length and complexity of MSc dissertations. Hopkins and Dudley-Evans (1988) adopted a similar approach to the discussion sections of both articles and dissertations. The fullest description of these moves comes in Dudley-Evans (1994). The list of moves in discussion sections is shown below:

Move 1 Information Move
Move 2 Statement of Result
Move 3 Finding
Move 4 (Un)expected Outcome
Move 5 Reference to Previous Research
Move 6 Explanation
Move 7 Claim
Move 8 Limitation
Move 9 Recommendation

The moves are essentially options open to the writer who will build his or her argument through the careful choice and ordering of these moves into cycles.

Research into the nature of the academic essay has been rather less fruitful. The academic essay is much less predictable than the genres discussed above and there appears to be relatively little consensus about what exactly constitutes a good essay, even within specific disciplines (O'Brien, 1992). A more tangible question is what stance a student should adopt. Should the student adopt a critical or uncritical stance to established theory? Should the student just report on this theory or develop his or her own position with regard to that theory? The answer to these questions depends on the level of the students, the discipline, the actual question and the lecturer for whom the essay is being written. Much can undoubtedly be done to help students write a clear and well-structured introduction or conclusion; to express guarded and appropriately hedged opinions; to refer to previous research. The broader question of the aims of writing an essay in a given discipline also need to be addressed.

In the area of EOP, Bhatia (1993) has shown that the techniques of genre analysis developed originally for the study of academic text can be applied to business letters and legal documents. He looks at two types of business letters which he calls *promotional genres* – the *sales promotion* letter and the *job application* letter – and finds that they use a virtually identical pattern of moves:

	Sales Promotion Letter	*Job Application Letter*
Move 1	Establishing credentials	Establishing credentials
Move 2	Introducing the offer	Introducing the candidature
Move 3	Offering incentives	Offering incentives
Move 4	Enclosing documents	Enclosing documents
Move 5	Soliciting response	Using pressure tactics
Move 6	Using pressure tactics	Soliciting response
Move 7	Ending politely	Ending politely

He also looks at the structure of legal cases, the 'abridged version of court judgements' (Bhatia, 1993: 118) and finds that they exhibit a typical four-move pattern with the following moves:

Move 1   Identifying the case
Move 2   Establishing the facts of the case
Move 3   Arguing the case
       3.1 stating the history of the case
       3.2 presenting arguments
       3.3 deriving *ratio decidendi (*the principle of law that the judge wishes to set down for application to future cases of a similar description)
Move 4   Pronouncing judgement

Thus far the research in genre analysis that we have reported has been very much text-based. It undoubtedly offers the ESP teacher a way into these texts, both for preparing reading and writing materials (see chapter 6), but there is a danger of becoming 'stuck' in the text, by which we mean being interested only in the surface features rather than the context and other outside influences on the text. One of the main advantages of genre analysis is its ability to relate textual findings to features of the discourse community within which the genre is produced. Swales (1990: 24–7) lists the following six defining characteristics of a discourse community:

1. A discourse community has a broadly agreed set of common public goals.
2. A discourse community has mechanisms of intercommunication among its members.
3. A discourse community uses its participatory mechanisms primarily to provide information and feedback.
4. A discourse community utilises and hence possesses one or more genres in the communicative furtherance of its aims.
5. In addition to owning genres, a discourse community has acquired some specific lexis.
6. A discourse community has a threshold level of members with a suitable degree of relevant content and discoursal expertise.

The concept of a discourse community is extremely useful, but it can be difficult in practice to produce real and concrete examples of actual discourse communities. An individual may be a member of many discourse communities, and the actual communities may be so large and amorphous that it may be easier to consider the concept of discourse community as a 'virtual' concept (Miller, 1994) that relates to the ways in which a writer or speaker producing a genre will be affected by expectations of that genre. At the individual level, writers or speakers construct their messages by imagining the needs of an imaginary reader or set of readers. They will, during the process of writing or speaking, constantly ask themselves the question 'what do I need to explain to make the message clear?' At the same time they will also ask themselves the question 'what does the discourse community expect me to do in terms of layout, organisation and structuring of the argument, or to include in terms of content?' Clearly, these two questions or processes overlap, but we think that it is useful to separate – albeit a little artificially – the role of writers or speakers as individuals and as 'social actors' in a community.

Consideration of these issues leads to the conclusion that genre analysis needs to take very seriously the academic and professional contexts in which genres exist and the sociological research into those contexts. Berkenkotter and Huckin (1995: 2–3) argue that genre studies have tended to 'reify' genres and see them as 'linguistic abstractions'. They argue for an approach based on 'case research with insiders' investigating the ways in which writers use the genre knowledge that they acquire 'strategically' to participate in a discipline's or a profession's activities. We discussed (in chapter 4) Charles' (1994 and 1996) findings on how the nature of the business relationship is reflected in the interaction of the event.

The more detailed sociological consideration of the context in which texts are written is important for ESP, especially in the professional and business contexts (Bazerman and Paradis, 1991). There is evidence that 'local' discourse communities either develop or adapt genres to meet the needs and expectations of the readership, and that there is a dynamic tension between the existence of models for a genre and the changes in the professional or business context that necessitate adaptation of the model (Berkenkotter and Huckin, 1995). Smart (1992, 1993) shows how the ESP teacher can play a role in helping writers understand this tension and adapt their writing, as well as in the on-going discussion of the suitability of the current models. The ESP teacher can be both a teacher of genre and a genre doctor.

What does this mean for teaching learners to use specific genres? We need to teach moves, but in a flexible manner (Dudley-Evans, 1995): In EAP, we need to introduce the idea that different departments expect students to adopt different stances. On British Masters courses in business, finance and banking, students are often expected in their essays to adopt the stance of the financial or business adviser making recommendations to an imagined client. In more 'mainstream' academic departments such as plant biology the stance expected is that of the critical reader evaluating the previous literature in the field of study and cautiously presenting claims arising from experimental results. In EOP, writers also need to be familiar with appropriate politeness strategies in making requests, complaints and in generally conducting business activities through letters, faxes and e-mail messages.

Our examples have come from written genres as most of the published research in genre analysis has been on written text. There is, however, growing interest in spoken genres, and the techniques that we have described are just as applicable to the analysis of spoken as of written text.

Reflection 5g

Choose a journal, either one in the area of applied linguistics or a subject area that you are interested in. Take the abstracts at the beginning of each article and see if you can devise a set of moves that capture the structure of the abstracts. Consider also any evidence of the ways in which pressures from the discourse community have influenced the texts.

5.5 Summary

In this chapter we have synthesised much of the research into the language and discourse of academic and professional English. We have moved from the grammar of academic English to the lexis of scientific, technical and business communication, to certain discourse features of spoken and written texts and, finally, to the genres used by academic and professional discourse communities. In all the analyses we have described, textual studies exist side by side with observations of insiders using rhetorical strategies. We believe strongly that both types of study are needed in ESP research. In fact, this balance between the more quantitative and the more qualitative types of study exists in other aspects of ESP work, for example in needs analysis, and we see no essential conflict between them.

5.6 Recommended reading

Peter Master (1986, 1991) writes about grammatical aspects of ESP; Huckin and Olsen (1991), Brieger and Sweeney (1994), Duckworth (1995), and Wilberg and Lewis (1990) can be used for reference. The Collins *Cobuild Grammar* (1995) is also useful; it is based on the same *corpus* as the *Cobuild Dictionary*. The volume edited by Lackstrom *et al.* (1973) has various studies of register features of EST. For vocabulary, Lewis (1993) and Carter and McCarthy (1988) are not specific to ESP but are interesting. Martinez (1994) lists semi-technical vocabulary in technical subjects, separating out Spanish cognates.

Swales (1990), Bhatia (1993) and Dudley-Evans (1987a) are good introductions to genre; Myers (1989) and Bazerman (1988) have been influential in this area. Halliday and Martin (1993) summarise the work of the Sydney school of genre analysis. Dillon (1991) has a good discussion of the rhetoric of the various social sciences.

6 The skills in EAP and EOP

6.1 Aims

In chapters 3 and 4 we looked at various linguistic features of EAP and EBP but we did not go into great detail on the skills of listening, speaking, reading and writing. We believe that the issues around these skills do not differ dramatically between EAP and EOP, and so here we will outline the key features indicating their relevance to both areas; we will also consider how the skills are taught. We shall, in fact, treat them as five skills: reading, listening (to monologue), listening and speaking, speaking (a monologue), and writing.

We opted for five skills because, when we discuss listening comprehension, we need to be clear about whether we are referring to listening to monologue, as in an academic lecture or a business presentation, or to listening as part of a group discussion, as in a business meeting or negotiation or a seminar in which the listener will also contribute as a speaker to the discussion. The same issue arises with speaking, which may be interactive in a two-way or group discussion or may be monologue, when the speaker is making a presentation.

The term 'skills' is used at two levels: there are five *macro-skills* of reading, listening, listening and speaking, speaking, and writing, each consisting of a number of *micro-skills*. Some (micro) skills such as 'using cohesive and discourse markers' will be associated with all the (macro) skills; others such as 'revising a first draft of a text' will be associated with a particular (macro) skill, in this case writing.

We will look at each of the five macro-skills in turn, but this does not imply that we should necessarily teach them separately; an integrated approach is usually desirable.

6.2 Reading skills in ESP

In this section we shall look at how the purpose of reading and the balance between skills and language affect the teaching of reading in ESP. We shall not discuss the micro-skills in detail; there are several excellent books and articles on this listed in the recommended reading. We shall then discuss three key stages in designing and teaching a reading course (or course component): the selection of texts, the extracting and recording of information, and the use of the information that has been gathered.

6.2.1 The purpose of reading: TALO to TAVI

One of the most important contributions to the approach to reading in ESP was the shift from Text As a Linguistic Object (TALO) to Text As a Vehicle of Information (TAVI) (Johns and Davies, 1983). Johns and Davies encapsulated the key principles that, for ESP learners, extracting information accurately and quickly is more significant than language details; that understanding the macrostructure comes before language study; and that application of the information in the text is of paramount importance. The reader first processes the language and then links the ideas to what is already known. Table 6.1 summarises their key points.

6.2.2 The balance between skills and language

Around the same time, there was a second significant contribution to teaching reading on ESP courses: the recognition that good reading requires language and skills. Hosenfeld (1977) had shown that less successful foreign language learners had a fragmented approach to text, while successful learners went for overall meaning, guessing or skipping language and information. Alderson (1984) tested several hypotheses about the role of language and skills and showed that poor reading in a foreign language is due in part to poor reading in the L1, together with an inadequate knowledge of the foreign language. He showed that learners need to reach a threshold level of language knowledge before they are able to transfer any L1 skills to their L2 reading tasks.

The reading component of an ESP course thus requires a balance between skills and language development. Some of the key skills to be learnt or transferred into the new language are:

- selecting what is relevant for the current purpose;
- using all the features of the text such as headings, layout, typeface;
- skimming for content and meaning;
- scanning for specifics;
- identifying organisational patterns;
- understanding relations within a sentence and between sentences;
- using cohesive and discourse markers (*ctd. p. 98*);

Table 6.1 *TALO and TAVI*

	TALO	TAVI
Principles underlying text selection	• texts illustrate syntactic structures • topics are of general interest • texts are specially written, modified or re-written • new vocabulary is controlled • texts are graded and short • texts are selected by teachers	• texts are chosen for their value in relation to students' needs • a range of authentic texts are used • grading is through tasks and support • texts are of different lengths, getting longer • texts are selected not only by teachers, but also by learners and others
Preparatory activities	• almost none • some translation of vocabulary	• always: important as direction finders, to awaken interest and to establish purpose
Working with the text	• focus on language and what is unknown • focus on detail and understanding all the sentences and words • questions on syntax	• focus on information and what is known • guessing unknown words • focus on links between meaning (function) and form
Type of teaching/learning interaction	• teacher monologue • teacher-centred: teacher questions, student responds, teacher evaluates	• students work in groups • reversal of roles: students ask questions, evaluate each other, reach agreement • model for self-study • learner and learning-centred*
Follow-up activities	• comprehension questions • grammar and lexis exercises	• using the information: transfer, application or extension • applying techniques

* the term 'learning-centred' was not used at this stage (1983) but with their discussion on modelling how students would study their subjects outside of the English class one aspect of the concept is present in Johns and Davies' approach.

- predicting, inferring and guessing;
- identifying main ideas, supporting ideas and examples;
- processing and evaluating the information during reading;
- transferring or using the information while or after reading.

Most of these skills are composed of several processes. We believe that it has been a misconception in some interpretations of ESP that skimming and scanning are *the* key skills (*cf*. the teaching of connectors in writing). Skimming and scanning are useful first stages for determining whether to read a document or which parts to read carefully. Once a document has been identified as relevant, then ESP readers need to read carefully, extract meaning and consider the author's attitude. Author's attitude is particularly important; it is another misconception that scientific discourse is attitude-free.

6.2.3 Designing and teaching reading courses

Where the balance between skills and language development lies in a reading course depends on the Present Situation Analysis (PSA) of the learners. The reading material will (i) be used for a given purpose – preferably some application or transfer of information; (ii) be designed to encourage the use (or teaching) of good skills; and (iii) have follow-up language work that concentrates on what is transferable. First though, there must be a suitable text to process.

Selecting texts

Who chooses? Traditionally, texts have mainly been chosen by institutions and teachers: by institutions through the textbooks available on the market; by teachers through the textbooks in their resource centre and any supplementary material they provide. However, learners and subject specialists also have an important role to play in selecting texts for reading. The texts they supply can become part of a regular course or be used just once.

The scenario where subject specialists contribute to text selection is most likely in EAP and English for Vocational Purposes (EVP) situations where there are set texts to study and to use. For instance, in EVP situations there may be a need to understand particular manuals for carrying out maintenance processes or for operating equipment. In some training situations the actual texts for work use may be brought into the language classroom; in others appropriate, interesting work-related texts may be provided. In deciding what to use, an ESP teacher will balance needs and motivational factors.

Learners may bring texts that they need to understand or texts they think would be interesting and valuable. The advantage here is that learners 'own' the texts and are involved and committed to them. These texts may be allotted classtime or self-study time according to whether they represent group or individual needs and interests.

What is chosen? The criteria used for selecting texts will relate to key features of both carrier and real content. We have already mentioned that the conceptual level of the carrier content must be neither trivial nor distractingly high and that there must be both value and interest to it. However, it is insufficient to satisfy carrier content criteria; our real purpose is with the real content and the chosen texts must clearly exemplify this. Table 6.2 summarises key criteria for selecting each text.

Table 6.2 *Text Selection Criteria*

Carrier content	Real content
conceptual level	significance
novelty	relation to objectives
value	exploitability
interest	clarity
	accessibility

In addition to the criteria that each individual text should meet, there are other factors to consider across a whole reading course or component (St John, 1992). These are summarised in table 6.3.

Table 6.3 *Text Selection Criteria across a Course*

Criteria	Comment
a range of sources	to reflect what is read and written
the full range of topic types	examples of all those common to the field (see Davies and Greene, 1984)
full range of purposes	to cover all purposes shown by needs analysis
non-verbal information	exploit realistically
dating	carrier content for on-going use must stand the test of time
varied text lengths	according to real reading; we process long and short texts differently

When using extracts from a long text, readers will need to know that it is an extract and to have one or two sentences (which probably have to be specially written) for orientation. These provide the context necessary for activating existing knowledge and accurate processing. If only the start of long texts were used, then all the reading would be of an introductory nature.

Once good texts have been selected, then activities can be written. These will relate to the overall purpose of reading the text and so the process begins from using the information gathered.

Using the information that has been gathered

Although this may be the final step in the process of reading a text, it is the one from which the design of activities begins. Knowing what students would really do with a text, and why, is necessary for setting the task that will guide the reading process and determine all the other activities. Whereas for EAP students it may be enough to make notes or to add to previous notes, EVP students may carry out an action while reading, for example when following instructions, and a BE student may have to write a response or make a telephone call.

The first stage for the ESP teacher is to know what kind of tasks and processing would be associated with particular texts or information. Can general principles be deduced, data analysed, situations appraised or problems solved? How would the expert set about understanding the text? What information would be extracted and in what format?

Reflection 6a

Think of different ESP learners (for example a doctor, a waiter, an engineering student, a secretary). For each one draw up a table showing: what type of documents they read, what they do with each type – purpose and task in reading and which skills and strategies are likely to be most used with each document. For example:

Hotel receptionist

documents	purpose	task	skills
fax/letter of reservation	extract booking requirement	check availability; write reply; record booking on form/computer	find details; relate to other information

---

Extracting and recording information

With a short document, highlighting the relevant information on the actual text may be an appropriate strategy. For instance, the facts in a business letter or fax could be highlighted in one colour and the calls for action in another. With longer or more complex documents extracting the information and reorganising it and fitting it in with existing knowledge is necessary. Visual representations can be very helpful for this – especially for right-hemisphere learners (see chapter 10). Key graphic representations include lists, columns, tables, matrices, tree diagrams, flow charts, bubble diagrams and mind maps. Then there are other two-dimensional representations such as maps, plans, pictures and different kinds of graphs. Which type is appropriate depends in part on the type of information.

Task 6b ●◆

For each item in column A suggest one or more suitable visual representation.

A Type of information	B Visual representation(s)
advantages and disadvantages	
cause and effect	
process	
physical structure	
numerical data	
location	
alternative procedures	
comparison/contrast	
how something works	

One indication of a good balance among our chosen texts is a full range of these visual representations. Flow diagrams in every chapter suggest an over-emphasis on process texts, tree diagrams on classification texts.

Having determined the overall task, the individual activities are designed to help the learner to process the language and relate the new information to existing schemata. These activities are not presented randomly but sequenced. A learner may decide just to do the main task, in their own way. If the learner carries out the other activities these should be building on each other so that at the end the main task has either been completed or is now easy to complete.

6.3 Listening to monologue

The ability to follow monologue, specifically the lecture, is particularly important in EAP situations and has received a great deal of attention in both research and teaching materials. In EOP situations, doctors and other professional people attend conferences and listen to presentations; technicians have to listen to and understand instructions; business people and other professionals listen to policy presentations.

Comprehension of a lecture, seminar or business presentation will involve the same two-stage process we noted for second language (L2) reading comprehension, the first being processing of the language, the second being the change to background knowledge of the topic that results from the understanding of the language. The process of listening to monologue has much in common with the reading process.

Orientation 6c

Draw up a list for ways in which:

a) reading and listening to monologue are similar;
b) listening to monologue differs from reading.

6.3.1 Micro-skills and language

A significant number of micro-skills related to listening are seen as necessary for effective comprehension of monologue. Flowerdew (1995: 12) quotes Richards (1983) who lists the following micro-skills:

ability to
1. identify the purpose and scope of monologue
2. identify the topic of lecture and follow topic development
3. recognise the role of discourse markers
4. recognise key lexical items related to subject/topic
5. deduce meanings of words from context
6. recognise function of intonation to signal information structure (for example pitch, volume, pace, key)

This research is drawn from the study of academic lectures, but it will equally apply to other monologues, and indeed to many conversational situations.

Both reading and listening thus involve a focus on the meaning of the text and on making links between meaning in different parts of the text. Both involve guessing the meaning of unknown words from the context and understanding the role of logical connectors. The key difference is that the listener does not get a second chance to catch the meaning of the listening text, whereas the reader can go over a text as often as s/he needs until the meaning is clear. As a result, a speaker includes much more redundancy in the text, more statements introducing and summarising the topic, and more repetition. If listeners can recognise the redundancy used in a monologue, this will improve their ability to follow topic development.

There are, we believe, five specific features of listening to monologue that influence the design of listening courses and materials.

6.3.2   Distinguishing features of monologue

1.   Phonology

One key feature which distinguishes listening to a lecture or seminar from reading a textbook or article is that listeners have to cope with phonological features of language as well as the other features of text. They have to be able to cope with the intonation patterns and to recognise unit boundaries (Brazil, 1985). They also need to be able to recognise phonological signals indicating both the main points of the lecture and the digressions into asides, jokes and other topics unrelated to the main topics of the lecture (Flowerdew, 1995).

2.   Speed of delivery

Listeners also have to cope with the speed of delivery; research (Flowerdew, 1994) indicates that a high speed of delivery causes comprehension difficulties for non-native speakers. Griffiths (1990), for example, found that a fairly fast speech rate of 220 words per minute led to a significant fall-off in comprehension amongst lower-intermediate learners. Interestingly, the use of a very slow speech-rate, 100 words per minute, did not lead to better comprehension than with the average rate of 150 words per minute.

3.   Real time processing

A monologue has to be understood as it is delivered. There is no opportunity to listen to certain sections of the lecture again in the way that a written text can be re-read until it is understood. Nor is there the possibility of skim reading or skipping certain sections of text (Buck, 1992). There is rarely a second chance to listen to the lecture. This creates the need for listeners to discipline themselves not to lose concentration on the main thread of the argument in sections of the lecture in which the lecturer introduces an aside in colloquial language that is difficult for the non-native speaker to comprehend (Dudley-Evans and Johns, 1981).

4. Note-taking in real time

The taking of notes is a complex task that requires a student to be assessing whether or not a point made by the lecturer needs to be noted down and how it can be taken down in such a way as to be understandable when the notes are consulted at a later stage. The student has to process the language, relate the new information to existing schemata and find a way to record that new, related information. Various descriptions exist in the literature (for example Chaudron *et al.*, 1995) of courses designed to help students develop a technique for taking effective notes from lectures.

In non-English-medium situations the note-taking skill may be much less important, and possibly redundant. Note-making (more concerned with summarising than just getting the information down) might form part of a reading skills course. In EOP situations, note-taking is likely to be more limited; a few key points or queries may be jotted down. The audience will often be given related material to take away.

5. Deducing the speaker's attitude

In some monologues it will be important to deduce the stance the speaker is adopting towards the information that he or she is reporting. Is the speaker favourable towards, neutral towards or critical of the work he or she is reporting? In EAP situations this is almost invariably done cautiously, using politeness strategies – certainly in the case of criticisms – and it is often difficult for non-native speakers (and sometimes native speakers) to deduce exactly what the speaker's attitude is. This may also be a problem in reading comprehension, but it is much more difficult to pick up attitudes in a talk.

6.3.3 *The teaching of listening comprehension*

There seem to be two questions that frame approaches to the teaching of listening comprehension. Should the teaching material focus on the micro-skills, building them up in an atomistic way until the student has control of each one? Lynch's (1983) *Study Listening* is an excellent example of such an approach. Or should the material adopt a task-oriented approach in which students initially listen for specific information (which may be required as part of a larger task that involves the use of other skills), for example as in *Executive Listening* (Waistell, 1993). Our experience is that a focus on extracting meaning from the listening text is the key micro-skill, and that learners, whether of EAP or EOP, need to have the experience of listening to monologue delivered at an authentic speed and try to extract the key information for a specified purpose. As with teaching reading, developing a control of the micro-skills should be secondary to the overall aim of extracting information.

What do we use for listening practice? As with reading, the listening text must be authentic in source and purpose. An orally delivered lecture is very different from a written text; reading aloud from a written text does not reflect normal use and such listening lacks authenticity of purpose. (The exception is the (poor) practice that is sometimes met when academics read out their written paper!) Similarly, a recording which involves, say, a business person talking about his or her area of expertise to non-experts will be different in content and purpose from how s/he would talk to peers and therefore not an authentic task for that context.

So how can we supplement published listening materials and retain authenticity of speech with its hesitations and redundancy, its less compact and complex grammar? Some suggestions include:

- choosing a topic, making notes and delivering a short talk from those notes;
- asking a colleague from the specific area to record a short talk on a relevant topic;
- recording discussions between academics or professionals;
- recording radio or television programmes and choosing a few short sections.

Task 6d ●◆

Consider the two extracts of listening comprehension activities, E1.2 (pp. 234–5) and E6.1 (p. 248).

a) What are the differences in their approach to teaching listening?
b) Which approach would be most suitable for your own situation?

6.4 Listening and speaking skills in ESP

6.4.1 Spoken interaction in EAP and EOP

This section concentrates on situations where listening and speaking are both required within the real time of the communicative event. In these circumstances participants have dual roles – as listeners and as speakers. We shall use the term 'spoken interaction' to cover situations where both these skills are employed, where to say the right thing in an appropriate way requires good listening skills as well as speaking skills.

In the earlier years of ESP development spoken interactions received almost no attention. In EOP teaching there has been more attention to spoken interactions. In fact, courses may concentrate entirely on this aspect, for example courses for students in the hotel and catering fields or for air traffic controllers.

Active listening

Good listening is vital in spoken interactions, particularly in business, and goes beyond understanding the words and the key points; it is a skill and an art. *Active listening* has been adopted from management interpersonal skills courses and is an example of an interdisciplinary crossover. Active listening includes the non-verbal and the verbal encouragement given to a speaker, for example, non-verbal physical expressions, gestures and movements, and verbal 'back-channelling' devices such as 'uh uh, really, right, that's interesting, tell me more' and questions.

Active listening also involves paraphrasing and summarising so that the speaker knows that their message has been heard. Thus active listening can involve speaking; it is about showing that we have been listening and understanding, and not thinking about other matters. The purpose is not to take over the turn but to encourage the speaker so that we find out more.

Reflection 6e ➡️

a) List some of the verbal encouragements and some of the non-verbal encouragements used in English and in another language – your L1 if it is not English.

b) With a partner, take turns in active listening. The speaker talks for up to five minutes on a topic of interest to them. The listener is active and summarises at the end. If, as the speaker, you do not feel the listener is actively participating, then stop and wait for encouragement. Does the summary give the same importance to points as you did? Has anything been missed out – or added?

An additional feature of good listening relates to body language. What body language conveys has a cultural dimension (see chapter 4). Scollon and Scollon (1995) discuss how a smile may be a sign of satisfaction in one culture (western cultures) and a signal of a potential problem in another (Asian cultures). Matching (but not mimicking) the speakers' body language and tone of voice can make them feel more comfortable and thus encourage them to talk.

For an effective spoken interaction it is not enough to be a good listener. It is also necessary to steer the interaction; hearing all about product specifications when you want to know about delivery dates is not efficient. An effective spoken interaction encourages talk (through active listening) and controls the direction of the interaction – and questioning is one way to achieve that.

Questioning

Orientation 6f

Brainstorm, and then try to group, different purposes for asking questions and different kinds of question.

Questioning is another skill and art needed for effective spoken interaction and, like active listening, it goes beyond just the words. Questioning is a powerful means of controlling communication. Questions can be asked for a range of purposes, using a variety of language forms. Questions may be about information – for detail, for reasons, for feelings; they may be about clarification – checking understanding, confirming; they can also be tactical – to stall for time, to disturb, to show the strengths or weaknesses of arguments. To ask questions, learners need to know several language structures:

1. use of the auxiliary with subject/verb inversion
2. 'Wh' words + auxiliary + inversion
3. statements and (rising) intonation
4. statements + tags (These are frequently not genuine questions: they can be used to confirm information but are often used merely to express a view or desire.)

In EGP and EGBP, these structures are generally taught separately as specific grammatical forms. However, in ESP situations a different perspective is useful; one based not on the format of the question but on the *response* the question will lead to. Three of the common categories of response are closed, limited and open:

Closed-response questions lead to 'yes/no' answers (grammatical structure 1). In social conversation, Grice's maxim of quantity (1975) means that responders often go beyond the yes/no and provide additional information. However, different maxims may operate in business or diplomacy and closed questions may result in a yes/no response with no additional information. Closed questions are a weak way to obtain information, but a powerful means of checking information or gaining commitment. For example:

> Did the order arrive on time?
> Will you be available on the 23rd?

Limited-response questions lead to specific information (grammatical structure 2) and are good for obtaining details. For example:

> What was last year's turnover?
> Which machine is playing up?

Open-response questions give a wider scope to the responder and do not bias the content of the response. They are vital for information gathering as they are the least directive. For example:

> In what ways is that a problem?
> How do you see this developing?
> How do you think we should . . . ?

They are mainly formed using 'Wh' structures with verbs of emotion or expansion, for example, 'what do you feel . . . ?', 'to what extent . . . ?', 'can you expand on that?'

Additional categories of questions are probing and building. Often questioners work from within their own frameworks and ask questions based on their own perspective and state of knowledge. That way information can be missed. The art of questioning is to work from the responder's framework which can lead to new insights. Careful listening gives rise to questions which are generated by the speaker's words.

Probing questions narrow down the information and generally concentrate on facts; they are often also limited-response questions. Probing can be cued as in the following examples:

> . . . everyone . . . Exactly who?
> . . . always . . . When?

Building questions aim to expand and may attempt to deal with feelings and values as well as facts; they are often open.

> What are your concerns about . . .?
> Why do you think that . . .?

The questions asked will depend on the purpose and the kind of response required and these may vary during an interaction. A technical discussion or a sightseeing tour may focus on detail and use limited-response questions. During a business meeting all types of question may be needed: For instance, at the start of a meeting a closed question may get the ball rolling but then open and building questions will establish interests and concerns. Limited response and probing may clarify details before commitment is sought through closed questions.

One-to-one spoken interactions

Many spoken interactions involve just two people; telephone conversations (excluding telephone conferencing) are one example. Many social situations, even where there are more people, also revolve around dialogues.

Telephone conversations can be difficult to handle mainly because of the absence of body language. Mehrabian's results (1971) showed that a listener's trust and belief in what is said can depend more on the body language than on the words.

An additional difficulty is that certain stages or types of telephone call are still quite conventional and can use phrases that will not be met elsewhere:

Stage	Phrase
getting going	X speaking. Who's calling?
getting the person you want	Can you put me through to . . .? Hold on, please.

A good deal of the speaking work carried out in Business English falls under the heading 'socialising'. The term encompasses the spoken interactions that surround the actual discussion of business matters. We prefer to use the term 'building relationships' as this expresses the real purpose of these interactions. A good business relationship depends on credibility, understanding, goodwill and trust. This is only partially generated through the business discussions. Building relationships is also to do with attitudes, as shown through features such as smiles, eye contact and topics of conversation – and the value of these is culture-dependent. Building relationships has a great deal to do with sensitivity to others' values.

Reflection 6g

What topics of conversation are good for building business relationships in your country, or others you know of?

Multi-person spoken interactions

One-to-one interactions also include meetings but issues such as turn-taking and control have greatest significance in multi-person interactions. Non-native speakers often complain that they have difficulty in getting into conversations, either informal, personal conversations or more formal discussions in meetings. Micheau and Billmyer (1987) have shown that NNS may use inappropriate strategies for entering a discussion in an American university.

One key skill lies in recognising when the speaker is giving signals that s/he is ready to finish the turn and 'hand over the floor' to another speaker. This may be done by the nomination of another speaker which can occur in meetings and in unstructured conversation. It is much more likely, however, that other participants will have to enter the discussion without being nominated. Listeners have to be aware of either syntactic, phonological or non-verbal clues that the turn is coming to an end. Syntactic clues are the approach of completeness of a given utterance, in other words the reaching of a natural grammatical and semantic break. The phonological signal of the willingness to hand over the turn is a drop in pitch (Brazil, 1985; McCarthy, 1991). Non-verbal clues include looking around at others, moving papers to one side.

A second skill is to then gain entry at the end of the turn. Sometimes a listener will anticipate the conclusion of a turn and complete it for the speaker as a way of gaining the floor. There are also various phrases (known as gambits) that can be used to facilitate entry, particularly in discussions and meetings. These range from informal expressions such as 'Hang on a minute' through 'Can I make a point here?' to the formal 'Madam chair'.

Other skills are to handle the turn effectively – to judge how long is appropriate and to prevent interruptions; to judge when a contribution will be most effective; to know who will support an idea and to get that support verbalised. These skills are developed in management training programmes and are part of effective business communication and Business English. They are also relevant for EAP seminar work. In the 1980s in the UK some work on seminar skills was reported and it was recognised that both the purpose and format of seminars could vary substantially. For instance, some students take part in seminars requiring the preparation and delivery of an oral paper and some are involved in discussing problem-solving exercises. Seminar discussions have much in common with other discussions and meeting situations – the need to turntake, to check and clarify, to question and respond, to give opinions. Seminar presentations share much with business presentation skills. Certainly the work reported on oral presentations, for both native and non-native university students, covers similar ground (see speaking monologue).

6.4.2 The teaching of spoken interactions

Whatever the focus of an ESP course, there can be a good deal of listening and speaking going on. This should not be confused with teaching effective spoken interaction. Task-based activities and group work generate discussion and provide learners with practice; but what of the input and feedback stages? Interestingly, these are often not an explicit part even of work which comes under the heading of 'speaking' or 'listening'. As a result some of the features discussed earlier may never be taught or discussed.

Speaking activities often just provide a scenario for interaction whereas learners might find it helpful to consider first what the features of a successful interaction would be. This would focus their attention on appropriate language and skills, and provide a basis for evaluation at the feedback stage.

On the listening side much comprehension work, particularly in EAP, has evolved around note-taking and showing understanding by answering questions on the content (mostly by writing information down, whether in prose or in a diagrammatic format). The listener is an outsider. In EOP spoken interactions, writing is rare. The point is to show that you have been listening actively and have really heard what is said. If a speaker does not feel s/he has been heard, then that speaker will keep repeating the point or withdraw from active participation. Once the speaker knows s/he has been listened to, then even if the topic or suggestion is rejected s/he more readily drops it.

Showing understanding is achieved through the use of paraphrasing, summarising and questioning, all of which require the listener to take part, to be an insider. However, listening practice provided in language teaching materials usually places the learner as an outsider. Thus learners fill in the blanks, take notes, answer comprehension questions. However, the listener can become an insider when we add questions with a different focus such as: 'You are present when [x] is being discussed. After (each stage of) the discussion summarise the key points as you understand them.' or 'You are present at the meeting. What questions would you wish to ask the speakers?'

Feedback

When students work on reading and writing, their efforts are tangible – words on a page – and can be discussed and revised. The equivalent tangibility in spoken interactions is gained through recordings, most specifically through video recordings. Equipment for video recording is more expensive than books, but as essential. Underlying our approach to the teaching of spoken interaction skills is the use of positive feedback (based on recordings) to enhance learning. Confidence is a significant factor for many people in speaking a language, and classroom feedback should be based on maintaining and increasing confidence.

Reformulation works well for spoken language and it is useful to take sections of an interaction and work through reformulating it. Likewise, some spoken interactions can be treated as some writing is – as a process of drafting; that is learners can be given an opportunity to speak, to obtain feedback perhaps with reformulation, and then to 'redraft' by repeating the interaction.

6.5 Speaking monologue

Spoken monologue, that is oral presentations, can be a feature of EOP and EAP work. Mostly the teaching of oral presentations in EAP occurs in English-medium situations (table 3.1 situation 1) with some examples in EAP courses of situation 2. In EOP, oral presentations feature particularly on courses for tour guides, sales representatives and professional people such as doctors and engineers.

6.5.1 Key features of oral presentations

An effective oral presentation is built on language and skills and requires confidence. ESP courses are likely to look at: structuring, visuals, voice, and advance signalling as well as language.

Structuring a presentation has much in common with structuring written communication in as much as listeners want a clear *map* to follow; there should be a start, a middle and an end. The adage, 'tell 'em what you're going to say, say it, tell 'em what you've said' still works well for the broad structure.

Genre analysis of written articles shows a limited range of moves in introductions and a more complex situation in discussions. Likewise, in oral presentations, the moves in the introduction and conclusion include:

Introduction	Conclusion
establish credentials	
state purpose and topic	summarise
indicate time	make recommendations
outline what is to come	call for action

The middle is more complex, but a good start gets listeners on board. A good end is essential; it is what remains with listeners. If only one stage is planned and practised it should be the ending. The moves in the middle section will depend on the type and purpose of the presentation. It seems likely that the natural and logical orders used to structure written information are valid. Thus the patterns of situation – problem – solution(s) – evaluation, general to specific, and most to least significant occur in oral presentations.

It is often said, '*Visuals* are worth a thousand words'. Yes, if they are good and used well, otherwise . . . ! Visuals can include a few written words but are hardly visual if they are primarily text and then get read aloud! However, there is specific spoken language associated with visual aids which will:

signal that a visual aid is coming
say what the visual represents
explain why the visual is being used
highlight what is most significant

Voice work may include pronunciation but intonation usually hinders comprehension more. Phrasing, pausing, speed of delivery, volume and tone variation all play an important role and may need as much attention as the actual words. Pausing is silence and often feels uncomfortable to a less confident speaker. It is though essential processing time for listeners. Silence is also a part of the language of visuals; the silent time when the visual makes its impact and the audience absorbs and processes the information.

Advance signalling or signposts help listeners follow both the structure of the information and argument, and recognise the significance of visuals. For instance through enumeration as in 'I've divided my talk into three parts' or advance labelling as in 'The next table helps us understand why' (Tadros, 1985).

6.5.2 Teaching oral presentations

For practical reasons, oral presentation work is often only a component on courses with restricted numbers. However, it is possible, with ingenuity, to include such work in large class situations (see chapter 10). At the Federal University of Technology, Minna, Nigeria, staff found a way in the mid-80s to develop oral presentation skills. Classes (minimum 40) were split and half attended taped listening comprehension work in an audio laboratory where a technician handled the equipment but there was no English lecturer present. She was with the other half where groups took turns to make small presentations and receive feedback (Fashola, personal communication). In other situations, oral presentations have been built into the outcomes of reading– and writing–based projects; the presentations are prepared and given by groups. Such a component has motivational value where learners want to improve their spoken English even though their main immediate needs are with the written word.

Oral presentation work often concentrates on the stand-up, prepared talk accompanied by visuals. However, for many business people the short, fairly *impromptu* presentation in a meeting is a more common event; they may be asked to state the current position of a project, to fill in details, to explain the need for extra resources. Most of the principles and language of a longer prepared presentation apply in these situations and fillers such as 'well, that's an interesting point' or 'thank you for asking about that' are useful devices as they give a second or two of thinking time.

Feedback

As with spoken interactions, the confidence factor must influence how feedback is handled. Strengths need highlighting and building on, positive features discussing first. Areas for improvement need concrete suggestions of ways and means of achieving it. The numerical rating of different features may be suitable in EAP situations where grades are an accepted part of life. We find them less appropriate, however, with business people.

Task 6h ●◆

While we do not like to use rating charts for feedback on oral presentations, it is useful to have a checklist of points to watch/listen for. Devise a checklist under the headings: voice, body language, use of visuals, structure of information, language, overall impact.

6.6 Writing skills in ESP

In this section we will summarise the main elements that constitute the writing skill. We will then discuss the various approaches to the teaching of writing, notably what are generally referred to as the *product* and *process* approaches. We will suggest that the *social constructionist* approach which builds on the results of genre analysis and sociological studies of academic and professional discourse, pulls together the merits of both the product and process approaches.

6.6.1   What is involved in writing

We have described genre analysis in some detail in chapter 5. We believe that knowledge of genre is a key element in all communication and especially significant in writing academic or professional texts. Knowledge of genre involves an understanding of the expectations of the discourse community that reads the text and of the conventions that have developed over time about the structure, the language and the rhetoric of the genre. It also involves an awareness of the fact that genres evolve with time and change in accordance with changes in the communities that use them. Genre awareness will help with all the five macro-skills, but here we focus on writing.

Developing writing skills also involves other skills, notably the skills of planning, drafting and revising so that the end product is appropriate both to the purpose of the writing and the intended readership. Writing starts with the individual writer(s), these days often using a word processor. S/he may begin by planning the piece of writing and then doing the actual writing. This writing will then be revised before the final draft is written. Alternatively, the writer may begin by writing as much as possible and then revising, polishing and adding further points.

In planning, writing and revising writers will have in mind a reader and will (or should) think about the needs of that reader and the purpose of the document. They will have a *map* to guide them – their *m*essage, *a*udience and *p*urpose. Writers need to ask themselves questions such as whether to expand a point, provide an example or define a term in order to help the reader understand the text or to persuade him/her of the validity of the argument presented. The reader may be a real person that is definitely going to read the text, for example a senior or junior colleague in a company, a client from another company, a supervisor in a university, an editor of a journal and so on. In other cases, however, writers have to construct an image of an imagined reader. In this situation writers need to ask themselves the same questions as above, but they will also consider the expectations of the discourse community.

For example, if we write an introduction to a business report or an academic article, we need, on the one hand, to consider how the text can be made clear and interesting to the people that will read the introduction. The introduction also has to meet certain expectations held by either the business or the academic community about how it should be set out. We may choose not to meet those expectations, but ultimately if we want to persuade the readership of the validity of our argument, we are likely to present the introduction in a form that matches their expectations. Of course an established person is able to break the conventions, and this may indeed add to the persuasiveness of the argument presented; a less established figure is unlikely to have that freedom.

We believe that the same process applies in any professional or academic writing. Successful writers are those who are able to persuade readers of the validity of their arguments by using or adapting the conventions of the genre they are using while showing an awareness of the needs of the readership.

6.6.2 Approaches to the teaching of writing

Orientation 6i

Consider how writing is taught in your institution. (a) Do you follow a particular approach, for example the process or product approach? Or a mixture of the two? (b) What kind of activities do you use? (c) To what extent does the writing take place in the class or as homework?

A distinction is often made between a product and a process approach to the teaching of writing.

The product approach

This term has generally been used to refer to concentration on the features of the actual text – the end-product – that writers have to produce. The product approach to writing usually involves the presentation of a model text, which is analysed and then forms the basis of a task that leads to the writing of an exactly similar or a parallel text. Robinson (1991) summarises the method in the following way:

Model Text → Comprehension/Analysis/Manipulation →
New Input → Parallel Text

In early days the use of a product approach often led to a rather simplistic copying of the model text by merely changing certain words from the original text to produce a new text. This was a purely mechanical task which involved no real thought about the purpose of the writing, the readership or the expectations of the discourse.

The use of models for text analysis and as a basis for thinking about the purposes and readership of a text can, however, have an important role to play in teaching writing. This is especially true where the teaching of writing is integrated with the teaching of reading. The situation where the writer looks at a model, or previous example, of a text s/he wishes to write and then adapts it for the specific purpose does, in fact, reflect what frequently happens in business or academic writing.

The process approach

The process approach began as a reaction to the simplistic model-based approach which focused only on the end-product. The process approach has emphasised the idea of writing as problem-solving, with a focus on *thinking* and *process*. It is most closely associated with the work of Flower (1985) whose textbooks show students how to identify the rhetorical problem, plan a solution or series of solutions to the problem and finally reach an appropriate conclusion. This is the *thinking* stage; the *process* stage involves translating the plan into paragraphs and sentences, reviewing the first draft and then revising the text to produce a number of subsequent drafts. In the actual teaching, the skills of editing and review are taught through peer review and group work, and the whole emphasis is on moving students on from over-concern with sentence-level accuracy. The first stage in the process approach is the thinking stage, which follows the sequence below:

Generate Ideas → Select Ideas → Group the Ideas → Order the Ideas

Robinson (1991: 104) characterises the subsequent writing stages in the following way:

Writing Task → Draft 1 → Feedback → Revision → Input → Draft 2 → Feedback → Revision → Draft 3

The social-constructionist approach

The process approach takes account of individual writers and readers. It does not take into account the broader context of the writing process. Writing is a social act in which writers have to be aware of the context in which they are writing. That context places certain constraints on what writers can write and on the ways in which they can express ideas. We favour an approach to the teaching of writing in which writers are shown how to take on board the expectations and norms of the community to which they belong (or which they aspire to join) and how these expectations shape the established practices of writing within a given community. As discussed in chapter 5, these communities are seen as discourse communities (Bizzell, 1982; Swales, 1990), and successful writing within a discourse community involves having an awareness of the community's values and expectations of text and an ability to resolve the tension between writers' creative needs and the norms for writing generated by the consensus within the community.

The approach based on these principles is generally referred to as the *social constructionist* approach to the teaching of writing and is closely associated with the development of *genre analysis* as a key approach to text in ESP and work on the *sociology of science* (see Bazerman, 1988; Myers, 1989). Work on various genres such as the academic article (Swales, 1990), the dissertation (Dudley-Evans, 1994) and business letters (Bhatia, 1993) have shown how the establishment of a number of *moves* can capture the regularities of writers' communicative purposes in certain genres. The social constructionist approach, however, does much more than teach these moves; it encourages writers to consider their role as members of a discourse community and what this implies in terms of the style and stance that they should adopt.

A synthesis of approaches

The process and the social constructionist approaches have generally been seen as two conflicting approaches to the teaching of writing. Certainly in ESP work the process approach, although extremely valuable in helping students organise and plan their writing, has failed to tackle the actual texts that students have to produce as part of their academic or professional work. Indeed, most advocating a process approach to the teaching of writing (at least in the USA) seem to regard the teaching of generalised strategies of planning, writing and revising as sufficient and the detailed analysis of the target texts as beyond the scope of the writing teacher (Raimes, 1993; Spack, 1988; Zamel, 1983). The social constructionist approach has reintroduced the idea of examining the end-product in a way that is much more acceptable than the old model-and-imitation approach used in early teaching of writing. It has also, as we have noted, extended the focus on the reader to take on board the discourse community. We therefore believe that it combines the strengths of both the product and the process approaches to the teaching of writing. The approach that we advocate follows the stages below:

- Develop *rhetorical awareness* by looking at model texts;
- Practise specific *genre features*, especially moves and writer stance;
- Carry out writing tasks showing awareness of the *needs of individual readers and the discourse community* and *the purpose of the writing*;
- Evaluate the writing (through *peer review* or *reformulation*).

Task 6j ◆◇

Consider the three writing exercises E6.2–E6.4 (pp. 249–251).

a) Do they exemplify the product, process or social constructionist approaches to teaching writing?

b) How well would the exercises work with a class of yours?

6.6.3   The teaching of writing

Types of activities

When we come to translate the approaches outlined in the sections above into teaching materials and actual exercises, we find that there are six main exercise types. These are exercises that develop:

- rhetorical awareness;
- particular skills or language features step-by-step;
- more extensive writing skills through *tasks* (the deep-end approach);
- editing skills through peer review;
- editing skills through reformulation exercises;
- more specific rhetorical and linguistic awareness through integrated teaching with subject specialists.

The writing class

How do we actually apply these activities in the writing class? We believe that the writing class differs in a number of respects from other skills classes. Firstly, we should recognise that learners are unlikely to want to spend the whole class actually writing. Writing is a difficult and tiring activity and usually needs time for reflection and revision, plus a peaceful environment, none of which are generally available in the classroom. However, the converse is also true: learners do not want all the writing practice as out-of-class work. They want help and ideas *while* writing, not only afterwards. A further distinction is that the teacher will have certain knowledge about the conventions of writing in business or academia, and such matters as the need for hedging in certain circumstances, that learners expect to be taught. So the teacher of writing needs to seek a balance between *talking about* writing and *setting up tasks* where students actually write, singly, or in pairs or groups, while in class.

6.7 Summary

We have in this chapter summarised the key elements involved in the five skills of reading, listening to monologue, listening and speaking, speaking, and writing, and discussed various approaches to the teaching of these skills. The fact that we tackled each skill separately does not imply that we favour the teaching of each skill in isolation. In fact, there are strong reasons for integrating the teaching of these five skills, or at least two or three related skills. Using one skill generally involves at least one more of the other skills; writing generally involves some reading, listening to monologue may be preceded or followed up by a discussion or a reading activity, a discussion may lead to a follow-up fax or letter.

Another reason is that skills are generally learnt more effectively when taught with other skills in an integrated manner. For example, research shows that following a written text when it is read aloud increases understanding and retention when it is subsequently read silently. Similarly, hearing the correct pronunciation of a vocabulary item helps storage of that item in the memory and retrieval when it is needed for speaking or writing.

6.8 Recommended reading

We include books or articles on each of the five skills:
Reading: Nuttall (1982); Grellet (1981); Alderson and Urquhart (1984); Carrell *et al.* (1988); Grabe (1993); St John (1992).
Listening: Flowerdew (1994).
Writing: Belcher and Braine (1995); Kroll (1990); Brookes and Grundy (1990); Allwright *et al.* (1988).
Spoken interactions: Furneaux *et al.* (1991) in Adams *et al.* Eds. (1991); Micheau and Billmyer (1987).
Speaking: Dubois (1980, 1981, 1985); Comfort and Utley (1995).

7 Needs analysis and evaluation

7.1 Aims

The key stages in ESP are needs analysis, course (and syllabus) design, materials selection (and production), teaching and learning, and evaluation. These are not separate, linearly-related activities, rather they represent phases which overlap and are interdependent. The simplicity and clarity of figure 7.1 is in reality more like figure 7.2.

This cyclical representation places evaluation and needs analysis, seemingly at opposite ends of a time span, in adjacent positions – and even allows them to overlap. Needs analysis is the process of establishing the *what* and *how* of a course; evaluation is the process of establishing the effectiveness. Neither of these are one-off activities – they both need to be on-going.

An initial pre-course needs analysis and a final end- or post-course evaluation have different aims and perspectives. On the other hand, on-going needs analysis within a course and formative evaluation have much in common. Robinson (1991: 16) comments that 'repeated needs analysis can be built into the formative evaluation' process. We support Brown's (1989: 223) suggestion that 'the difference between needs

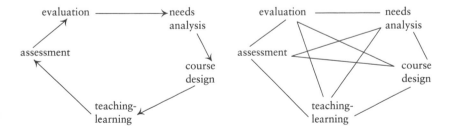

Figure 7.1 Stages in the ESP process: theory

Figure 7.2 Stages in the ESP process: reality

analysis and program evaluation may be more one of focus than of the actual activities involved'.

In this chapter we will look at both needs analysis and evaluation. We will look at the fundamentals of each, focusing on the similarities and differences between them. We will look at the issues in actually carrying out needs analysis or evaluation and show that the three steps involved in each, mainly collecting data, analysing data and implementing the results, are very similar.

7.2 Needs analysis

Needs analysis is neither unique to language teaching – needs assessment, for example, is the basis of training programmes and aid-development programmes – nor, within language training, is it unique to LSP and thus to ESP. However, needs analysis is the corner stone of ESP and leads to a very focused course.

Within ESP the definitions of needs and needs analysis have broadened with experience and research. For instance, in the 1960s and early 1970s, literature and language trained English teachers, faced with teaching science students English for their subject studies, knew very little of the 'what' or 'how' of those studies and concomitantly little about the language of science and technology.

Data collection therefore began from first principles, and language analysis was influenced by the General English stance and by approaches in linguistics and register analysis which helped to define needs as discrete language items of grammar and vocabulary. When Munby (1978) published his *Communicative Syllabus Design*, the English language teaching world had begun to recognise that function and situation were also fundamental. Munby provided detailed lists of microfunctions in his communicative needs processor; what he did not include was how to prioritise them or any of the affective factors which today, with our broader knowledge and understanding of language and language learning, we recognise as important.

Teachers or trainers setting out nowadays to determine learners' needs begin from a different and broader base. Before they approach clients and students they can trawl the literature for previous needs analyses, available materials, research findings. Not only are they able to do so but we believe that they must. The information obtained from clients and students will only be as good as (a) the questions asked and (b) the analysis of the answers. For example, neither of us have ever worked with police forces or on board ship and we know nothing about how either group operates. If we went straight to them, we would have to ask a great many questions, we would probably not distinguish the relevant from the trivial, and we would probably have as many questions at the end as we began with.

Instead we would do some groundwork which would include checking the literature for relevant articles, looking for ESP teaching material, contacting colleagues and organisations who might have experience of such groups, reading material about the subject or discipline. We would want to be as knowledgeable as possible beforehand because then we would:

- know what we did not know – that is, we would know what to ask;
- not waste our clients' or students' time;
- appear much more professional;
- know how we should analyse the data.

A crucial point, whenever data is being collected, is to know beforehand what will happen to the raw data and to the information derived from it. Much time and effort can be wasted in gathering responses that cannot be interpreted or lead to more questions rather than answers. As ESP practitioners we need to know exactly what we are trying to find out and what we will do with the answers before we start (Berwick, 1989: 62).

7.2.1 What is meant by needs?

One difference between now and the 1960s is what we understand by the concept of needs and needs analysis. A confusing plethora of terms exists: needs are described as *objective* and *subjective* (Brindley, 1989: 65), *perceived* and *felt* (Berwick, 1989: 55), *target situation / goal-oriented* and *learning, process-oriented* and *product-oriented* (Brindley, 1989: 63); in addition, there are *necessities, wants and lacks* (Hutchinson and Waters, 1987: 55). These terms have been introduced to describe the different factors and perspectives which have helped the concept of needs to grow. Each of these terms represents a different philosophy or educational value, and merits careful thought.

Briefly, objective and perceived needs are seen as derived by outsiders from facts, from what is known and can be verified, while subjective and felt needs are derived from insiders and correspond to cognitive and affective factors. Thus, 'to be able to follow instructions accurately' is an objective/perceived need. 'To feel confident' is a subjective/felt need. Similarly, product-oriented needs derive from the goal or target situation and process-oriented needs derive from the learning situation.

These pairs can be seen as corresponding to a *target situation analysis (TSA)* and a *learning situation analysis (LSA)*; a third piece of the jigsaw is what learners already know, a *present situation analysis (PSA)*, from which we can deduce their lacks. Thus, a TSA includes objective, perceived and product-oriented needs; an LSA includes subjective, felt and process-oriented needs; a PSA estimates strengths and weaknesses in language, skills, learning experiences.

Task 7a ●◆

Group the following statements under the headings target situation analysis (TSA), learning situation analysis (LSA) and present situation analysis (PSA).

1. I need to see vocabulary written down.
2. I have occasional meetings with British colleagues.
3. I find it difficult to write persuasively.
4. I pick things up by listening.
5. Student X needs to read more widely.
6. I like problem solving.
7. I get my tenses mixed up.
8. I hate group work.
9. I have to write reports.
10. My problem is finding the right word.

To establish a workable course design, means analysis is suggested (Holliday and Cooke, 1982: 133) as an adjunct to needs analysis. Means analysis looks at the environment in which a course will be run or, as in the original metaphor that generated the term, the environment in which a project will take root, grow healthily and survive. The two key factors considered are the classroom culture and the management infrastructure and culture. An important perspective is that these are viewed not as negative constraints but as relevant features. The negative-constraints view corresponds to: 'ideally we would do . . . but it is not possible so we will compromise and do . . .' The relevant-features perspective is a positive approach which says: 'what will be best in this particular and given situation?'

Means analysis is an acknowledgement that what works well in one situation may not work in another. While hotel staff around the world may share some similar language needs, how they learn the language, the conditions in which they are learning and where and how they apply the language are not the same. So the needs, and how they are prioritised, ordered and then met will be different.

7.2.2 A current concept of needs analysis

We see today's concept of needs analysis including aspects of all these approaches. Needs analysis in ESP, figure 7.3 below, now encompasses determining:

A. professional information about the learners: the tasks and activities learners are/will be using English for – *target situation analysis* and *objective needs*

B. personal information about the learners: factors which may affect the way they learn such as previous learning experiences, cultural information, reasons for attending the course and expectations of it, attitude to English – *wants, means, subjective needs*

C. English language information about the learners: what their current skills and language use are – *present situation analysis* – which allows us to assess (D)

D. the learners' lacks: the gap between (C) and (A) – *lacks*

E. language learning information: effective ways of learning the skills and language in (D) – *learning needs*

F. professional communication information about (A): knowledge of how language and skills are used in the target situation – *linguistic analysis, discourse analysis, genre analysis*

G. what is wanted from the course

H. information about the environment in which the course will be run – *means analysis*

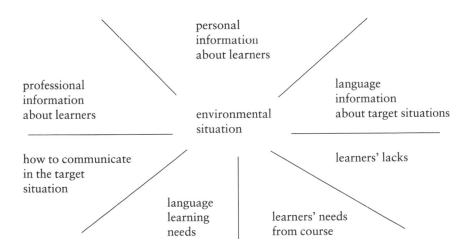

Figure 7.3   What needs analysis establishes

The aim is to know learners as people, as language users and as language learners; to know how language learning and skills learning can be maximised for a given learner group; and finally to know the target situations and learning environment such that we can interpret the data appropriately.

7.2.3 *The non-uniqueness of needs analysis*

The findings from a needs analysis are not absolute but relative and there is no single, unique set of needs. The findings depend on who asks what questions and how the responses are interpreted. What we ask and how we interpret are dependent on a particular view of the world, on attitudes and values. Berwick makes the point that 'our perceptions of need develop from what we believe is educationally worthwhile, that needs are not simply "out there" waiting to be counted and measured' (p. 56). Users of needs analysis must recognise this and try to ensure that the view of the world which is applied is congruent with the situation rather than in conflict with it. This view will also affect what, at the course design stage, is prioritised within a given set of needs.

7.2.4 *Matching needs analysis to situation*

In theory, needs analysis is a first step carried out before a course so that a course outline, materials and other resources can be in place before teaching begins. Practice may be rather different.

The way in which needs analysis is actually approached and conducted will differ according to each situation. Needs analysis and courses are not mounted in a vacuum and must be developed around available human and material resources. (The four case studies in chapter 8 illustrate this.) Other variables that are influential can be represented on a course cline of:

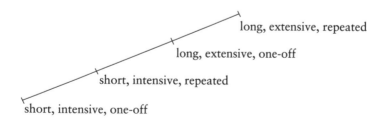

long, extensive, repeated

long, extensive, one-off

short, intensive, repeated

short, intensive, one-off

The amount of data collected and when it is collected may be very different at opposite ends of the cline. In a situation where the course is repeated, with large numbers of students, substantial advance needs analysis may be possible and justified. This often happens in EAP situations when a new course is devised or an existing one revised (Hewings and Dudley-Evans, 1996; Rea-Dickins and Lwaitama, 1995).

In contrast, many EOP courses are one-off, cater for a handful of people and may be held at quite short notice. Often, participants can provide some pre-course information (see Extract E.7.1, pp. 140–41) that provides a framework for course design. However, sometimes there is no opportunity to obtain information from participants until they arrive. These are situations where trawling for as much background on the Target Situation as possible, asking pertinent questions on arrival, and evaluating and adapting throughout the course is the practical approach. The initial framework may have to change. Certainly the detail will have to be negotiated jointly while the course is running.

A word of warning: we must distinguish between overall needs and course needs. This is our point (G) in the list of what constitutes needs analysis (p. 125). The following cautionary tale indicates why. In the mid-1980s, as part of a joint research project between a British and a Spanish university, an analysis of Spanish science researchers' English needs was carried out. The needs analysis showed that all the researchers needed to read English-medium journal articles, some of them needed writing. On the basis of that, a one-week course (10 hours, 2 hours per day) was devised around skills and language development for reading scientific articles. After the first session, the participants all said it was very interesting but that what they needed from the course was writing; if necessary, they could read a text over and over again with a dictionary and work out the meaning for themselves. The result? On-the-spot planning and an instant writing course – with some long late nights of preparation – and all because one question had not been asked:

What do you need/want *from the course?*

The questions had all been around:

What do you need English for?

An additional factor is that an ESP course is rarely long enough to cover all that learners need. Thus, both at the needs analysis stage, and when we meet with the learners, we need information that will help us select and prioritise. For example: What could cause communication breakdown? What are the absolute essentials? (see chapter 8).

Task 7b ●◆

At the end of the chapter there is a pre-course questionnaire E.7.1 sent out to participants who will attend short EOP courses.

a) What questions will help most in designing the course?
b) What else would you want to know?
c) Could you include additional questions to obtain that information?

7.3 Evaluation

7.3.1 What is evaluation?

There are many definitions of evaluation; fundamentally evaluation is asking questions and acting on the responses. For us, evaluation is a whole process which begins with determining what information to gather and ends with bringing about change in current activities or influencing future ones. We believe that evaluation must be more than collecting and analysing data: to have value the evaluation process must include action.

Evaluation is usually described as formative or summative. As ESP practitioners we are most likely to be concerned with formative (on-going) evaluation which takes place during the lifetime of an activity (a course), and the findings help to shape the course during its life-time. Formative evaluation is typically undertaken at intervals and will consist of a series of 'mini-evaluations'. Summative evaluation takes place at (or after) the end of an activity and so does not influence that version of the activity. Its purpose is to assess impact and to provide information that can be fed into repeat versions or related activities. Summative evaluation is therefore valuable for durable courses. Ideally we would also evaluate sometime after the course and determine its longer-term impact; this has rarely been possible in practice.

Evaluation can be both qualitative and quantitative. Tests and objective-question questionnaires provide numbers and percentages for individual items. They provide answers to *what* questions but cannot easily address the *how* or *why*. More qualitative methods such as discussions and interviews cover a wider picture, but may be less comparable (*cf.* objective : subjective and perceived : felt needs).

Evaluation involves making judgements which means that we must have criteria for comparative purposes; what the criteria are will depend on which aspect of work is being evaluated and why, and are likely to relate to the course aims and objectives. If there is no clear objective for a particular activity or material, how can its success be measured? For example, a learner says at the end of a course: 'I enjoyed the course; I am much more confident in face-to-face interactions; there were some excellent activities.' We may think we have a good course. However, if a key objective was to improve telephone interactions we may have to think again. Thus, evaluation is also systematic: a set of random questions does not amount to an evaluation.

Evaluation can be very threatening; it suggests change and change is often resisted. The threat is greatest when evaluation is seen as an imposed external act, over which there is no control. In fact evaluation is a very constructive and powerful activity and a very stimulating one. There is the chance to focus on what has been going well and to ask what have been the most significant contributing factors so that less successful aspects can be modified. Evaluation will also show weaknesses or features that were just not suitable for the particular group of learners. Evaluation should not be used only negatively to comment on perceived problems. A good evaluation emphasises the successes *and* discusses less successful aspects. It also addresses the crucial *how* and *why* issues. Knowing how well something has worked is not significant on its own. Understanding *why* will enable us to repeat success and avoid the less successful.

7.3.2   What do we evaluate?

Evaluation in ESP situations is concerned with the effectiveness and efficiency of learning; with achieving the objectives (assuming that the needs analysis has set valid objectives). Has learning been maximised? Have resources been optimally employed? Our focus in this chapter is on evaluation as used by teachers and learners and on formative evaluation; we are less concerned with large-scale project evaluation involving outsiders (the recommended reading refers to some interesting work with valuable results).

To be an integral part of a course, evaluation has to be built in as part of the course design. To evaluate everything is unrealistic; priorities can be set, the type and timing of data collection can be planned together with the resulting actions. At different times evaluation might focus on the materials used, the classroom activities, the out-of-class support, the course design, methodologies, the role of assessment, that is any aspect of the teaching-learning situation.

For one-off courses the important questions are those asked part-way through; and they must focus on change that is feasible and immediately implementable. If you ask about the hours of contact time, can you change them? This is where evaluation overlaps with, and can be equivalent to, on-going needs analysis. If you ask about the balance of activity types can you actually change it? Could you focus more on, say, spoken skills?

On courses that are durable, evaluation questions may be asked for a range of different purposes. Some may evaluate in order to modify the existing situation, some to provide information for the next version while others could be support for longer-term change. Comments on how effective group work is relate to the current course; comments on new material will mean it can be revised for the next group. There will be a benefit for the current group only if the comments can also be applied to material still to come.

Evaluation results can be used to influence decisions and bring about long-term change. A successful argument for more hours per week on an EAP course needs to show positive achievements within the existing time plus a general demand for more. Evaluation questions can show whether this is the case. If a policy decision and money are sought for adopting a new coursebook, teachers and learners need to identify the deficiencies in the current one and show how they would be overcome with the new. Again, evaluation techniques can provide evidence.

Evaluation can have a variety of unexpected spin-offs. Jansen (1995: 69) found students responded positively because of the involvement. St John (1995) reports that EAP lecturers in Nigeria found evaluation encouraged more change; it 'showed the way' through the sharing of different approaches, it motivated and encouraged both students and staff, and exerted influence through an increase in communication and awareness leading to better relationships and professional respect from other colleagues.

Some of the questions to ask before an evaluation are:

Audience and purpose

- Who are the stakeholders? The term 'stakeholder' is used to cover all those who have an interest or concern with the course. The client who requests the course, the learners and the teachers are the main stakeholders but there can be others (sponsors, organisers).
- What do you want to evaluate?
- What do you want to change?

Criteria for evaluation

- What are the objectives you are evaluating against? In some situations these are not clearly set out and need to be defined before planning an evaluation.

Criteria for analysis of results

- What will you do with the answers? What can *you* change? What requires the authority of others? And what will convince them?

Sources of information

- Who can provide useful information?
- When would it be appropriate for them to do that?

7.4 Collecting data for needs analysis and evaluation purposes

7.4.1 Who collects the data?

For both needs analysis and evaluation, outsiders or insiders could be involved. Outsiders can be perceived as more objective since they provide a fresh or alternative viewpoint and are not stakeholders. However, as outsiders, they do not know the situation and the environment so they may miss or misinterpret data. Holliday (1995: 124) stresses how important it was that he knew the educational system of the country in which he was asked to carry out a company needs analysis. Without taking cultural and micropolitical factors into consideration his recommendations would not have been realistic. This constitutes a real problem for a complete outsider who may find that there are hidden agendas and that their support is being sought for a decision that has already been made.

On the other hand, insiders will have a feel for the situation but can be too close and involved, or lack expertise. A known, respected outsider working together with insiders is one alternative (Alderson and Scott, 1992: 36/37). The outsiders can be others in the same institution who are not involved with the course that is being evaluated.

Complete outsiders are most likely to be used both for needs analysis and evaluation on large-scale projects with external funding. External evaluation is also used for accreditation and inter-institutional comparison. For instance, in recent years BALEAP (British Association of Lecturers in EAP) has established a system whereby members visit pre-sessional courses to validate them. They are insiders in the sense that they are involved in the same or very similar work in their own institution, but outsiders in the sense that they do not belong to the actual institution being validated. The system combines the perspective of both insiders and outsiders.

7.4.2 *Who provides the data and how?*

Orientation 7c

Brainstorm on *methods of gathering data*, for example questionnaires, and then try to group the suggestions. Draw up a separate list of *sources of data*, such as employers, and also try to group them. What categories did you think of? Can you make any links between items in the two lists, that is, are some methods more suitable for certain sources?

For needs analysis the main sources are:

• the learners
• people working or studying in the field
• ex-students
• documents relevant to the field
• clients
• employers
• colleagues
• ESP research in the field

For evaluation the main sources are:

• the learners
• people the learners work or study with
• documents and records used
• ourselves
• colleagues

The main data collection methods for needs analysis are:

• questionnaires
• analysis of authentic spoken and written texts
• discussions
• structured interviews
• observations
• assessments

For evaluation useful methods are:

• checklists and questionnaires
• assessment
• discussion
• record keeping

A brief discussion of these follows; the recommended reading suggests more detailed sources.

Checklists and questionnaires

Questionnaires are generally more wide ranging than checklists and, as they are used for quantitative information, they need careful construction. Checklists are narrower in scope and more commonly used for a qualitative feel. They can determine facts or attitudes.

Constructing good questionnaires is not easy (see the recommended reading for help). When used with large numbers then only objective responses can be analysed which restricts the information collected. Striking the balance between enough answers and data, and time/boredom for responders is difficult. Wording the questions so that they and the responses are unambiguous takes time. All questionnaires should be piloted before extensive use, and statistical techniques should be used to analyse the results. In large-scale projects they can have a valuable role as one among several methods. For small-scale work other methods may be more informative and reliable.

Task 7d ◆◆

Each of the following items is likely to cause problems. For each item:

a) decide what the problem(s) is (are) and their causes.
b) write a better item.
c) use your answers to construct a 'Beware the Following' checklist.

1. Do you need spoken and written language?   yes/no

2. Do you use a lot of English in your work?
   ☐ a lot   ☐ a little   ☐ not much

3. Do you prefer a friendly student-centred approach to a rigid teacher-dominated one?   yes/no

4. What qualifications do you want your teacher to have?
   ☐ PhD   ☐ MSc   ☐ BA

5. If your utterance is linguistically deviant do you want:
   ☐ peer correction   ☐ a metalinguistic signal
   ☐ language correction

6. How much individual consultation with the teacher do you think you should have on this course?

For evaluation purposes, attitude scales (much used in market research, for example Tull and Hawkins, 1976) such as paired comparisons, the Likert scale, balanced non-comparative rating scales and adjective checklists can quickly assess views – but not the reasons behind them. Of the attitude scales the easiest to construct is an adjective checklist. The Likert scale consists of statements that respondents agree or disagree with. It reveals useful information and is easy to administer but the statements need careful thought, particularly when the language is not the L1 (St John, 1988). Rating scales are easier to use and useful for broad distinctions. The respondent ticks on a numbered descriptive scale as in:

> The text for this task was   1   2   3   4   5
> where 1 = extremely easy, 3 = suitable and 5 = extremely difficult.

The more positions there are, the finer the distinctions responders are asked to make; between five and seven positions is normal for most rating scales.

Task 7e ●◆

We have begun a rating scale for use after any lesson.

a) Devise a suitable scale for points 3, 4, 5, and 6.
b) Think of a particular lesson (such as reading, writing, expressing cause and effect . . .) and devise an additional four points and scales.

Please give your views by ticking a box for each point.

1. Teacher's presentation of the lesson   ☐ poor . . . ☐ excellent
2. Usefulness of the exercises   ☐ low . . . ☐ high
3. Interest of the topic
4. Amount you learnt
5. Pace of the lesson
6. Overall assessment of the lesson

Structured interviews

The structured interview is extremely useful in evaluation and needs analysis. Structured interviews consist of questions which have been carefully thought out and selected in advance. Because the interviewer has key questions which everyone is (and must be) asked, comparisons can be made (and numbers crunched). Additional questions may be asked to follow up responses for clarification and more detail. Structured interviews are time consuming but provide valuable information that we may not otherwise obtain. There should be an agreed time limit for the interview, and where possible it should be recorded so that the interviewer can really listen rather than take lots of notes. The art is to gain the maximum relevant information in the minimum time. Key skills for interviewers are active listening (combining both hearing and processing), summarising and asking open questions. Interviewing takes up other people's time so it is good policy to let them know the results and what action will follow from their help.

Observation

For needs analysis, observation can cover a range of activities from watching a particular task being performed to shadowing individuals at work. (To shadow someone is to follow everything they do for a block of time such as a day, several consecutive days or one day a month.)

Observation and particularly shadowing are sensitive issues. People in business may feel the content of events are commercially sensitive; anyone may feel a personal threat at having their movements watched and their words noted or recorded. Good groundwork beforehand is a crucial part of the process so as to explain the purpose, give confidentiality assurances, possibly show the results of previous observation or shadowing and thus gain people's confidence. We want to observe or shadow because that world is unfamiliar to us; we must remember that ours is equally unfamiliar to them. We need to carefully explain what we are looking and listening for, and why; equally, what does not concern us and why not.

EAP examples of observation for needs analysis include sitting in on subject lectures or practical sessions. In places where English is only a medium of education, such observations have led to an understanding of how and when English and the L1 are intertwined, of the code-switching which often goes on. In EOP situations, any relevant work processes may be observed. As well as carrying out workplace observation, ESP practitioners have also attended subject conferences and seen how slide presentations, poster presentations and read papers are used in different fields (Dubois, 1981, 1985; Shalom, 1993; Rowley-Jolivet, 1998). Most observation or shadowing is for Target Situation Analysis (TSA) purposes but it could be for the Present Situation Analysis (PSA) of a particular individual. In situations where English is not a medium of communication, observation and shadowing are still very useful for understanding work patterns, although they cannot provide language data for materials production.

Most observation for evaluation is of classroom activity, but it could also include seeing how well a learner was coping with using the language in their work or studies. Teachers are often reluctant to have others observe their classes. Perhaps this stems from unfortunate experiences in teaching practice and a misunderstanding of purpose. Classroom observation requires careful groundwork and handling. For peer evaluation, we believe the focus must be on the learners and the material and not on the colleague, the teacher. The observer and teacher should talk about and agree on the purpose of the observation beforehand. Is it concerned with the learners' behaviour, for instance, their interactions in group work, the way in which they approach tasks, or is it to determine how well some (new) material works, for example, to note when learners are interested or bored, involved or passive, clear or confused; to see whether any parts are difficult to teach?

After the session, observer and teacher should share their perceptions of what was happening. As always, the early comments must focus on positive features. When these have been noted and discussed, then attention can turn to where improvements might be introduced. It takes discipline to carry this approach through, particularly where there has been a culture of observation meaning negative comments. It is important to avoid this because it is easy to take things personally, even when the focus is not on the teacher. Also, beginning with negative comments sets up the wrong perspective. It is more productive to build on the positive.

Analysis of authentic texts

Analysing authentic texts is a crucial stage of needs analysis. The texts can be written documents or audio and video recordings of events such as lectures, meetings, telephone interactions, classroom activities. The logistics of obtaining spoken data for needs analysis mean that it is less accessible than written documents. As with observation, confidentiality is an important issue; people may wish to white-out information such as figures and company names. The analysis may be for TSA purposes, to determine the key linguistic features of a communicative event or genre that is new to us. Alternatively, the texts may be samples of participants' language and help us to carry out a PSA.

Authentic texts are invaluable for learning about real and carrier content. They can also form the basis of classroom materials, with three provisos: the client/source has given permission; fictitious facts replace confidential ones; and anything which can directly identify the author is removed.

For evaluation, the texts learners produce in class can be looked at to evaluate progress towards the objectives and to identify needs that have not yet been met.

Assessment

Assessment includes formal and informal judgements of students' performance and progress through classwork, assignments and tests. Testing or assignments may form part of a pre-course PSA or evaluate progress. Issues of assessment and testing are covered in chapter 11.

Discussions

All the other methods require advance preparation and planning. Discussions are more informal; they can be planned but are often more spontaneous. Discussions can pave the way in both needs analysis and evaluation to other methods such as interviewing and observing or be an end in themselves. Talking informally to students over coffee or taking a few minutes of classtime can provide insights into how activities went, what was most beneficial, where difficulties arose, what else they would like to cover – but it is important to check whether the views are representative of everyone or only reflect the vocal minority.

Record keeping

For evaluation, record keeping is a must. This can include teacher records of what actually happened in lessons, and learner records such as diaries and journals. What is needed in record keeping is systematicity: records must be made immediately, as other events dull our memories. Information on similar points over time is essential for comparative purposes so it is useful to devise evaluation forms even as a sole teacher (exactly what is recorded depends on what is being evaluated). But a record-keeping system will only work, if it is simple, quick, easy to use and suits the culture.

7.4.3 How do we analyse the data?

We made the point that the results of a needs analysis are not unique. Even with the same raw data different interpretations are possible. First though, the raw data must be converted into information. With small amounts of quantitative data manual methods can be employed to process the data into information – a simple tally system. Some data, such as written comments, will be more subjectively processed.

Large scale needs analysis for business or EAP using questionnaires can generate the quantities of data that require statistical analysis and the help of computer software. Several statistical techniques can be useful. Jones (1991) described how Principal Component Analysis (PCA) provided insights into the needs of FRANCE TELECOM employees who carried out technical assignments overseas. He had a 70-item questionnaire that gathered data on skills and functions on a four-point scale. With 400 completed questionnaires a simple tally and ranking was inappropriate. By using PCA, which is a type of correlational analysis that can resolve data into underlying factors, he was able to identify clusters of variables. By talking to management he could then match each cluster to a significant speech event.

Nelson (1994) has devised a computer-generated system for Business English course design which starts with a placement test and a needs analysis questionnaire completed by students. The questionnaire covers both the TSA and Learning Situation Analysis (LSA). All the information is fed into the computer for processing and charts are drawn to show needs and wants of both students and sponsors. The program is designed to search out the areas most needed for study. There is a manual override to the system at all stages so that teachers can influence the process.

LANA (LAnguage Needs Analysis) (Reeves and Wright, 1996) is another tool intended either for individual needs analysis or as part of an audit. The complete system uses interviews, modelling and a computer-based questionnaire. An individual responds to the LANA cues concerning his/her function, tasks, topics, language. The software analyses the responses and presents the results in a series of three-dimensional histograms.

A characteristic of ESP situations is limited time, and needs will invariably exceed the available time, so the analysis must help in selection and prioritisation. The original design of the data collection and analysis has to allow for this. Will statistics be used? If so, which techniques will be used? These questions need answering before data collection.

There are dangers in interpreting data, especially when a little knowledge has been gained. We believe that needs analysis must result in an understanding of a target situation such that we, the ESP practitioners, could be efficient communicators in it. If we do not know how to communicate in the target situation, we run the risk of passing on misconceptions or false information. We illustrate this with a real case which shows: (a) why our concept of needs analysis (see p. 125) includes F, information on how language and skills are actually used; and (b) how a view of the world affects the questions asked and the interpretation of the answers.

The English teachers at a tertiary institution wanted to revise a course and materials which included writing skills. They carried out a needs analysis, and essay writing was identified as a priority. The literature-and-language-qualified English teachers had a great deal of experience in writing essays and teaching essay writing, so they were confident about revising the objectives and materials for this section of the course. However, no analysis of student essays was carried out. This was unfortunate as the students were science students who write structured, factual essays, with restricted content and a different purpose from those introduced into the revised course. The essays in the language class were expository, asking for opinions and quotations, and allowing a wide range of content. The essays are two different genres. In science, facts, ideas and theories are important, not quoted words.

7.4.4 What happens to the results?

Results either feed into course design (initial needs analysis), course re-alignment (on-going needs analysis / formative evaluation) or future activities (summative evaluation). We would like to suggest that, whatever the purpose was, some feedback of the results to those who provided data is important – and often neglected. The feedback may be how a text is to be used, how the design of a course component has been influenced, the overall results of a mini-evaluation. Feedback is good PR (public relations), good for the quantity and quality of future cooperation.

Reflection 7f

At the end of the chapter there are two questionnaires, E7.2 and E7.3, used to evaluate short courses. What are the significant differences between the two questionnaires and what are the advantages of each? Consider the stakeholders who may see the results, what is being evaluated, how the results may be used. Do both approaches have validity for your situation?

7.5 Summary

Behind successful ESP courses is a continuous process of questioning. Ascertaining what a course should contain, how it should be run; checking throughout how valid the original answers were and how effective the ideas they led to are; discovering what works best and why.

Initial needs analysis	On-going needs analysis formative evaluation	Summative evaluation
set objectives	revise objectives	inform future
determine approach	modify teaching and materials	justify measure

As a multi-disciplinary field the questions range over resource management, communication skills, language use, ways of learning, genre conventions:

7.6 Recommended reading

Richard West's (1994) survey article is not just about ESP, but includes a wide range of relevant references. Richterich and Chancerel (1980) is also about needs for language teaching in general, but has been very influential. Chambers (1980) introduces the concept of Target Situation Analysis, now widely used in ESP. Holliday (1995) has introduced the idea of an ecological approach to needs analysis, taking the constraints of the situation as a given and possibly exploitable feature of the situation. Other reading concerned with evaluation, or the construction of questionnaires is Celani *et al.* Eds. (1988); Alderson and Beretta (1992); Rea-Dickins and Lwaitama (1995); Bell (1987); Tull and Hawkins (1976).

7.7 Extracts

E 7.1 Pre-course information questionnaire

PERSONAL DETAILS

Family name _____ First names _____

Nationality _____ Main language _____

Date of birth _____ Female/male _____

Contact address_____

Contact numbers _____ e-mail address _____

PROFESSIONAL DETAILS

Name of organisation _____

Length of time with organisation _____

Job title _____

Length of time in current job _____

Working language of organisation _____

CURRENT USE OF ENGLISH

Do you use English in your current job? _____

If yes, is this mainly spoken, written or both? _____

How many hours a week are you likely to use English? _____

Do you use English mainly in-company, externally or both? _____

Do you use English mainly with native speakers (for example Americans), non-native speakers or both? _____

Please give details of previous English studies. _____

_____

Please give details of extended visits / stays in English-speaking countries.

_____

_____

FUTURE USE OF ENGLISH

Do you want to improve your English for your current job or a new one?

_____

Is there a particular reason for wanting to take a course at this point in your life?

_____

If yes, please specify? _____

_____

_____

Will your future use of English be different to your current use?

_____

If yes, please specify in what ways. _____

_____

YOUR JOB

Please describe the roles and responsibilities of your job.

_____

_____

_____

_____

_____

E 7.2 *Evaluation of the workshop: English for research communication*

The course participants contributed to the content of this evaluation form.

1. Please rate your experience in writing articles for publication.
   a) You have drafted   o   1–3   4–6   7–9   10+
   b) You have had
      published   o   1–3   4–6   7–9   10+

2. How useful was this workshop for you?

            o   1   2   3   4   5
           (not)   (extremely)

3. What language is your mother tongue?

4. Please fill in the table.

most useful	unnecessary	could have been improved

5. Please indicate your feelings about the following (a to i):

	very satisfied	satisfied	fairly satisfied	not satisfied
a) achievement of objectives				
b) amount of input				
c) level of input				
d) participants' contribution				
e) handouts				
f) number of exercises				

g) duration of workshop				
h) the room				
i) other facilities				

When you tick 'fairly satisfied' or 'not satisfied' please give your reasons.

6. What were the best sessions/aspects of the course?
   _____

7. What were the least satisfactory sessions/aspects?
   _____

8. What improvements would you suggest for repeat courses?
   _____

9. What would you suggest for follow-up to this course?
   _____

10. Please list the outcomes of the course for you personally.
    _____

11. Please add any other comments.

E 7.3 Course evaluation student questionnaire

This was devised by teachers who had been trying new approaches and new materials in a course.

New approaches to learning and writing

Tick only the appropriate box, thus:

a) How did you find group activities in the classroom?
   very interesting ☐   interesting ☐   not interesting ☐

b) Did you find the activities before the actual writing exercises
   very interesting ☐   interesting ☐   not interesting ☐

c) Did you
like ☐ tolerate ☐ dislike ☐ hate ☐
discussing and correcting errors in your draftwork with your colleague(s)?

d) Editing each other's written work was
very useful ☐ useful ☐ not useful ☐

e) How did you find sharing the teacher's comments in your marked work with your neighbour?
very useful ☐ useful ☐ not useful ☐

f) How did you find working in pairs in class?
very useful ☐ useful ☐ not useful ☐

g) Did the pre-writing activities make it easier for you to produce better pieces of writing?
Yes ☐ No ☐

h) Did you find the passages used for comprehension and summary relevant to your area of study?
Yes ☐ No ☐

i) Did you find the passages and exercises
extremely difficult ☐
above your level but challenging ☐
within your level ☐
below your level ☐

8 Course design

8.1 Aims

In this chapter we will discuss the steps and the criteria for an integrated approach to course design. Needs analysis asks questions about students' needs and wants, the expectations of the institution, the features of the actual teaching situation. In developing a course outline, there are additional questions to ask and issues to face. We shall discuss these, illustrate their implementation through four case studies and finally suggest an organisational framework for grouping and ordering course items.

Orientation 8a

Consider the situation where you are redesigning your existing ESP courses. You have invited an ESP expert to come for a week's seminar to help with this process. What are the issues that you want him or her to address? What are the questions you want to put to him or her?

8.2 Parameters of course design

There are a number of parameters that need to be investigated in making decisions about course design. Our questions, as presented here, show these as choices between two poles of a dichotomy. However, our discussion illustrates that these choices represent the ends of a continuum and that there are, in fact, a number of positions along that continuum. Some of the positions are pre-determined by circumstances – the client, the environment – others are determined by the course designer.

1. Should the course be *intensive* or *extensive*?
2. Should the learners' performance be *assessed* or *non-assessed*?

3. Should the course deal with *immediate* needs or with *delayed* needs?
4. Should the role of the teacher be that of the *provider* of knowledge and activities, or should it be as a *facilitator* of activities arising from learners' expressed wants?
5. Should the course have a *broad* or *narrow* focus?
6. Should the course be *pre-study or pre-experience* or *run parallel with that study or experience*?
7. Should the material be *common-core* or *specific* to learners' study or work?
8. Should the group taking the course be *homogeneous* or should it be *heterogeneous*?
9. Should the course design be *worked out by the language teacher* after consultation with the learners and the institution, or should it be *subject to a process of negotiation* with the learners?

8.2.1 Intensive or extensive

During an intensive ESP course the learners' time is totally committed to that ESP course. In contrast, an extensive ESP course occupies only a small part of a student's timetable or a professional person's work schedule.

ESP courses, both EOP and EAP, are frequently intensive. Companies send their managers, secretaries or technicians on short intensive courses in the expectation that an exclusive concentration on certain skills or language for the period of the course will greatly enhance their performance in activities that require English. Similarly, intensive EAP pre-study courses are very common in English-medium situations. Students are given language improvement and study skills sessions for between one and six months (or even one year in a few cases) before they actually begin subject courses. The assumption is that they need to reach a certain level of proficiency before they actually begin their subject course.

Advantages of intensive courses

There are clear advantages in the intensive course. The students are totally focused on their purpose for learning English and, if the course is residential, they can be immersed in an English-language environment, even outside the actual class sessions. They have no distractions and, because of the availability of time, a great deal of variety in the activities can be introduced. Learners can, for example, spend time preparing an oral presentation or writing a report, and then get feedback on their performance. This total focus on the ESP course and the absence of other distractions can mean that the intensive and residential course makes the most effective use of time available for English and study/communication skills.

Disadvantages of intensive courses

There are, however, dangers with the intensive course. Without reinforcement, what is learnt on the intensive course may lie dormant. With longer courses the total concentration on English and the absence of academic or professional activity may become increasingly artificial. We once visited a university where students followed a year-long intensive English course before beginning their subject courses. Students' motivation seemed to decline over the year, in some cases quite dramatically. When we ran such courses in the UK we found that we needed to make the courses more and more specific as the course progressed and to bring in activities that were more related to students' disciplines.

Advantages of extensive courses

There are advantages of extensive ESP courses. The course can run in parallel with the subject course or the professional activity and can relate to it, adapt to it as the learners' experience or needs change, and generally remain flexible. In EAP situations where the ESP course is part of the timetable and learners are assessed, the profile of ESP as a subject is raised, thereby increasing motivation.

Disadvantage of extensive courses

The main disadvantage of the extensive course is the potential lack of continuity between classes, particularly if the classes are infrequent (Robinson, 1991). Each class and the material for it may have to be self-contained in terms of both the aim of the class and the material used, which does not allow for carry-over between classes.

The choice between intensive and extensive courses is generally determined by circumstances within the institution or company for which the course is being run. With extensive courses, however, it may be possible to incorporate some intensive elements into an essentially extensive course. Periods of time can be blocked for intensive work on a particular skill, for instance listening comprehension at the beginning of an EAP course, meeting skills in a company if an important series of meetings are coming up. Indeed, it may be important that ESP course designers push for some intensive components of this kind when it has been decided that the overall course should be extensive.

8.2.2 *Assessed or non-assessed*

Assessed courses in EAP

A compulsory EAP course, where learners' performance in English is assessed along with other subjects at the end of a semester or academic year, has definite advantages: It raises the status of the subject and should ensure that it is taken seriously by both students and the departments. It does, however, bring responsibilities. Where different groups are taught by different teachers but take the same test, it is vital that teachers coordinate to ensure that the testing is valid and fair. This inevitably means some loss of freedom in the choice of topics and material used on the course.

Assessed courses in EOP

Short intensive EOP courses are not usually concerned with testing learners' proficiency. There are, however, various standardised tests of proficiency in business and professional communication and many learners will find that passing one of these examinations enhances their career prospects (chapter 11). It is clearly possible for such a test to be built in on longer intensive and extensive EOP courses.

8.2.3 *Immediate or delayed needs*

By *immediate needs* we refer to those needs that students have at the time of the course, while by *delayed needs* we refer to those that will become more significant later. Any pre-experience course, whether EAP or EOP, is by definition a course that deals with delayed needs.

However, many EAP courses fall on the continuum between these two points: the English course runs parallel with subject courses in the first or second years of students' subject course, but the students' actual needs for English become more pressing in later years of the course, or once they have graduated. For example, where the subject courses are taught and assessed in the students' L1, students often do not need English much in the early years of the course, but may well need to consult English sources when they write a dissertation in their final year (see Bates for a discussion of Iran, 1978). Similarly, in English-medium situations students may be required to make an oral presentation in their final year. Is there any point in including a component on oral presentations in the EAP course two or three years beforehand?

We believe that there is a strong case for running EAP components in the final years rather than in just the first or second years, or at least ensuring that the course continues till the final year. There is certainly a case for running a short intensive course on presentation skills or writing in the final year if that is when such skills are needed. Interestingly, we have noted that running courses in the final years of the academic course is another factor that contributes to the raising of the status of ESP courses.

We also believe that there is a strong case for concentrating on professional skills where the subject course is taught in the students' L1 or students are coping well with the academic courses taught in English. Students often seem to be much more motivated by a course that prepares them for oral and written communication in their future professional world. Again there is logic in running such a course in the final years of the course, especially where there is the possibility of integrating the course into subject courses that also prepare students more specifically for professional work (see Dudley-Evans, 1984).

8.2.4 Teacher as provider or as facilitator/consultant

Teacher as provider of input

The question of the role of the ESP teacher is a very important and a controversial one (Hutchinson and Waters, 1987; Swales, 1988; Johns and Dudley-Evans, 1993). In many situations the teacher expects, or is expected, to control the class, to provide information about skills and language, to control the activities, possibly moving into pair or group work for part of the class, but always at the suggestion of the teacher. In these situations the role for the teacher generally matches the expectations of the learners. We define this teacher role as *teacher as provider of input and activities*.

Teacher as facilitator or consultant

In other situations the ESP teacher manages rather than controls. S/he may not make decisions about the course design but will negotiate with the learners about what is most appropriate to include, and when to include it. S/he will often get members of the class to bring material for exploitation in class. We see this role as *teacher as facilitator* or *teacher as consultant*. A development of this is where the teacher knows relatively little about the content or the skill that is being taught in the

ESP class, and proceeds by pulling together and organising the information that the learners, and – if possible – their lecturers or instructors, are able to provide about the language or skill. A good example is the British team-taught session or the American adjunct class where the role of the English teacher is to act as a kind of intermediary between the specialist teacher and the students. In a sense, the ESP teacher becomes an equal with the students, but uses his or her greater knowledge of the language and the nature of communication to help them interpret what is happening in the specialist course or training.

This role is a difficult one to adopt for any teacher, especially an inexperienced one. In many cultures it is a role that is alien to traditional views of the role of the teacher. However, where it is possible, it is a role that is very appropriate and productive with sophisticated learners who have a clear and specific set of purposes.

The two teacher roles we have described are at opposite ends of a continuum that goes from teacher as total 'controller' (or dictator, Swales, 1984) to one as a total facilitator. There are many positions on the continuum between these two ends. In many situations the role of the teacher may constantly move between that as 'provider of knowledge' and that as 'facilitator' or 'consultant'. A good ESP teacher will have certain information to impart to the students; there is no harm in sometimes doing this in a traditional way, provided that room is also allowed for less teacher-centred activities, such as pair or group writing, or problem-solving activities. At other times the teacher may move towards a stance in which s/he as an equal works out a strategy for a reading or a writing task together with the students.

The institutional and cultural expectations of the learners must be taken into account. One group of learners may welcome the teacher's adoption of a facilitator role, another may find it completely alien; but this does not mean that attitudes cannot change or be changed.

8.2.5   Broad or narrow focus

Broad focus

By a *broad focus* we refer to a situation where we concentrate on a range of target events, such as study or professional skills, or a variety of genres. The focus is broad because of the range of target events covered, but this does not imply that the skills are taught in a general and superficial manner. Skills will be dealt with in great detail, and the teaching material may even include some specific carrier content.

A broad focus has the advantage that it allows us to deal with a number of skills even if the actual need is one skill. This may be especially useful if motivation is a problem. Learners may be basically happy with a specific focus in the ESP course, but will still welcome, as a change to normal routine, some general conversational work, or some presentation of background information about Britain, the USA, or other English-speaking countries. Introducing some variety of this kind provides a broad focus for the course. In other situations there may not be the time for such variety or learners may find it distracting.

Narrow focus

By a *narrow focus* (Williams, 1978) we mean that we concentrate on a few target events, for example just the listening skill, or just one or two genres. A narrow focus does not necessarily mean that we only use specific carrier content for teaching material. We may focus narrowly on one or two skills, but use a wide range of general and specific carrier content to teach those skills and related language. A narrow focus is appropriate where the needs are limited and the learners are convinced of the importance of concentrating just on those needs.

8.2.6   Pre-experience or in parallel with experience

By *pre-experience* we mean that the learners do not have experience of the target situation at the time of the ESP course. By *parallel with experience* we mean that the English course runs concurrently with the study course or professional activity.

The course designer does not always make the decision on this parameter. Institutions or companies often send groups for English training before they have had much professional or academic experience. In this case we have to bear in mind that we cannot assume too much subject knowledge in the materials and need to focus on more common-core study or professional skills.

We would, however, argue that there is always an advantage in teaching ESP to learners who already have some subject or professional knowledge. The teacher is able to draw on the learners' knowledge, to ask them to give examples from this knowledge and to make use of certain learning strategies that are familiar from learning about their subject or profession. This is the case whether the course is extensive or intensive. In EAP situations timetabling usually means that we teach students with experience on an extensive course; in EOP situations the nature of business and professional work means that learners with professional experience may only be able to follow intensive courses.

8.2.7 Common-core or specific material

By *common-core material* we mean material that uses carrier content which is either of a general academic nature or of a general professional nature. By *specific material* we mean that the material uses carrier content that is drawn directly from the learners' academic or professional area, such as topics that EAP students are following in their subject course, or case studies related to the professional work of EOP/ EBP learners.

Specific material

We have discussed specialist EAP work in chapter 3 and specialist EOP work in chapter 4; our main conclusions there were that introducing some specific work into the ESP class, either as the main focus of the course or to supplement the common-core features of the course is generally beneficial. However, the opportunity to introduce more specific work depends on the timing of the course and other institutional constraints as well as the motivation of the learners.

If the ESP course is pre-experience, it is much more difficult to make the course specific. Learners will have little or no knowledge of the topics that will be introduced in a subject course or the activities that they will be undertaking in their work. It is therefore impossible to draw very much on their knowledge or experience. They will probably have some generalised knowledge of the way their discipline or profession works so some limited specific ESP work may be possible, but, in general, the ESP course will need to focus on the underlying competence needed (Hutchinson and Waters, 1987), general EAP or EOP skills and language.

8.2.8 Homogeneous or heterogeneous groups and motivation

Another factor to consider is whether the ESP class is made up of a *homogeneous* group from one discipline or profession, or a *heterogeneous* group of learners from different disciplines, professions or levels of management. Even a group from one company, or even one department of a company is unlikely to be homogeneous if it contains senior managers, junior managers and secretaries, as each sub-group will have different needs.

If the group is heterogeneous, it is difficult to introduce much specific work, and it is again more appropriate to look for topics and activities that are common to the various interests in the group.

If the group is homogeneous, it is possible to undertake more specific work. The main question here is that of the motivation of learners (see also discussion of this point in chapter 1). Most will be enthusiastic about ESP work that relates directly to their needs, helps them with writing assignments or reports that they are actually having to write at the time of the ESP course, or helps them understand the lectures or meetings they are attending.

There are, however, situations where learners may be less enthusiastic about specific work; in an EAP situation they may be looking for a change in the English class from what they are doing in their subject course while in an EOP situation they may feel – rightly or wrongly – that they are competent in the main skills and language related to their everyday work, but need help with a less immediately important skill. This might be something like drawing up a contract with a foreign company or negotiation skills for people who, in fact, rarely have to attend meetings.

We believe that it is important to take account of motivational factors and, as in needs analysis, we ignore learners' wants at our peril. We do feel that, if we have the option, it is better to set up homogeneous groups for ESP classes. If this is not possible for all sessions, then we should push for the opportunity to break groups down into homogeneous groups for at least some of the time. Where groups are homogeneous, the ESP teacher has much more flexibility and choice about whether to use more specific materials, or to incorporate some specific materials into an essentially common-core course.

It would, however, be wrong to think of the choice as being solely between totally common-core material and totally specific material. In those situations where it is possible to use specific material it may be desirable to seek a balance between some common-core and some specific carrier content in the material. In other situations it may be desirable to use only specific carrier content.

One other aspect of the homogeneous/heterogeneous question is the language level of the students. In ESP work, especially if we are trying to run the ESP course with groups homogeneous from a study or work point of view, it may be very difficult to ensure that groups are also homogeneous in their language level. It is generally advantageous in language learning to divide groups by level – but in ESP homogeneity in the learners' specific purposes is more important.

8.2.9 *Fixed course design or flexible negotiated course design*

A *fixed course design* is laid down in advance of the course and is rarely deviated from; a *flexible and negotiated course design* allows room for change based on feedback from learners (Nunan, 1988). Many of the points we have made about the role of the ESP teacher also apply here. Many learners expect to follow a fixed syllabus and worry if that syllabus is deviated from. Others really welcome the opportunity to have a say in or even some control over what they are taught.

Institutional constraints are also relevant. Where an EAP course is part of the subject timetable, and is assessed, it is important to ensure that all students have covered the same material. This will lead to a need for a more or less fixed course design. If, however, teachers or the institution follow the philosophy that learners need to be involved in making decisions about their learning and in assessing their own progress, then a flexible negotiated syllabus is important. It is often the policy with such courses that a record is kept of the decisions made by the group about what should be taught and what skills and language work this entailed, and how much time was spent on each aspect of the course. Such records have been referred to as 'retrospective syllabuses' (Nunan, 1989).

Again we have described two positions at opposite ends of the continuum. A middle position on the continuum may well be used with a course following a more or less fixed design that also allows for some time to be spent on topics and issues that learners raise themselves. Similarly a negotiated course may well include some pre-planned components.

Courses can also be *repeatable (durable)* or *one-off*. Repeatable courses are those that are taught again after a specified period of time, for example every term or year with EAP courses, every so many months with EOP courses. The course outline and materials are prepared and, although they may be revised after a course, they remain essentially similar each time they are used.

One-off courses are run for a particular course or group and are not repeated. A course outline and materials may be prepared, but it is more likely that the course uses particular sources provided by the learners or by the teacher to meet an expressed need or want.

8.3 Balancing the parameters

In planning a course, ESP teachers should first be aware of the options and of the limitations arising from institutional and learner expectations.

In some circumstances, course design may be carried out before the course takes place and the details may be revised either during the course or, more likely, after the course has been run. Initial revisions may be major, but thereafter the details may only need fine-tuning. In other circumstances the teacher may be designing the course while teaching takes place or negotiating the course with the learners and reacting quickly to the needs as expressed at the beginning of the course and as they change over the period of the course. It is generally important in such situations that the ESP teacher has a good deal of experience in both teaching, and materials provision and writing. It is also important to have a range of materials available.

8.4 Case studies

We will now look at four case studies which illustrate the implementation of the parameters described in this chapter.

8.4.1 Case study 1: residential intensive non-assessed EOP course – GEC Management College, Dunchurch

This example illustrates a situation where the course is designed in advance, taught and then evolves gradually over time through evaluation and shifts in client needs.

Background

A British and a French company merged, adopting English as the company language and language improvement programmes, both French and English, were initiated.

Needs analysis procedure

The client provided a brief of their aims for English and a management college commissioned three draft course designs based on different features of the brief. After a number of negotiations a course design was agreed on. This was a team-taught, one-week residential course to simultaneously develop management skills and English language for conducting effective meetings and discussions in English.

There are about 35 hours of formal tutor contact plus preparation, self-study, meal times and evenings. The participants, a maximum of 10, are European business people, mainly with French as their L1. Their background is varied: some are in technical departments, others are in commercial, financial or legal work.

Course framework

The course was designed to be team-taught and experiential. The cycle of activities is:

⌐ perform (video recorded) ⌐
prepare   feedback
⌐ input / language practice ↵

There are two tutors: one, a Human Resource Development expert, who leads the interpersonal skills work; the other, a language expert, leads the language work. Their role is to facilitate learning through providing task frameworks, directing discussions and giving input at a suitable level (Berger and St John, 1993). At the design stage, a number of mini language practice situations were planned. In fact, all the language practice has been built into the skills tasks. The course is designed around these and the language supports rather than determines them. The course materials, which are common-core, consist of in-house handouts and tasks plus Business English: an individualised learning programme (Wilberg and Lewis, 1990).

Adaptations were made during the first and subsequent courses based on tutor and participant evaluations. At the client's request the course was further adapted to take account of cross-cultural issues, not just French and English but more broadly as the company has business around the world. The current language components comprise original components (•) and new aspects or aspects covered in a different manner (• •):

- use of notes
- language guidelines relevant to first meetings
- conventions and expressions for saying 'yes' and 'no'
- language for discussing change, that is dealing with data-based facts and figures
- guided self-study
- • language for introducing visual aids
- • language for structuring a presentation
- • daily vocabulary development work
- • intensive listening practice based on video extracts of meetings
- • input and practice in questioning techniques, particularly asking open and building questions
- • specific practice on summarising what you have heard and checking on mutual understanding
- • most of the language feedback is combined with the skills feedback. During feedback some work on pronunciation / intonation is built in plus 'common errors'.

8.4.2 Case study 2: an extensive, repeated, assessed EAP course for students at the Jordanian University of Science and Technology (JUST), Irbid, Jordan

This example illustrates a situation where teaching and course design happen simultaneously and a satisfactory course is achieved over time (several years) through a number of revisions.

Background

Arabic is the main language in Jordan; English is a foreign language. Some secondary schools provide English-medium education. At JUST, English is the official medium of courses. There is a compulsory under-graduate course in English which all students must pass. The purpose is to raise their level of English language and to try and ensure that no student fails their subject studies because of English-language problems – the entry levels are very different; some students are quite fluent, others almost beginners.

The original courses and materials did not meet student needs and so JUST established a project to develop new courses, write materials and train English staff in ESP.

Needs analysis procedure

An initial Target Situation Analysis (TSA) was conducted using questionnaires with students and staff, plus structured interviews with subject lecturers. Formative evaluation during the next years refined the needs and provided valuable feedback on materials and methods. Lesson record sheets, focus groups with students, staff discussions, questionnaires, test results and observation were all used for evaluation.

Broad results of needs analysis procedure

All faculties have prescribed reading and there are often handouts or laboratory instructions in English (although Arabic was used too). Subject lecturers felt students did not read widely enough, either in subject areas or more extensively. The faculties also require writing, from note-taking to short reports, laboratory reports, problem-solving assignments, project reports and examinations. The major area of difficulty was considered to be at the macro-level, understanding the conventions, rhetorical awareness and organisation of ideas. (However, a substantial proportion of students also have problems at the basic sentence level.) Students have to listen to lectures, demonstrations and instructions and comprehension was generally considered acceptable although the speed of delivery by subject lecturers was seen as problematic. Speaking about their subject areas was generally acceptable but students were less confident in other situations.

Course framework

The groups are fairly large, about 40, and heterogeneous in level (some have attended English-medium schools) and subject disciplines, so the courses are mostly common-core and focus on broad EAP skills areas. The course materials were originally a mix of published selections and in-house. One of the initial problems was lack of ESP experience. The aim was to have in-house learner-centred material but staff did not have experience of teaching ESP materials or of the desired learner-centred approach. Without such experience, producing local materials is difficult. With time the team became proficient ESP teachers and sound materials adapters and writers. They produced, revised and published full sets of in-house material.

Two courses are offered each semester:
Course 111, compulsory for all new undergraduates. Duration 12 weeks, total length 36 hours. Course content: Units 1–5 Strategies for reading: topic sentences, paragraph organisation, paragraph development, dealing with unknown words, finding information quickly; Units 6–7 Writing laboratory reports; Units 8–12 Explorations in reading, listening and writing.

Course 112, compulsory before graduating. Duration 12 weeks, total length 36 hours. It was felt that this course needed a different format and focus so it is designed around the written and spoken presentation of a term paper. The first units cover skills for gathering information, the second block deals with organisation, language and skills for the written version, the third group of units looks at editing for meaning, coherence and accuracy while the last three units cover oral presentations.

8.4.3 Case study 3: extensive EAP specific course for students studying international banking and finance at MBA level, University of Birmingham (non-assessed)

The students are following a fairly intensive course in the Business School which combines elements of training for work with an introduction to the academic field appropriate to a Masters level course. The English course focuses for the first term on essay writing, thereafter by negotiation with the students on oral presentations and/or dissertation writing.

Background

The University of Birmingham places great emphasis on running international courses and funds an English for International Students Unit to run classes for such students. The course is also supported financially by The Business School.

Needs analysis procedure

Discussions with department and students. The banking and finance students originally followed the same English course run for the core MBA group. This was not completely effective for them and so a separate group was formed. The needs of this new group were determined through discussion with students and follow-up discussion with the lecturers teaching the course. Essentially the same material as for the core MBA group was used, but it was given a different emphasis.

Course details

Course duration:	two academic terms
Course length:	20 one-hour sessions plus one-to-one tutorials on writing
Size of group:	10–20
Resources:	a prepared course, plus all the resources of a British university
Participants:	students shown by the Birmingham assessment and diagnostic test to need extra help with English plus others who come voluntarily. Most students are from South East Asia and the Far East (Taiwan, Hong Kong, China, Indonesia and Japan); others are from Latin America, Europe or the Middle East. Most will have obtained Band 6 in the IELTS test, and some will have attended the pre-sessional language course run by the English for International Students Unit.
Objectives:	
First term –	to write assignments that meet the departmental requirements; to enable students to use sources for their assignments without plagiarism
Second term –	to help students with oral assignments (if required); to help students with dissertation writing (if required)

The materials used include:

specific materials prepared by Martin Hewings and others focusing on:
- adopting an academic style through the use of appropriate lexis and grammar;
- techniques for quotation and citation;
- describing and discussing data;

- the Visitron video (a published video-based course on oral presentations in a business context);
- materials on writing an introduction, a method section and a discussion section of a dissertation.

The carrier content is from general academic business and finance topics and is common to various groups, for example those following international business, accounting, and money, banking and finance courses. Student performance on the course is not assessed, but all their subject examinations are in English.

The major change in the syllabus as a result of experience has been a move away from a focus on writing an introduction for an assignment to a concern with the appropriate academic stance for a student to adopt in writing. This has led to a much greater emphasis on the reasons for citation and quotation and acceptable limits of drawing on sources rather than just setting out the bibliographic references. In other words the teaching of writing has moved from a procedure that combined aspects of the product and process approaches to one that incorporates social constructionism.

8.4.4 Case study 4: an intensive one-off EOP course for research scientists, India

This example illustrates a very specific ESP situation where a draft programme is drawn up based on very little pre-course information, and great flexibility is needed in implementing it. Such situations call for experienced ESP practitioners.

Pre-course information

Course duration: $3\frac{1}{2}$ days
Course length: 20 hours
Size of group: 20–40
Resources: photocopying
Participants: post-doctoral agriculture and science researchers from universities and research institutions
Assessment: none
Course objectives: for participants to (i) produce more effective journal articles; (ii) to increase the rate of acceptance of articles by journal editors; (iii) to spend less time on the whole writing process

Background

India is a multi-lingual society; English is a mother tongue for some, a second language for many, the official language of the judiciary, a medium of some education and widely spoken. India has a large scientific research community but is under-represented in international research journals.

Needs analysis procedure

It was not possible to conduct a pre-course needs analysis directly with participants, so no PSA or LSA was possible. The broad TS was to get articles accepted in international, English-medium journals with minimal revisions. A list of the target journals was provided. The TSA which could be conducted pre-course consisted of:

- reading research into the process of writing
- reading research on scientific articles
- analysing articles in a selection of target journals
- building on previous experience

Sources of published teaching materials included:

Writing up Research by Weissberg and Buker (1990)
Academic Writing for Graduate Students by Swales and Feak (1994)

Course framework

An outline programme was drawn up in the UK and modified on delivery. The major changes that took place on the spot were:

- re-ordering – covering Introductions before Results
- introducing a new topic at participants' request – Abstracts
- spending more time on feedback and revisions
- omitting one task – writing a Procedure section.

The major changes for a later course were:

1. more on the reading and writing process; looking at why and how articles are read, leading to reader orientation versus writer orientation
2. more language work, particularly tenses and associated meanings, and creating good links and transitions; areas where even those with wide exposure to English felt unconfident
3. more on writing a good abstract; readers use this to decide on the value of the article
4. more attention to learning strategies because of knowing more about the local environment.

Task 8b ◆◇

We show below a set of diagrams showing the positions on the various course design continuums for the last of our examples, the intensive writing course for research scientists in India. Reread the course description for our other three examples and draw similar diagrams for each cline.

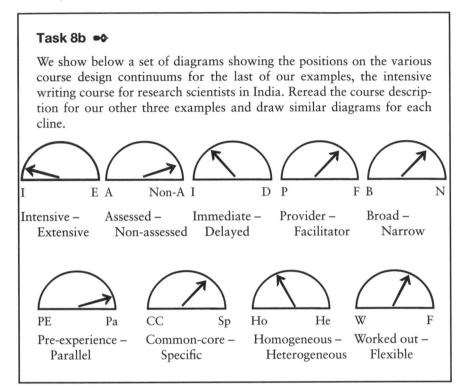

| I | E | A | Non-A | I | D | P | F | B | N |

Intensive – Extensive   Assessed – Non-assessed   Immediate – Delayed   Provider – Facilitator   Broad – Narrow

| PE | Pa | CC | Sp | Ho | He | W | F |

Pre-experience – Parallel   Common-core – Specific   Homogeneous – Heterogeneous   Worked out – Flexible

---

8.5 Developing a course outline

Coming up with a course design is a dynamic mix of juggling and doing jigsaw puzzles. Juggling because there are a lot of different aspects to keep in mind and keep moving between – the balls a juggler has to keep in the air. Jigsaw puzzles because we are taking different pieces and shifting them around until they fit to make a satisfactory picture.

We have shown that there are many factors to consider and a variety of situations in which courses are designed. Whatever the situation, choices have to be made so criteria have to be clear. As Swales (1989) put it, course design should be about what *and* why.

With the range of ESP courses that have been taught around the world and the materials published, even for a new course, we should not have to start from scratch – to invent a wheel. As with needs analysis, an important part of the process is to learn from what else we and others have done. Evolution rather than revolution or invention may be the route for innovation.

Whatever the circumstances are, there are so many pieces to fit together that we like to be fairly systematic in our approach and to have an organising framework. This is a matrix or grid of related components. The first of these comprise the target events and tasks that the ESP learners need and want to perform, together with the associated rhetorical awareness needs. From these we can consider the associated skills areas and linguistic realisations – genre moves, grammar, vocabulary requirements – and micro-skills. However, the course is not just about linguistic realisations and skills. It is also about materials, carrier content topics, learning processes and classroom interactions. These must all have their place within the grid.

A first stage may be to fill in whatever information we have, without attempting to order it. Some of the items are the results of the needs analysis (and because we take a broad perspective on needs analysis, many of the features that are sometimes described as course design variables were actually discussed there). Other items stem from existing courses and available materials. The practicality of course design is that it is affected by materials as well as determining them (see figure 7.2). When we believe we have all the key items, we attempt to group and order them in a way that enhances learning. When we have ordered and shifted we should have a grid that helps us check that everything is included and well-balanced (a completed jigsaw).

8.5.1 Ordering: criteria for prioritising

(a) Beginning with target events and rhetorical awareness

Our starting point is the macro-level – the target events in which the learners want to operate successfully and the necessary rhetorical awareness. Those target events need to be ordered, so we need criteria with which to order them. One criterion is according to when the target events are needed by the learners (this can only apply when the needs are immediate rather than delayed). Thus at JUST, writing laboratory reports was originally taught in the last two or three weeks of the semester because writing is a more difficult skill. However, it was realised that students were having to write reports for their subject tutors well before the end of the semester, so that section of the course was moved to weeks six and seven.

A second key criterion is that using or learning certain language or skills is dependent on others. The linguistic building blocks must therefore come before or at the same time as they are needed. This building block criterion applies to learning as well as to use. We can ask of two events, which is easier to learn? We can also ask, what is needed to learn x? (Hopefully, we are already aware of these because of our needs analysis – E + F, p. 125.) For instance, the passive uses the verb *to be*; many 'if clauses' use the *would/should/could* modal verbs; the metaphorical meaning of expressions may derive directly or indirectly from their literal meaning.

These two criteria of 'when needed' and 'building' do not usually order everything. Some items will now be in specific places in the jigsaw, others could, at this stage fit in more than one place. They will fit into a specific place either because of other related variables in the grid or because of the materials or according to additional criteria such as: building confidence. For instance, at Dunchurch presentations come before meetings partly because it is easier to speak a prepared monologue than to take turns in a meeting. (Also, taking part in a meeting may mean giving a brief presentation so the building block criteria also applies to some extent.)

Task 8c ●◆

Look at the case studies and deduce some of the target events.

Case study	Target events
JUST course 111 Research scientists, India Dunchurch University of Birmingham Masters in IBF (International Banking and Finance)	

(b) From target events and rhetorical awareness to skill areas to language

The target events will have been broken down into skill areas and the appropriate rhetorical awareness considered as part of the needs analysis. For the Birmingham IBF students, the needs associated with writing their assignments broke down into four skill areas:

- writing a good introduction
- citing sources and attributing ideas
- writing in an academic style
- discussing data

Within those the students needed to develop an awareness of how to handle others' ideas, what it was acceptable to use, what should be attributed, what should be quoted and what could be termed plagiarism. At the course design stage these skill areas also have to be ordered and the same criteria apply: what is needed first, what is a building block, what increases confidence?

Orientation 8d

In what order would you place the rhetorical awareness and skill areas for the IBF course above? Can you think of any associated language?

Because *writing in an academic style* is the most general of the skills, and will be used throughout the assignment, it is the first component. Rhetorical awareness of how to handle others' ideas is also fundamental and so the second component is *citing sources and attributing ideas*. Banking and finance are heavily dependent on *interpreting and presenting numerical data* and so this is the third component. The data has to be attributed and so this component can build on and recycle ideas from the second component. *Writing a good introduction* is the final component (largely by default – the others need to come earlier).

Associated with each of the four skill areas are particular functions and language. We can find that particularly the micro-skills and also some of the grammar, and even lexis, occur more than once, that is, they match with more than one target event or skill area; there is no one-to-one relationship between target event and skill area, or skill area and function, or function and grammatical realisation. We do not want to teach the same point more than once (although we do recycle for practice) so this means that sometimes we must choose when to teach that point and whether to recycle. The criteria for that choice are again need: What does not occur elsewhere? Which of the various language items will be most useful early on? Putting all this together led to the grid shown in table 8.4.

Task 8e ●◇

For the Dunchurch course (case study 1) one target event is handling meetings effectively:

a) Decide what some of the skills areas and associated rhetorical awareness, language and micro-skills are for that event.
b) Draw up a partial course grid for these components.

Table 8.4 *Partial course grid for Birmingham IBF course*

Target Events	Rhetorical Awareness and Skill Areas	Language — Usage		Functions	Materials	Interactions	Topics
		Grammar	Vocabulary				
Writing good assignments	writing in academic style		choice of lexis; use of nominalised structures		in-house	teacher input leading to class discussion; writing activities done singly or in pairs; pair evaluation of each other's writing	general business and finance topics, for example relative commercial performance of supermarket chains, management styles
	citing sources and attributing ideas	tense and mood: x claims, it is claimed, x has claimed	reporting verbs: show, claim, suggest and so on	conventions about quotations, citation and references			
	discussing data	tenses	verbs of increase/ decrease; quantifiers and modifiers				
	writing a good introduction			moves functions: cause and effect, compare/contrast			

8.5.2 The role of materials

We stressed in the chapter on needs analysis the process of discovering, through reading, analysing texts, observing interactions, and asking questions of experts, exactly what is involved in communicating effectively in the target situation and in learning to do so. Looking at existing materials, published and unpublished, is part of this process; we can learn about skill areas and associated language from materials. The final choice of some features to be taught and the order they are taught in will come from the materials we select.

For example, if you do not know what is important for *interpreting and presenting numerical data* then a look at materials such as Wilberg and Lewis *Business English* (pp. 84–95) or Swales and Feak *Academic Writing for Graduate Students* (pp. 77–102) or Williams *Panorama* (each unit) would provide plenty of ideas. What you select for your course will depend on the precise aims, language levels and your overall approach.

Reflection 8f ●◆

Look at two or three books that deal with data comment (for example Wilberg and Lewis, Swales and Feak, Williams).

a) List what each does / does not teach about data comment.
b) Consider the main difference(s) in the approach of each one.
c) Consider the effect of choosing one book rather than another.

8.5.3 Timetabling

Through timetabling a final order for the course outline and a time allocation are reached. In some circumstances – courses with few hours or little time for course design – this may be part of the initial juggling. Thus, for the India course we did not draw up a matrix of variables. Instead we drew up the timetable of sessions and fitted the items in directly. This 'shortcut' was possible because the course was short and because we had a good deal of experience to draw on. We knew what the main items under each variable were likely to be.

With the Dunchurch course we considered the timetable after drawing up the first grid of what we wanted to teach. Much discussion and information exchange went on in order to establish the course content because this was the first course of its kind (dual purpose / team-taught). In addition, there was time and finance for this. When the course content was outlined, we began to think about how to teach it and how long different activities would require. That gave us a feel for whether everything could be included and which items had to have less time allocated to them. The final order (the timetable) was also influenced by practical learning issues such as: (a) varying the kind of activities throughout the day, (b) not having heavy input sessions at the end of the day, (c) having interactive rather than 'passive' work immediately after lunch.

8.5.4 The role of assessment and evaluation

Other factors to be built into the course design and timetabling are assessment and evaluation. Both take up course time which must be allowed for. Building them in ensures that (a) they happen and (b) they are planned and effective.

At JUST, the course is extensive, with 15-week semesters. However, little teaching takes place in the first week when registration is still in progress; there is time out in the middle for testing and again at the end when classtime is lost through subject examinations. The original design of 15 weeks material was unrealistic and did not take account of institutional activities. Now the course contains 12 weeks material and staff find that they can cover everything.

Grading We have discussed criteria which we use to prioritise and order items in a course. We have mentioned building blocks which are about grading. What we have not used as a criterion is to go from easier to more difficult. That is something which we address through the materials and how we handle them in class. There is not enough knowledge and evidence about language learning for anyone to order all features of language according to simplicity / difficulty. Even if there were, this would not necessarily help an ESP learner. The present perfect may be trickier than the past simple but if both are needed to write a good introduction or discussion then it is no good leaving the present perfect until later.

Grading is achieved not through the course order / outline but through the materials and methodology. When the language learning will be difficult, the carrier content needs to be easy (but interesting and not trivial). The more difficult an area of language, the more guidance and support a learner needs in exercises and tasks as well as more practice.

Reflection 8g

For a course you are teaching or have taught, draw up a current or retrospective course grid.

8.6 Summary

We have in this unit looked at the parameters for course design, illustrating these with four case studies from our own experience. We have also looked at the questions of ordering and grading. In our final remarks we will restrict ourselves to two points. The first is to emphasise the importance in course design of looking at other examples from other situations. As we noted in chapter 2, a significant part of ESP literature is concerned with describing course design. A considerable amount of time and energy can be saved if we learn from these examples, by looking at the decisions other course designers made and at the materials they selected, and then adapt these other approaches to match the particular parameters in our own situation.

Our second point is about what we have not included in this chapter: We have not described in detail either the theory or the practice of the various approaches to syllabus design such as functional/notional, task-based, lexical. This is partly because we looked at the issues involved in these types of syllabus in chapter 2. It also reflects our view that course design is based on intelligent juggling of all the course parameters and on experience of how best to match them with learners' needs.

8.7 Recommended reading

The British Council ELT Document (1980) contains interesting articles about a number of important ESP projects in Sudan, Saudi Arabia, Mexico, plus one of the first of the articles by Hutchinson and Waters challenging the existing ESP orthodoxy. The Hewings and Dudley-Evans volume (1996) looks at course design for EAP in British universities while the Kenny and Savage volume (1997) looks at the role of language in development projects. The Nunan book (1988) is a standard reference for learner-centred courses.

9 The role of materials

9.1 Aims

Materials are used in all teaching. The core materials are usually paper-based but, where possible, ESP teachers also want to use audio and video cassettes, overhead transparencies, computers and, occasionally, other equipment or real objects. In this chapter, we will consider how we can make the most of existing material or add our own. We will also discuss how we can involve our learners and use learner-generated material. We begin by considering why we use materials as this has implications for what material we use and how we use it.

9.2 The purpose of materials

Orientation 9a ••

Before you read on: Brainstorm reasons for using materials. Then, for each reason think of the implications that follow. Note these in a table or as an 'octopus' as in these examples.

reasons	implications

reason source of language —*implication –*

implication – use real not invented examples

Four reasons for using materials which seem significant in the ESP context are:

1. as a source of language
2. as a learning support

3. for motivation and stimulation
4. for reference

9.2.1 Source of language

In some situations, where English is a foreign not a second language, the ESP classroom may be almost the only source of English. Materials then play a crucial role in exposing learners to the language, which implies that the materials need to present real language, as it is used, and the full range that learners require.

Consider the situation where learners need to extract information from English-medium subject textbooks. A reading-only course could be suitable. However, if nearly every text comes from magazines such as *Time* or the *New Scientist*, content and style will be journalistic. The language differs substantially from the didactic/pedagogic style of textbooks. So, the language is real but it cannot provide the range of features that learners require.

Where the classroom is the primary source of language, the materials also need to maximise exposure to the language, for instance, by providing additional material: not everything needs to be studied in detail; interested learners will use it for their own learning practice. Another source of language in materials are the rubrics (instructions). In monolingual situations, the L1 may be used in the materials for instructions and explanations. If learners have very little exposure to English, having up to 50 per cent of the material written in the L1 seems a lost opportunity. When learners begin with a low level of language, one solution is to use both languages and gradually remove the L1 version.

9.2.2 Learning support

As a learning support, materials need to be reliable, that is, to work, to be consistent and to have some recognisable pattern. This need not mean a rigid unit structure; we would argue against a fixed format. There have been materials published where each text is followed by ten comprehension questions. Such a constraint is an imposition that takes no account of either the real or carrier content of the materials. The text may lend itself to detailed study and the asking of more than ten questions. More likely, the questions that arise naturally will be fewer. The other questions become trivial fillers and distract from the real objectives.

To enhance learning, materials must involve learners in thinking about and using the language. The activities need to stimulate cognitive not mechanical processes. The learners also need a sense of progression.

9.2.3 Stimulation and motivation

To stimulate and motivate, materials need to be challenging yet achievable; to offer new ideas and information whilst being grounded in the learners' experience and knowledge; to encourage fun and creativity. The input must contain concepts and/or knowledge that are familiar but it must also offer something new, a reason to communicate, to get involved. The exploitation needs to match how the input would be used outside the learning situation and take account of language learning needs. The purpose and the connection to the learners' reality need to be clear.

9.2.4 Reference

Many ESP learners have little time for class contact and rely on a mix of classes, self-study and reference material. For self-study or reference purposes, materials need to be complete, well laid out and self-explanatory. The learner will want explanations (possibly in an L1, as well as in English), examples and practice activities that have answer and discussion keys.

The materials will need to take account of different learning styles and allow for the explorer, who will follow through a train of thought; the browser, who will pick and choose at random; and the systematist, who will work through methodically. This implies that an important feature is the overt organisation of the material – through informative contents pages and an index. Contents pages such as: Unit 1 – Reading: The four Ps; Listening – Total Quality Control; serve little purpose. Those that provide a matrix (or grid) of objectives, skills, language, activity and topic are far more helpful.

9.3 Writers or providers of materials?

All this places high demands on the materials and great pressure on materials writers. Not surprisingly, producing one hour of good learning material gobbles up hours of preparation time. Each stage of finding suitable carrier content, matching real content to learning and real world activities, composing clear rubrics, planning an effective layout, is time-consuming. Estimates vary but 15:1 can be considered a minimum. Preparing new materials from scratch for every course taught is clearly impractical, even if every teacher actually had the ability. One of the myths of ESP has been that you have to write your own materials. This then leads to the myth that every ESP teacher is also a good designer of course materials. We would dispute that; only a small proportion of good teachers are also good designers of course materials. What all ESP practitioners have to be is good providers of materials. A good provider of materials will be able to:

1. select appropriately from what is available;
2. be creative with what is available;
3. modify activities to suit learners' needs; and
4. supplement by providing extra activities (and extra input).

The balance between these will vary from course to course, situation to situation.

9.3.1 Selecting from what is available

Selecting materials, like selecting a partner, involves making choices and decisions. To make good choices we need to have good criteria on which to base our decision. Numerous criteria, such as factors about the learners, the role of the materials, the topics, the language, the presentation, have been put forward for the analysis of materials and each of them has validity. There are checklists for evaluating a whole book which are useful when thinking of purchasing a set or using the book as core course material (Cunningsworth, 1995). Operating with so many possible variables is difficult. Our approach would be to use two or three key criteria in the first instance. We would then apply others to reduce the selection or to identify some of the weaknesses we would want to address in our use of the material.

From our discussion of the purposes of materials we would suggest that initial questions to ask when selecting materials include:

a) Will the materials stimulate and motivate?
b) To what extent does the material match the stated learning objectives and your learning objectives? (It is rare for a single set of published material to match the exact learning needs of any one ESP learner group; and activities do not always meet the stated objectives.)
c) To what extent will the materials support that learning?

Very often it is not a whole book we need to evaluate but a unit or just an activity. Identifying and separating the real content (exploited and exploitable) and the carrier content of particular activities is crucial to this process. The carrier content must be appropriate and the real content must match the course objectives. In our experience, the only way to check this is to 'be a student' and do the activities, thinking carefully about what we are actually having to do to complete them successfully.

9.3.2 *Being creative with what is available*

Often, being creative with what is available is crucial, especially if the work environment is heavily constrained. Situations can vary along the cline of:

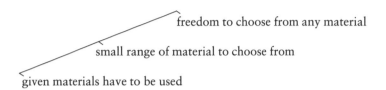

freedom to choose from any material

small range of material to choose from

given materials have to be used

For instance, on a recent in-service development course one teacher was very frustrated because she had to work with a set book which she and her computer science learners found dull and out-of-date. This was a situation which called for two simultaneous strands of action: preparing a persuasive case to change the situation and being creative with the existing situation. As the carrier content was computer science, the situation was particularly extreme because that is a field in which technical developments have been so rapid that carrier content dates rapidly.

Orientation 9b

Suggest ways in which a teacher could have exploited the dated carrier content, mentioned above, to the benefit and interest of the learners.

Where possible no one would use unsuitable carrier content but there can be situations where there is no alternative. Until we have succeeded in changing the situation we have to be creative. The very act of being creative can put a new perspective on material and reveal possibilities such that it is no longer 'making the best of a difficult situation'. With input where the carrier content is out-of-date, learners could:

- extract what is no longer true (and explain why);
- separate what they already know from what is new;
- extract what is true and re-write or re-tell it.

With carrier content that seems irrelevant, the focus must be clearly on the real content. The purpose of the material needs to be explicit and why this carrier content is being used could also be made explicit.

9.3.3 *Modifying activities to suit learners' needs*

Modifying activities is generally for when the input and carrier content are adequate but some or all of the exploitation is unsuitable. There could be many reasons why the exploitation seems unsuitable and each requires different action.

Orientation 9c

Below are five reasons for modifying materials. For each reason, suggest the kind of modification you could make.

1) There are too many activities, so either there is repetition or too many different objectives are dealt with at one time.
2) The activities focus too strongly on carrier content.
3) The activities are too mechanical.
4) The activities focus too quickly on the detail of the carrier content.
5) An activity is linguistically flawed.

What action would you take?

Possible modifications

Reason 1 Select the activities that are central to the core objective. With a mixed group these could be carried out by everyone while other activities could be selected for weaker learners to practise later (repetition) or faster learners to work on in spare class time (additional objectives).

Reason 2 Replace them with activities which focus on real content. This may mean preparing a new activity.

Reason 3 Change the rubric to change the focus or drop the activity. Examples are activities which require learners to manipulate grammar constructions without reference to meaning. For example, 'Convert the following sentences into (or out of) the passive'. Ironically, we have seen more rubrics which require learners to convert into the passive but spent more time on writing courses helping them to switch to active!

Reason 4 Add in an activity or two before those given in the material.

Reason 5 With an established, high-level group, ask them what the problem is. Otherwise omit the exercise.

9.3.4   Supplementing by providing extra input and activities

There is no black-and-white dividing line between modifying materials, supplementing with extra input and activities, and preparing materials from scratch. In each case it is a question of degree and perspective. To supplement with extra activities can be viewed as a form of modification. Changing the input is more likely to be viewed as supplementation or preparing new material. The skills ESP practitioners need in order to provide different input and extra activities, that is to write materials, include:

- matching carrier content to real content;
- providing variety;
- grading activity level to learning and language level; and
- presenting the material well.

We discuss each of these in the next section on teacher-generated material. Preparing materials benefits from a co-operative effort because the exchange of ideas, availability of different abilities and strengths, and piloting that can take place are invaluable for the quality of the final material.

9.4   Teacher-generated material

9.4.1   Matching carrier content to real content

The development of new material along traditional lines could be from one of two directions: one starting point (A) is having some good input / carrier content. This may come from a client or from the learners or be something we have come across. When the starting point is good carrier content, the next stage is to analyse it to determine what real content it could be exploited for. Then it is a question of whether, where and how that real content fits into the course. The other starting point (B) is where there is a gap in the course material; that is, there is a course objective, some real content for which there is, no suitable material available. In this case, the first stage is to search for some suitable carrier content.

These two possibilities can be represented as:

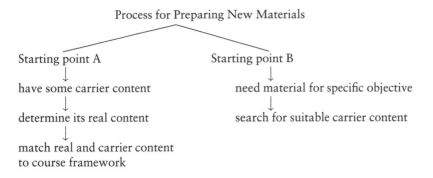

Process for Preparing New Materials

Starting point A

↓

have some carrier content

↓

determine its real content

↓

match real and carrier content
to course framework

Starting point B

↓

need material for specific objective

↓

search for suitable carrier content

When the real and carrier content are matched, the next stage is to draft activities. The (likely) resources, group sizes, approaches to learning and target activities must be considered when selecting activities so that they are appropriate for the learning environment. In ESP, the learners are not primarily language learners; they are or have been learners of other disciplines and this has to be a major consideration in the devising and delivering of a course. To maximise learning means activating all existing learning strategies (see chapter 10).

9.4.2 Providing variety

Variety is essential in any language class, but we feel that it is particularly important in an ESP class as there is sometimes the danger of the ESP class becoming rather a dry affair that fails to motivate learners. We need to practise a number of micro-skills in one class, we need to introduce a range of activity types and we need to vary the type of interaction taking place during the class.

Variety in the micro-skills

A class may have as its aim one particular macro-skill, such as writing, but the use of other macro-skills will both help the learning of the target macro-skill and provide variety for the class. In the same way we feel that we should ensure that we focus on a number of micro-skills in a class; a reading class dominated by, say, deducing the meaning from context is likely to be less effective and motivating than one that focuses on a number of related micro-skills, for example deducing meaning from context, learning certain key core business vocabulary items and investigating collocations.

Variety in activity types

Many textbooks use a relatively narrow range of exercise types but we have always found that the use of a wide range of types increases motivation, for both the learners and the teacher. Learners welcome this variety, but, when we use a new exercise type, we must familiarise learners with it so they know what they are expected to do. A visual element in an exercise is often effective as it both increases variety and avoids the danger of too much writing to be read and understood as input for a task. We can use visuals for language work, to generate spoken or written production, and as a comprehension check on a reading or listening passage. Visuals include diagrams, flow charts, graphs, bar and pie charts, matrices, photographs and sketches.

We should also make learners think when they do an exercise. An exercise that requires some pulling together of ideas from different sources, some drawing on the learners' own knowledge, or even some simple calculation is much more challenging than a purely mechanical exercise, and can both increase motivation and improve the chances of retention of the target language or skill. Again this should not happen all the time: we also need to vary the amount of challenging material and the demands that it makes on the learner.

Consider the exercise E6.4 (pp. 250–51) taken from Swales and Feak (1994). It asks the student to read a data commentary and then judge whether some imaginary comments made by a supervisor are valid or not. In our experience the exercise certainly leads to a lively discussion, and also makes students realise that they can question evaluations of their writing.

Reflection 9d

Consider a published coursebook or your own in-house materials and look at:

a) the number of different activity types in each unit;
b) how often certain exercise types appear over three or four units;
c) how visuals are used.

Draw conclusions about whether there is sufficient variety and whether the activities make learners think.

Variety in interaction

We need to ensure that the ESP class is varied in the nature of its interactions. Changes from teacher input to individual work to pair work to class discussion can provide this so long as they are not overdone. We should also build in choice as far as possible: some students would rather work on their own than in groups or pairs, so we can allow them to do so for at least part of the class. Class size and learners' expectations of how they should be taught will affect how successful these changes are and the teacher should be sensitive to these issues.

9.4.3 Grading exercises

Grading is concerned with the amount of support provided to enable learners to do a set of exercises, and with providing learners with tasks at different levels of difficulty. Many ESP practitioners find themselves in the situation where their groups are of very mixed abilities. Such a situation requires an approach to material which to some extent caters for everyone. One way this can be achieved is to present each task or set of exercises at three levels: unsupported / partially supported / fully supported (Nunes, 1992). In addition, activities differ in their conceptual level (Nunan, 1989) and can be graded according to complexity of processing.

9.4.4 Presenting the material well

A final, important step is to present the material well. This includes writing good, consistent rubrics, planning layout and proofing. Consistency helps learners to focus on learning rather than working out what to do. A unit of material might have the following broad format.

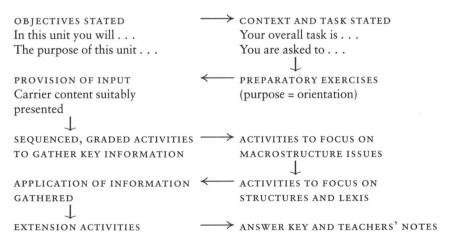

OBJECTIVES STATED   ⟶   CONTEXT AND TASK STATED
In this unit you will . . .   Your overall task is . . .
The purpose of this unit . . .   You are asked to . . .
                        ↓

PROVISION OF INPUT   ⟵   PREPARATORY EXERCISES
Carrier content suitably   (purpose = orientation)
presented
 ↓

SEQUENCED, GRADED ACTIVITIES   ⟶   ACTIVITIES TO FOCUS ON
TO GATHER KEY INFORMATION   MACROSTRUCTURE ISSUES
                        ↓

APPLICATION OF INFORMATION   ⟵   ACTIVITIES TO FOCUS ON
GATHERED   STRUCTURES AND LEXIS
 ↓

EXTENSION ACTIVITIES   ⟶   ANSWER KEY AND TEACHERS' NOTES

When modifying or writing materials, a checklist of different exercise types and another one of prompts used in rubrics can be invaluable for achieving variety in exercises and consistency in rubrics.

Reflection 9e

Go through some ESP textbooks and make a checklist of:

a) good exercise types;
b) key words and phrases used in rubrics.

9.5 Learner-generated material

Learner-generated material can provide both carrier content and activities: in chapter 6, we mentioned some advantages of using texts which have been chosen by the learners. Another way in which learners can provide carrier content is through framework materials.

9.5.1 Framework materials

Most materials provide carrier content and activities for input and practice, and one of the major difficulties ESP materials writers face is balancing the levels and appropriateness of carrier content and real content. Framework materials remove that difficulty. They do not provide carrier content. Neither do they provide language input. Instead they set a context, a framework, within which the learners fit their own carrier content and their existing language competence.

What do framework materials look like?

In chapter 6, we gave examples of frameworks into which learners could fit the ideas they extracted from reading and listening, such as tables, matrices and flow diagrams. Framework materials take the same concept of visual, diagrammatic representations but use them for the production of language. So the ideas that are fitted into the framework are the learners' and the framework is a device for organising those ideas.

Frameworks that have already occurred in this book are: a flow diagram (p. 250) and a classification tree (p. 6). With a flow diagram a learner might describe the whole of a process or just state the purpose of the process and then focus on a stage which is problematic or particularly crucial. A classification tree might lead to justifying why items are grouped together, or explaining differences.

The framework below is useful for comparison, contrast or the listing of advantages and disadvantages. Within a mixed business group the topics discussed might range from the advantages and disadvantages of a modified production process (production engineers), a proposed promotional campaign (marketing personnel), a new product idea (research and development), a structural re-organisation (personnel officers) or the opening of a new agency (strategic managers). The learners fit their own content into the framework.

Compare and Contrast

Relocation of head office to a new site		
London		Midlands
prestigious		space to expand
close to Heathrow airport		some loss of personnel
traffic congestion		more flexible layout
more expensive		good road and air communication
		short-term relocation costs

Advantages and Disadvantages

Production Process		
Advantages		Disadvantages

A key aspect for using framework materials is what Ellis and Johnson (1994) refer to as 'the setting box'. The setting box establishes the criteria for a particular interaction by asking for each interactant 'Who am I?' (*a*), 'What are we talking about?' (*m*) and 'Why are we talking about this?' (*p*). (This parallels the *m.a.p.* we referred to when learners are writing, chapter 6.) An additional significant feature of the setting box is the question, 'Where are we?'. In the light of Charles' (1994) research (see chapter 4), we would wish to add, 'What is our business relationship?'. The setting box establishes the context for the interaction. Our framework map or setting box for spoken interaction would be:

Framework m.a.p. / setting box for a spoken interaction

Who are we?
What is our (business) relationship?
Where are we?
What are we talking about?
Why are we talking about this?

Using framework materials

Framework materials supplement rather than replace more traditional materials. They may be used at a practice stage after specific language input or as a starting point for a deep-end approach. Some frameworks are designed to be completed by an individual while others require two or more people. Since the language is from within the learners' own competences the same framework can be used by learners with different language abilities. (However, some frameworks are more suitable for advanced learners and others for elementary students.) Likewise, the same framework can be used with professionals from different backgrounds and a session can generate the same language or same interaction but with a variety of carrier topics.

The frameworks can also be used for specific language practice. With a flow diagram the grammatical structures used with 'before', 'after', 'while', 'when' can be introduced and practised, as can the active and passive; by using an old, a current or a future process, different verb tenses can be worked on the comparative (and superlative, if a third column is added) can be practised using the frameworks on p. 181).

Framework materials are enjoyed most by people with right-brained learning styles because they use visual representation (see chapter 10). With groups where learning styles are mixed, they complement the more left-brained materials and provide a more balanced mix. Learners who have only experienced traditional, teacher-centred education, may need help and time to adjust to the concept of framework materials. The very fact of having responsibility and choice over the material can be both stimulating and intimidating.

Devising frameworks

In keeping with our earlier discussion on materials, we recommend first using published frameworks devised and tested by others. When modifying or devising additional frameworks the golden rule would be 'Keep it simple'. The visual variables within the frameworks are: shape, size, colour, relative position and connections. The content variables are primarily whether the framework generates particular language such as cause and effect, process and sequence or generates particular interactions such as presentations, decision making, problem solving, brainstorming, evaluation. (For a fuller discussion see Ellis and Johnson, 1994.)

Task 9f ●◆

Consider the problem-solution pattern discussed in chapter 5.

a) Devise a framework for learners to present two alternative solutions to a problem, evaluate the strengths and weaknesses of each and make a recommendation for action.
b) Devise two setting boxes to accompany the framework: one for a learner giving an oral presentation; the other for a learner writing a report.

9.5.2 *Activities that are devised by the learners*

Creativity and learner involvement is also possible using traditional materials through adopting a non-traditional approach to some of the activities. It has been traditional for teachers (materials writers) to ask all the questions. In ESP situations, teachers may not know what the most appropriate questions are while their learners may. We illustrate some ways in which learners can devise the activities and hope that you will develop others.

Text comprehension

Working with a partner, learners prepare comprehension questions (and the answers) on a text. They exchange with another pair and answer the questions they are given. This can be extended to language work around the wording and phrasing of the questions. A further class activity is to compare all the questions and discuss which they think are best. The discussion usually helps to distinguish main points from minor issues. The group can select the best ones and then there is a set of questions the teacher can use for another group!

Note-taking/information transfer

Similarly, learners can devise information transfer activities for their peers (and the teacher) to complete.

Vocabulary development

We discussed techniques for vocabulary development in chapter 5. Learners can generate their own sets or word partnerships; they can devise matching and grouping activities and try them out on each other.

Reflection 9g

Take a text you use with learners (or one of our extracts, although they are rather short) and consider what activities learners could carry out on it. Write the rubrics that instruct them to generate their own questions, notes, vocabulary or other exercises.

9.6 Materials and technology

Technology offers the possibility of alternative materials and classroom interactions (chapter 10). After audio and video cassettes, the next major technological change, in the 1980s, was the use of computers and the opportunities for Computer-Assisted Language Learning (CALL). CALL programs are largely linear, constructed along certain thought patterns, with a single or limited response. The development of CD-ROM has brought more interactive packages. For the learner, CD-ROM offers information and the opportunity for repetitive practice.

CD-ROM offers greater interactivity than paper-based materials, but is still more constrained than when working with people. The more open-ended the activities, the more need there is for interaction with someone. The Internet is bringing further changes as courses can now be downloaded from all over the world. For the teacher as provider of material, the concern will largely be with evaluating and using rather than preparing materials – and they nearly all require more time to preview than paper-based materials.

9.7 Summary

It has often been noted that ESP is a materials-led movement and that part of the role of the ESP practitioner has been to write teaching materials to meet the specific needs of learners. We have suggested in this chapter and at other points in this book that the ESP teacher is mainly a provider of materials – selecting material that is available, adapting it as necessary and supplementing it where it does not quite meet the learners' needs – although in some cases it is more appropriate to use the authentic materials that learners can provide.

We have also described the use of framework materials. These provide a simple structure for use with any carrier content that is of interest to the group or individual that we are teaching. Because of the lack of restrictions on topics that can be introduced, they also allow an unpredictability in communication that reflects the natural situation at work. Framework materials also have the advantage that the teacher spends less time writing materials and more time actually planning the use of those materials!

Further developments we would like to see include:

- more flexible materials;
- material which provides explanations, practice and reference in separate blocks;
- fewer linear courses and more banks of resources and ideas;
- material that takes more account of the sociological frame – of audience status, old/new relationships, cultural expectations;
- material which is founded on a sounder knowledge of just what language is used, when, with what effect;
- core material that builds knowledge and awareness which is then applied in more specific material, preferably the learners' own.

9.8 Recommended reading

Swales' (1980) thoughts on ESP materials, although perhaps a little dated, are still worth reading and Nunan's (1989) ideas are relevant to ESP. On materials evaluation, Cunningsworth (1995) includes a section on ESP; the Sheldon (1987) volume also provides an interesting discussion. Ellis and Johnson (1994) and St John (1996) describe the range of published materials for Business English. Nolan and Reed (1992) offer framework materials for photocopying.

10 Classroom practice and beyond

10.1 Aims

We suggested in chapter 1 that ESP teaching can be very different to EFL teaching and that there is a distinguishable ESP methodology. This arises mainly from two factors associated with the learners:

- the specialist knowledge that they bring – both conscious and latent; and
- the cognitive and learning processes that they bring with them from their experience of learning and working within their specialist field.

One of the major corollaries of these two factors concerns the kind of activities through which learning takes place:

- in addition to language-learning activities, the ESP classroom uses tasks and activities that reflect the learners' specialist world.

There is a further factor which, while not unique to ESP, has a significant effect on ESP methodology and that is:

- the numbers of learners.

In this chapter we shall discuss the influence of these four features and their impact on ESP classroom practice. We shall not look at the classroom teaching techniques that all language teachers need; these are well covered in other texts (Brown, 1994; Nunan, 1991; Willis, 1996).

In considering which approach to take, it is most important to remember that *there is no best way*; all techniques and methods are a response to a particular situation. One of the skills ESP teachers need is the ability to assess a situation from a variety of viewpoints and then to select and adapt their methodology to match the learners' needs. Flexibility and a willingness to take risks are the name of the game!

The classroom is only one place in which learning takes place and so we will also look in this chapter at more autonomous ways of learning. Increasingly, developments in technology, such as computers, word processors, CD-ROM and interactive video are influencing when, where and how we learn. So we shall look at how the hardware and software are beginning to be used in ESP situations.

10.2 Learners' specialist knowledge

10.2.1 Latent communication knowledge

ESP learners bring to their language learning some knowledge of their own specialist field and the communication within it. Those who are still students or apprentices to the specialist field bring less than those who are already experienced and practising specialists. Some of this knowledge, such as content knowledge, will be conscious; this can also be true of certain aspects of communication such as form, for example how the tense system in English works or format, for example the IMRAD sections of a scientific report or paper (Introduction, Method, Results And Discussion). Some knowledge will only be latent and learners will not have the ability to control the use of that knowledge.

One aspect of the ESP teacher's job may be to develop a conscious awareness so that control is gained, whether over language, rhetorical structure or communication skills. St John (1987) described how, in context, the words 'The aim of this investigation' triggered the latent knowledge of Spanish science researchers (see p. 127). They recognised that this signalled the last move in the introduction section of a paper; they could not actually verbalise that knowledge. Similarly, while people may 'know' that standing in front of the overhead projector and turning your back on the audience is poor technique, they may still do just that when concentrating on their English. Until these aspects are ingrained, familiar carrier content and/or a familiar format are important. When everything is unfamiliar the learner is overloaded.

10.2.2 Content knowledge

Teaching ESP is different from teaching EFL because learners have knowledge that they need to use which we, the ESP teachers, generally do not have. This can seem threatening until we realise that our learners do not expect us to have such knowledge. Business people do not expect a Business English teacher to know how to run a business; they expect a knowledge of how language is used in business – which involves some understanding of business concepts and contexts. Doctors do not expect English teachers to diagnose, prescribe, prevent or cure illness; they expect some understanding of the patient-doctor or nurse-doctor inter-actions so they can learn appropriate language.

In EFL the carrier content is selected from a stock of shared knowledge and concepts. In ESP it is also necessary to include more specialised carrier content. One of the skills an ESP practitioner has to acquire is the ability to balance content level and language level and to 'see' the real content.

An ESP teacher provides a bank of English for learners to use. Any judgement of appropriacy, versus accuracy, can only be made jointly. The ESP teacher is often more of a 'consultant' than a 'teller', giving advice, suggesting alternatives and allowing the learner to make informed decisions.

10.2.3   The impact of learners' knowledge

How do these aspects of knowledge influence ESP classroom practice?

Roles and relationships

One effect is on the kind of relationship that is appropriate between teachers and ESP learners. We discussed (in chapter 8) the negotiation that takes place and how an ESP teacher has to play the role of a 'consultant' not a 'font of all wisdom'. The ESP teacher must acknowledge and use the learners' greater knowledge of the carrier content. An appropriate diagrammatic representation of many ESP situations would be figure 10.1 not figure 10.2.

ESP teacher ⟺ ESP learner   ESP teacher
                                         ↓
                                    ESP learner

Figure 10.1   *Figure 10.2*

Exactly how this role is developed depends on the learners' experience, cultural expectations and what status a teacher has and how status is awarded.

Reflection 10a

In chapter 4 we discussed some intercultural differences and in the next section we discuss learning styles. Consider how easy or difficult different learners may find it to accept the role as represented in figure 10.1.

Teaching and learning materials

Another effect is on the kind of teaching materials used. Framework materials (discussed in chapter 9), which use learners' experience, are a good example. The carrier content comes from those with that knowledge – the specialists, the language learners. The use of owned authentic material from the learners' job or studies is another example. By owned authentic material we mean material which the individual learner uses or produces versus authentic material from the discipline. Thus the business report that is being written or the taped lecture or recommended reading text on which notes need to be made have an immediacy and focused purpose that published material cannot have. The immediacy affects both teacher and learner; the ESP teacher will not have hours to mull over the input and determine activities. Learners sometimes ask for an instant response but it usually works best to take at least a few minutes of time while they work on some other material.

Methodological approaches

The above examples illustrate why language awareness work is integral to successful ESP learning and why the deep-end strategy, certainly for intermediate plus students is often more appropriate than the PPP (present, practise, perform) tradition of EFL. PPP can work effectively for beginners to intermediates or when both the language and the communicative event are new to the learner. The deep-end strategy takes performance as its starting point. The learners use their existing L2 competence, discovering where it is adequate and where it fails them.

The extreme of the deep-end strategy is to set a task and ask students to perform. In practice the deep-end strategy involves providing preparation time before performance. In the PPP tradition a prior decision is made by the materials writer as to what language and skills (a) should/will be needed and (b) will be lacking. Communication is not this predictable. The strength of the deep-end strategy is that the approach to the task is the students' and is likely to reflect their personal and professional world. The deep-end strategy is particularly effective on short intensive courses and where learners are proficient in the communicative events in their L1.

The main input stage may come after the performance, based on comments from the teacher and from the learner and peers. As the preparation phase is controlled by the learners, another effective approach is to develop materials that support each learning stage but to supply them only on request, as an option.

10.2.4   *Harnessing learners' cognitive and learning strategies*

Psychological research has shown that there are quite different ways of viewing the world and approaching learning. For instance, some people are divergent thinkers; others are convergent thinkers. Our general approach may be predominantly right-brained (global/holistic) or left-brained (analytical) or a mix. Analytic, left-brained thinkers are highly verbal, linear, logical and temporal whilst global, right-brained thinkers are highly visual and spatial, intuitive and relational (parts to whole) (Kinsella, 1995).

Our culture also affects our learning styles. Learning is a social process and so attitudes to learning and views of language have a cultural dimension to them, determined by national culture, professional culture and individual culture. For example, it is suggested that Asian students look for structured learning, with a teacher as an authority figure and are less comfortable with autonomous learning and situations where there are several acceptable answers (*ibid.*, p. 208). Hispanics are more likely to develop a global learning style and accept flexibility and negotiation while Anglo-Americans are more analytical wanting planned, methodical approaches (*ibid.*, pp. 204–8).

In language learning significant factors are also the extent to which an individual is visually, aurally or kinaesthetically oriented. Visually oriented learners need to see words to remember them and will read and write a lot; auditory oriented learners can recall pronunciation and meaning from hearing only. Kinaesthetic learners are stimulated by touch and movement and benefit from learning through games and drama.

In addition, in the ESP situation we also need to activate and build on the learning styles and strategies which have been developed through the specialist field, that is through the academic and professional culture. If observation and deduction are central to the learning style of scientists then in helping them to learn language we can attempt to activate those same processes. For example deducing grammatical patterns can be more effective than being told about them. Extracting information into tables, flowcharts and other diagrammatic formats is often more natural for EST learners than for their teachers.

Learning style is different from learning strategies which are specific behaviours or techniques learners use such as grouping words, holding mental conversations with themselves, getting someone to read aloud to them, watching TV. The strategies chosen are often linked to the individual's learning style. Following a text while it is read aloud is helpful for visually oriented learners, while watching TV can suit auditory learners.

Research studies have shown that learning can be enhanced by teaching in ways that encourage students to activate their own learning styles (Dunn and Griggs, 1990). This suggests that teachers need both to ascertain their learners' styles and to recognise similarities and differences with their own. Questionnaires (examples in Reid, Ed., 1995), interviews and discussions can be used to raise awareness and an understanding of these issues.

Teachers can also work to extend their own style, particularly to take account of any major differences between their style and their learners', whether these arise through national culture (teaching in another country) or through another discipline (humanities-trained teachers working with science or medical students). This will make it easier for a teacher to select and adapt activities to match learners' styles. Learners can also be helped to extend their style, to stimulate the use of both sides of the brain, to adapt to the approach of a new discipline.

10.2.5 Integrating the methodologies of other disciplines

One specific way in which cognitive learning processes can be harnessed is through the methodologies of other disciplines. A strength of ESP methodology is the way in which language learning and subject learning approaches can be integrated. Widdowson (1983) referred to this when he wrote 'ESP is (or ought logically to be) integrally linked with areas of activity (academic, vocational, professional) which . . . represent the learners' aspirations' (pp. 108–9).

Two particular examples of subject learning approaches that have been adopted in ESP situations are case studies and project work.

Case studies

Case studies are a feature of many professional courses such as business, law, engineering and medicine. Their purpose is to present students with some aspect of a real-life scenario, through which they can apply and integrate knowledge, skills, theory and any experience. The role of case studies varies from one profession to another: in law, cases establish precedent; in medicine, case conferences can take the form of an enquiry as to whether there is anything else that can be done. On business courses, students are presented with data concerning some aspect of an organisation's business and a brief which could comprise some questions, a specific problem or a decision about 'where would you go, what would you do now?'. These case studies are carried out in 'syndicates' which provide experience of teamwork and develop students' abilities to fulfil various team functions and roles. The results may be written up as a report or poster and/or presented orally. Evaluation considers the accuracy of the analysis, the appropriacy of any models applied and the business rationale behind the proposed solution.

The business case study approach fits comfortably within ESP principles since it is activity based, often uses authentic material and involves learners in both individual and group work. There is challenge, participation and the use of professional know-how. It is a multi-skilled approach in which learners' attention is directed towards the task more than the language (Krashen, 1981).

On the negative side, business case studies can involve a large amount of background reading, difficult texts and difficult concepts. Data overload is a feature of their construction, so the time to read, understand and absorb the data can be over-long when the students' aim is to develop language and skills. On EAP courses, where the students are being prepared for the use of case studies in their subject courses, the use of long case studies is clearly justified (Charles, 1984). On other courses, the use of mini-case studies may be the best option. Some of the case studies for introductory business courses can be adapted and used with both EBP and non-EBP students. The tasks below are examples from a book of mini-case studies suitable for students on introductory business courses (Huggett R. 1990. *Business Case Studies*, CUP); they could easily feature as ESP tasks:

• Design an advertisement / a market research questionnaire / a poster;
• Write a letter / a report;
• Draw up a business plan;
• Design an announcement for display on computer screens.

The briefs are one to two pages long and the language is not difficult. On the negative side, experienced business personnel would find them very simplistic. Another word of warning – many have been prepared around western concepts of life and business; more serious adaptation will probably be required to use them in other cultural situations.

The case-study approach can be broken down into three main stages: data input, data processing and output presentation. Both the case and the way it is used can reflect the learners' professional world (Charles, 1984). However, each of the three stages may be handled slightly differently for ESP purposes: there may be more structuring of activities than usual and more of the work may be carried out in class so that language work can be undertaken as required. Table 10.1. illustrates some of these differences. (The data processing stage can be further broken down into several phases such as understanding and manipulating the data, analysis, the application of knowledge and skills, and

Table 10.1 *Using case studies*

Stage	Business Course	ESP Course
1. Data input	Data presented through paper documents – scope for CD-Rom.	Data presented through paper documents, audio and video recordings. Good scope for CD-Rom in the future.
2. Data processing: for example – understanding and manipulating data	No specific help given. Syndicate members apply experience and learning from subject modules.	Guided questions on the input to focus attention on key aspects and areas where language could hinder understanding; checking comprehension.
3. Output presentation	No specific help given.	Oral presentation planned, rehearsed, videoed for language feedback; support and feedback for planning, drafting and revising written reports.

weighing up alternative solutions – we have given just one phase.) The case-study approach is a deep-end approach with the ESP teacher making decisions about what language and skills to feed in as it becomes apparent that without input or practice learners will be hindered in their work.

An issue with case studies is the degree of subject expertise required by the ESP teacher. Some understanding of the concepts behind a particular case study seems essential: experienced professionals do not require specialist guidance from the ESP teacher but they will have more confidence in, and respect for, a teacher who has a grasp of the relevant concepts. Students on or preparing for a subject course may benefit from some guidance as to the approach they should adopt and the issues they should take into consideration. As always, the carrier content needs to be within the realms of their experience. The need for an understanding of relevant subject or business concepts suggests that, in the first instance, it is advisable for an ESP teacher who does not have the subject or business background to work with a specialist somewhere on the cooperative:collaborative:team-teaching continuum (see discussion in chapter 3).

Project work

In a case study, the resource materials and brief which generate the language and skills development are given to students. In project work it is the students who find and assimilate information for a brief that, preferably, they have generated for themselves. The degree of involvement and ownership is thus much higher. When students are well prepared for project work and understand what is required of them, the purpose and the benefits, their motivation can be very high. Project work can be very rewarding but it is also a high-risk activity. Students have to search out information for themselves, so there is a good deal of out-of-class activity. The project begins in the classroom, moves into the outside world and then back into the classroom, and provides an opportunity for real world and classroom experience to overlap.

One of the first examples of project work was that used most effectively by Herbolich (1979) with his Box Kites. In the late 1970s he was working with engineering students at the University of Kuwait on a Technical Report Writing course, one component of which was Manual Writing. To successfully write manuals authors need to know how to operate the machinery or produce something themselves, so it was decided that the students should construct something and box kites were selected. This was because:

- they were new to most people
- they required engineering skills
- the work was enjoyable
- the language involved was relevant
- there was little available information on them so there were no short-cuts

The project worked well, an additional reason being that most of the kites did work – they 'flied and flied' (Herbolich, 1979, reproduced in Swales, 1985). In this project, there was a tangible object created from the carrier content as well as that of the real content manual; the students worked in pairs but the topic was selected by the ESP teacher.

Project work has become a standard feature of much EAP work as most students have to carry out a project during their undergraduate studies (in postgraduate studies the project is the dissertation) and EAP practitioners have devised work to parallel these. In subject projects students generally have to:

1. generate a hypothesis
2. carry out a literature review
3. test the hypothesis

4. write a report
5. give an oral presentation or seminar.

A number of disciplines set library projects which involve stages 2, 4 and 5 but do not require the setting and testing of a hypothesis.

While many EAP courses now include input on all these aspects, the EAP project rarely runs in parallel time with the subject project. Therefore, ESP teachers have to devise project situations. Few of us are as creative as Herbolich and most projects do not have a tangible object as their outcome, although projects can involve students in real research as individuals, pairs or groups. Mini-research projects for individuals or pairs can be formulated around interviews or questionnaires. More often projects are based on library research, engaging individuals in extensive purposeful reading followed by a written report and oral presentation (Bloor and St John, 1988). Which of these three approaches is most suitable depends on students' goals, the circumstances of the course and cultural considerations.

In many situations in life we gather information from more than one source, collate it, select from it and then transform it into spoken or written format to transmit to someone else. In ESP, it is appropriate to provide opportunities for this, for example by giving several texts for reading or listening and setting a task that exploits them jointly. The gathering and then transmitting process involves a minimum of two skills and probably all four, thus it is also often appropriate to use an integrated skills approach. These are features common to both project work and case studies which can also be built into smaller scale activities.

10.3 Class size

Class sizes can vary immensely: an ESP teacher could have just one student, for example a business person; an ESP teacher could also have several hundred students, for example in a first-year tertiary level class. While this variation is not unique to ESP it seems to occur in ESP more frequently than in other areas of English language teaching.

Orientation 10b

a) What is the average size of classes you regularly teach?
b) What class size is uncomfortably large for you?
c) What is your ideal class size?
d) What class size is uncomfortably small?

If you can, plot your and other people's results on a bar graph.

10.3.1 When is large large?

The notion of when a class is large is not an absolute, that is, there is no given number of learners above which a class is large. Rather the notion of what constitutes a large class depends on situation, purpose and experience. In primary and secondary education a class of over 35–40 pupils may be a large class; in private EFL schools, over 15 students could be large. Some of the largest classes are found in tertiary EAP situations – 150 students is not uncommon in some countries, such as Nigeria or Indonesia. For lecturers in these countries, 50 is a small group.

A survey (Coleman, 1988) conducted under the Lancaster-Leeds Language Learning in Large Classes Research Project (LLLLLC Report no. 4) confirmed that the perception of large is related to the size of the largest class teachers regularly teach. Table 10.2 shows how the size of the usual largest class regularly taught (column one) affects your view of when a class becomes intolerably large (column two) and when problems actually begin (column three).

Table 10.2 *Large class size*

Largest class taught	Large becomes intolerable	Large, problems begin
1–20	33.3	25.0
21–40	44.5	34.1
41–60	50.0	37.4
61–80	60.5	42.1
81–100	64.5	44.5
101–120	85.0	62.9
121–140	80.0	55.0

A large class cannot, therefore, be defined numerically. It is probably best thought of as a size that requires a conscious and substantial alteration to approach. The same can be said of a small group: teaching two or three students also requires adaptation.

The term 'large class' generally sets up negative connotations of undesirable consequences and problems. However, a consideration of aims and opportunities can lead to a more positive viewpoint. Bolton (1988) outlined how he chose to combine three groups of 25 into a megasection of 75. The purpose of the megasections could then be different from the conventional class and, for the same total contact time, more small group conferences and office hours (one-to-one work in the USA) were offered. He found benefits for himself and students did just as well, and in some cases better, than their counterparts in conventional classes.

A similar approach was adopted at a Federal University of Technology in Nigeria. Students were combined for sessions where the input could be handled in plenary fashion so as to free some time and space for discussion and activity in smaller groups.

10.3.2 Challenges of large classes

The difficulties teachers of large classes around the world feel they face are similar, although circumstances and culture can introduce additional or specific problems and each situation will have a unique constellation of factors that require a particular solution. For instance, in Nigeria the design of handouts had to take into consideration both costs and shortages of paper and duplicating materials; a distinction had to be made between those handouts which would be kept by students – a limited number – and those which would be collected and re-used with parallel groups and subsequent years. In that situation, physical-resource constraints were highly significant.

In other cases the challenge may be less tangible: For example, for a teacher with responsibility for several hundred students and perhaps two classes a week, learning names is extremely difficult. How problematic this is may be a matter of culture. In some cultures the use of names is important and so this is a significant issue requiring an innovative approach.

Orientation 10c

a) Brainstorm a list of challenges which you and your colleagues have faced or which you imagine may arise in a large class.
b) Consider different ways of grouping and categorising them.
c) What are some of the solutions that you have or might try?

The challenges which teachers around the world have listed during workshops revolve around the issues such as control, for example of behaviour and noise; assessment and feedback; individual attention; mixed abilities; and use of the mother tongue. They are issues which perhaps arise when (a) a teacher takes on all the responsibility for a class, (b) teaching is equated with learning, and (c) personal attention is seen as direct teacher-to-student time.

The solutions that teachers have proposed and practised generally involve a shift of attitudes and an encouragement of the strategies that the students themselves use to cope with large classes. The problem of large classes may be greater through a teacher's eyes than it is for the students, and this may be because teacher training uses ideas and textbooks devised in situations where classes are smaller (Coleman, 1997).

10.3.3 Meeting the large class challenge

'Large classes are not an aberration; they are a fact of our teaching experience and they require practical solutions' (Alimi, personal communication). Dealing with large classes to our own satisfaction as teachers and to our students' benefit presents us with opportunities for innovation. When investigating how best to meet the demands of large classes, consulting and observing learners may be the first step. Learners know they cannot rely solely on the teacher and so they cope by asking each other for help and sharing notes and ideas; they use a cooperative approach. We describe below some of the innovations that teachers we have met have introduced.

Changing the numbers

- Run classes at alternative times: Lecturers at FUT Owerri gave classes before and after the standard day, when suitable rooms were free.
- Combine and split classes: At the Federal University of Technology, Minna groups were combined for taped listening practice, under technician and student control, so that oral presentations practice could be introduced.
- Split classes: Lecturers chose to teach additional hours so that they could split groups up.
- Team-teach: Lecturers at FUA participated in each other's sessions, helping with group work, observing and evaluating procedures and materials. (This is different from the subject-and-language lecturer team-teaching described in chapter 3.)
- Get the authorities to increase resources – teachers, rooms, materials – so that class size can be reduced or out-of-class support be increased.

Changing the approach

- Allow learners to consult each other.
- Introduce pair and group work.

- Introduce new feedback procedures, for example:
  instead of a full report from each group, students should mention just one, new point (good for listening and thinking);
  posters on the wall;
  one or two groups only write up their ideas on the board, one additional point, question or comment is elicited from other groups;
  self-checking using teacher checklist;
  self-checking through consultation with other groups; snowballing (check answers in pairs, then fours, then eights);
  peer assessment of written work;
  taking questions instead of giving feedback and answers;
- Have core and alternative/additional activities.

The essence behind most of these approaches seems to be the four 'I's:

Involvement
Interaction
Individualisation
Independence

with a modified teacher role as manager rather than controller.

Involvement can actually reduce rather than raise noise levels as the buzz of active *interaction* is different to that of noisy boredom. *Individualisation* is not one-to-one attention but allowing each person to be an individual and work and contribute in their own manner. *Independence* results from the teacher allowing students to learn in their own ways rather than controlling them through teaching.

The four 'I's are one way of sharing responsibility within the class. We mentioned earlier that learning is a social process. Left to ourselves we naturally ask each other questions. The load on teachers is dramatically reduced when they see themselves as responsible only for answering what the class as a whole cannot solve. The four 'I's are a route to dealing with learning and feedback constraints; they may not be able to affect the physical constraints.

What is also clear from teachers is that success is neither immediate nor guaranteed and that learners need time and training to work differently but that most of them enjoy the switch. What will work in one situation will not necessarily be suitable in another but there is only one way to find out: by trying, by experimenting, by modifying and by trusting – ourselves and our students. Participants in the COMSKIP-TECH Project in Nigeria summed it up, 'we have learnt that managing change requires a lot of tact and patience; when introducing a new idea don't be discouraged if initial results are not brilliant' (St John, 1995, p. 152).

10.3.4   When small is small – one-to-one

One-to-one teaching also offers unique challenges and opportunities. Broadly speaking it can be divided into two categories: intensive and extensive.

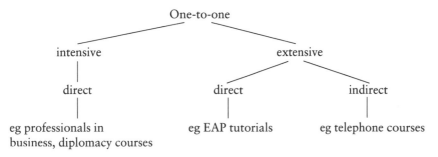

Figure 10.3 One-to-one teaching situations

Intensive courses equate almost exclusively with professional people in the business and diplomatic worlds. Extensive one-to-one, where contact is occasional or spread over several weeks or months, is found in EAP and EOP situations. In most situations there is direct contact between the tutor and learners. In the case of e-mail and telephone courses there may be no direct contact, although they are also used as an adjunct to contact courses.

Telephone courses

For people in jobs, taking time out for language learning can be difficult; there is no guarantee of when the working day will end or when travel may intervene. Classes in working time can solve some of this for the student and place the burden of travel time on the teacher.

Another solution to some of this is telephone teaching. This provides one-to-one contact with no travel time and minimal disturbance to the work routine – half an hour on the phone. If you are on the phone when someone enters your office, they usually go off and come back later; if you are with the teacher, others usually interrupt. So one-to-one on the telephone is less prone to interruption!

One of the first successful telephone courses was set up by Telelangue in Paris. The system involves testing and conducting a needs analysis on the phone. From this the teacher can select units from a large bank (Mascull Ed., 1993). These units are then worked through on the phone. The teacher calls at set times and the class can last from 30–60 minutes, either daily or a few times a week for a period of several months. The one-to-one telephone sessions can be self-standing, although many people combine them with attendance at a group class.

e-mail and the Internet

Indirect one-to-one contact is also possible through e-mail and Internet which take us beyond the classroom (the final section of this chapter).

10.3.5 Challenges and opportunities in one-to-one teaching

Orientation 10d ●◇

Brainstorm ideas of what you can do in one-to-one teaching that you cannot do in group teaching situations.

One-to-one teaching is definitely different from class teaching. It can be seen as ESP in its purest form: the needs of the single student can entirely determine the learning, the carrier content can all be provided by the student and the teacher can provide the real content through continuously increasing the student's awareness of language.

A key role of a teacher in a group situation is to manage: to manage time, to manage materials, to control activities, to monitor relationships yet remain apart. One-to-one teaching is different because the key role of the teacher is to respond – it is not possible to remain apart. To respond (as opposed to react) involves observation, processing and interpreting – and then acting.

The one-to-one teaching situation is much more personal than the class situation. In one-to-one the aim is to establish an interpersonal learning dialogue. Interpersonal because communication is essentially personal; learning because both participants will be learning: the teacher about the individual, their work, their communication style, their language and style; the student about language and language use; and dialogue because it is a two-way process of negotiated give and take.

Within this interpersonal learning dialogue we as teachers need to match, rather than mismatch, our student's style. Listening actively and responding to him/her means matching in terms of both behavioural and learning style. On an EAP course students may be encouraged to modify and experiment with their learning style – particularly if these are very different from those of the environment in which they will study their chosen subjects. On a short, intensive one-to-one course a student wants to learn language, not a new learning style. Wilberg (1987) gives an example of how mismatching in learning style was ineffective: For four days he mismatched his learner's immobile style with excess energy. On the fifth day he matched stance and mood and 'for the first time in the week, we began to get somewhere' (p. 15).

A major advantage of one-to-one teaching is that you can – should, must – go at the student's pace. Wilberg (p. 9) likens the one-to-one class to a partnered dance: You do not have to like or be liked by your dance partner, only to adjust, to respond. 'As dance partner your job is to guide but not to rush, grip too firmly, confuse, tread on your student's mental toes'.

10.3.6 Meeting the challenges in one-to-one

In the class situation students can often 'take a mental break' when they need to, for instance by taking longer on one exercise and less time on another, by skipping an exercise. This gives them time to pause, to process. Likewise, they may be able to take a physical break by, for instance moving around during pair or group work. A danger in one-to-one, particularly in the intensive situation, is that the learner can feel pressurised because there is no one else to deflect the teacher's attention. All learners need time and space so, although one objective of one-to-one classes is individual attention, that should not be equated with undivided, constant attention.

One-to-one does not mean having to be there 100 per cent of the time; giving the learner physical and mental space by becoming involved in something else, such as the preparation of some materials or leaving the room, is essential.

Variation in pace and type of activity can be extended through where and how learner and teacher sit in relation to each other; even by shifting furniture, playing music, altering what is on the walls. In class situations teachers try to watch TTT (teacher talking time); in one-to-one it is SSS (student silent space) that needs watching (Wilberg, p. 19).

We have discussed how in one-to-one situations what is required is not so much a teacher as a partner to work with. To create this rapport, it is necessary to be aware of power relationships. One way of reducing teacher power is for the teacher to share information with the learner and share decision making.

ESP teachers may also find themselves working with just two or three learners. The principles behind one-to-one interaction still apply; the advantage is that a wider range of interaction is possible: the learners can negotiate among themselves.

10.3.7   One-to-one in EAP

In EAP situations the one-to-one tutorial is usually offered to help students with written work, either class assignments or dissertations. The tutorial may work at the correction level, for aspects such as faulty grammatical constructions, infelicitous wording, and inappropriate citation and referencing. At an earlier stage in the writing process (see chapter 6), there are opportunities for more in-depth discussion. All-wright *et al.* (1996) discuss how one-to-one tutorials can contribute to a critical approach to study. Focusing on one student's approach to citation, they discuss how the tutorial system went beyond the rather remedial level of describing different citation systems (as practised in Austria and the UK) to a more developmental role of enabling the student to find his own voice. Through discussion and reformulation, they reached a point of 'That's it! That's the sort of thing I want to write' (Allwright *et al.*, p. 77).

10.4   Beyond the classroom

Developments in technology, increases in demand but not in resources, and research into learning are all changing the face of how, where and when people learn. In this section we look at how ESP has adopted new approaches and might adopt more.

Two factors coalesce – the understanding that learning is exploring and the ability of technology to provide wide spaces for exploration. In these two senses the use of technology complements and extends the learner-centred methodology that predominates in ELT and ESP teaching. The main advantage is that learners can access the source material in their own time, work through the material at their own pace, choosing topics and subject areas to match their own interests and do all this without necessarily having to interact with a teacher. In other words, learners are in control of their language learning and have increased choice.

One aspect of this increased choice is that the new technology is blurring the distinctions between self-study outside the class, distance learning and institutional self-access centres (Moore, 1996).

10.4.1   Five modes of technology

Essentially there are five modes that are being used in language learning and, to some extent, in ESP teaching. They are the use of video discs, the use of CD-Rom, the use of the Internet or World Wide Web, the use of e-mail and the use of the computer for either CALL (Computer Aided Language Learning) work or Data Driven Learning based on corpora held on the computer.

Video Discs and CD-Roms

We will take video discs and CD-Roms together. They can be used (Sharma, talk given at a BESIG seminar held 1996):

1. to *support a course* by, for example, revising basic skills or language;
2. to *enhance a course* by providing extra topics for the course;
3. as *free-standing material*. The CD-Rom or video disc presents a self-contained unit or set of units, and no other material is provided;
4. to *provide data* which can be exploited for language purposes;
5. to *provide authentic material* originally designed for a purpose other than learning language.

Two particular features of CD-Roms make them invaluable in helping learners with oral production and in listening to monologue. It is possible to record yourself speaking and then compare very small features of pronunciation, intonation or lexis with a model much more easily than it is when using a cassette recorder. With monologue it is possible to examine very closely a particular feature of a lecture or presentation, for example an intonation feature, by clicking onto a split second of the recording and playing it again and again until you have grasped completely what the speaker is doing. Cauldwell (1996) has shown that 'zooming in and out of sounds on a CD' can improve learners' understanding of fast speech.

The Internet

The Internet provides the opportunity for courses to be used by all learners with access to the Internet. This means that a language school or a language centre can place an ESP course on the Internet, and that course may then be used by any student. It is even possible for institutions to charge for access to their courses.

The general format for such courses is that learners follow them on their own, in their own time. In other words, the sole interaction is between the learner and the computer screen. Nesi (1996) argues, however, that such courses can also be used with whole groups, with or without a tutor, and for pair/group or whole class work. Nesi suggests that where the course involves an aspect of communication, the presence of a tutor acting in a 'moderator' role can be very helpful, if rather expensive in terms of institutional costs.

Of the English language courses available on the Internet few were relevant to ESP at the time of writing. One of the few EAP related courses is 'Purdue University On-Line Writing Lab (http://owl.trc. purdue.edu) which mainly provides handouts on writing skills. Purdue students can arrange face-to-face tutorials to discuss their work.

The Internet can also be used as a source of material for ESP classes, generally where students are involved in project work or case studies. Here the students can either access the relevant web-page and use the information, or they can download the actual pages for use in the ESP activity. In the latter case the format of the web-page may well be rather different from that of a document written in the traditional paper-based format and may therefore need to be adapted. Material for down-loading can be purely investigative with no feedback on the language and use of the program. Other material has pre-set interaction and can provide answers to discrete item work.

Perhaps of most interest to ESP practitioners are interactive courses with tutor presence and peer interaction. The patterns of interaction possible are:

- participant to text
- one-to-one participant-to-participant or participant-to-tutor
- peer-to-peer in pairs or groups
- whole group
- whole group plus tutor

Nesi and Studman-Badillo (work in progress) suggest thinking of these within figurative locations such as: the café for social interaction, the bulletin board for course information, the lecture theatre for tutor-only input.

Electronic mail (e-mail)

E-mail communication has become widespread in communication between educational, administrative and business institutions. ESP learners will almost certainly need to become familiar with the conventions of writing e-mail messages (see Gains, 1998), but this is a different question from that of how e-mail can be used in ESP teaching. We have read of e-mail being used for commenting on students' writing and also for student-to-student peer commenting. A writing course for business people was launched in Brazil in 1998 (CEPRIL).

CALL materials

CALL materials have all the advantages of self-access materials; learners can work on their own and can carry out tasks without support or feedback from the teacher. Materials for CALL are generally produced using authoring packages which enable the teacher to introduce exercises into an existing exercise framework and use the same exercise types. Flowerdew (1995) describes how a principled ESP approach to course design was used to develop a CALL program to help Hong Kong students acquire job seeking skills, such as writing application letters and preparing CVs. Flowerdew's article provides a very practical introduction to the use of various authoring programs.

A similar approach has been taken to materials for grammar and academic writing at the University of Birmingham. The materials, known as the CALLCO materials, are available on the campus network (Warren, 1997). Unlike the Hong Kong course developed by Flowerdew, the materials are seen as supplementing the taught courses in grammar and writing.

Computer-based corpora

As discussed in chapter 5, the establishment of a number of computer-based corpora of texts relevant to both EAP and EOP provides an extremely useful resource for ESP researchers, teachers and ESP learners (Biber, 1988; Biber *et al.*, 1994; Johns, 1991; Scott and Johns, 1993). For researchers and teachers there is the opportunity to look in detail at lexical features; one example is to investigate the frequency of lexis in a text or a corpus, and, using the techniques developed by Yang (1986), to determine which are technical terms, semi-technical lexical items and general vocabulary items.

For ESP teaching the corpora provide a resource for students wanting to check whether they have used the correct collocation in their writing, a question that frequently occurs when feedback is given on writing. Students or professional writers usually do their writing themselves on the word processor; they thus have the opportunity to check collocations very easily with the use of a program such as Microconcord. This type of activity has been referred to as Data Driven Learning (Johns, 1991).

Thurstun and Candlin (1998) show how MicroConcord (Scott and Johns, 1993) can be used to teach the lexico-grammatical patterning of certain key semi-technical words related to various functions used in academic writing. Flowerdew (1998) shows how the concordanced output from a corpus taken from students' own writing can be compared with that taken from a corpus of 'expert' writing to see what the deficiencies are.

These activities usually involve some deduction from printouts of collocations, and are therefore consistent with the problem-solving approach we have advocated for ESP teaching. Another advantage is that the investigation of the collocations presents vocabulary in authentic contexts and provides actual uses rather than native speaker intuition about the use of vocabulary which can often be wrong (Sinclair, 1991).

Programs such as MicroConcord and a recent version *of Wordsmith* (Scott, 1996, available electronically from OUP) are undoubtedly useful research tools for ESP learning. The question is how useful they are for teaching and self-directed learning. Such programs can provide challenging and empowering activities for the learner that involve finding out about the way that vocabulary or grammar works, and there is considerable evidence that vocabulary and grammar learnt deductively in this way is retained for longer than that learnt in a more traditional manner.

The question is whether the time needed for such activities is fully justified by the end-results. An activity that can take up to 30 minutes to present various collocations deductively could be replaced by a short 5-minute presentation by the teacher. With learners who are curious about language and enjoy working with computer programs the extra time spent using data-driven learning techniques is justified. For learners who are less curious about language and computers the benefits are considerably fewer. We can talk in this context of *technophiles* and *technophobes;* clearly technophiles will generally gain a lot from data-driven learning programs while technophobes may not.

Our final point above leads us very neatly into our conclusion. The five modes we have described have undoubtedly widened choice in ESP teaching, and provided the means whereby learners can do more on their own and can control their own learning; but these activities generally supplement the regular ESP class and the role of the teacher. They do not normally replace the class and the need for the teacher. Moore (1996) reports how the establishment of self-access centres in Mexico and Poland using multimedia of the various types described above proved extremely popular and motivating when they were first introduced but were actually used less and less over time. There was undoubtedly a Hawthorne Effect when the centres were first introduced. (The Hawthorne Effect is where an innovation is initially seen as popular because of its novelty value and the attention paid to the new idea. Over time the popularity decreases as the novelty wears off.)

The use of the devices is most successful where it is integrated with the classroom courses, and the learning activities are consistent in methodology with those of the classroom courses. They appear to be particularly successful with lower-level students on extensive courses who need support with some of the more mechanical aspects of language learning, such as learning grammar and vocabulary.

We support Sharma's conclusions (BESIG seminar talk, 1996) that ESP teachers should have at the same time a positive attitude towards and a healthy scepticism of these technological devices.

10.5 Summary

In this chapter we have provided examples of how ESP teachers can exploit the methodology of the disciplines and occupations that learners are following through the use of problem-solving techniques, case studies and project work. We have also shown how the role of activating learners' passive knowledge of the conventions of communication in their discourse community is a key one for the ESP teacher. We have emphasised that there is no one methodology for ESP. In some cases, especially in the more 'common-core' EGAP or ESAP classes, a more traditional methodology based on PPP (present, practise, perform) may be appropriate. This will depend on the learners' expectations and preferred learning styles as well as on the materials being used.

We have also summarised the role of various technological innovations in ESP teaching. There are many 'technophile' ESP students who gain independence through the use of CD-Rom, the Internet and Data Driven Learning programs based on computer-based corpora. We have suggested that the great value of such techniques, especially combined with sociolinguistic analysis (Stubbs and Gerbig, 1993), lies in research possibilities, particularly for ESAP and ESBP.

10.6 Recommended reading

We include Hutchinson and Waters (1987) because they take a different view of methodology from ours and Holliday (1995), Kinsella (1995), Oxford and Anderson (1995) because they address cultural contexts. Charles (1984) discusses case studies, Coleman (1997) and Allwright (1989) deal with large classes while Wilberg (1987) tackles one-to-one. On the use of technology, there is Higgins and Johns (1984), Johns (1989), Stevens (1991) and two web pages: Tim Johns' web page: http://sun1.bham.ac.uk/johnstf and an EST web page started by Roy Bower and now managed by Tom Robb. The address is http://www.wfi.fr/est1.html. Wordsmith can be downloaded from the Internet at http://w.w.w.oup.co.uk/elt/catalogu/multimed/4589846/4589846.html.

11 Assessment: Continuous assessment and testing

11.1 Aims

Assessment is a process of measuring, and one formal method of measuring is to test. There are less formal, more qualitative methods of assessing which are particularly important for feedback on learning. In this chapter we will look at assessment procedures, ranging from formal tests through tutor-assessed assignments to peer- and self-assessment. We discuss some key features of public ESP examinations and show how practices and examples from these can assist with the design of in-house tests. (We use the term 'test' except when referring to these examinations.)

11.2 Why assess?

The reasons for assessment can be grouped under two main headings: for feedback to aid learning and for a comparable measure of competence. Comparable measures are the reason for public examinations and regular assessment or testing within educational institutions. Assessment as an aid to learning encompasses benefits such as reinforcement, confidence building, involvement and building on strengths. Self- and peer-assessment can also help to develop the independence that ESP learners require for their continued progress.

The ultimate proof for an ESP course is how well the learners fare when using English in their target situation; after the course they should be more effective and more confident using English in their target situations. In many ESP situations tests may be inappropriate: on a short intensive course the time is needed for input and practice; the real effect is likely to show itself some time after the course. That said, clients often want immediate, tangible evidence of course outcomes and improvements; learners benefit from recognising their progress and teachers can plan better when the learning is assessed. In addition, some organisations will want to use assessment as a part of the Present Situation Analysis, to help with course design and allocating learners to groups.

11.3 Classroom assessment

Classroom assessment and formal testing are both methods of assessment but the circumstances in which they take place are often very different.

Orientation 11a

List ways in which formal tests differ from classroom assessments.

Most tests are conducted under supervision and require candidates to answer questions in a given time limit, without reference to books or other people; the learner is not involved in setting or grading tests. In contrast, continuous assessment can be based on work carried out over a period of time and is more flexible and formative; the learner may have some say in what the assessed task will be and can use additional resources to complete the work. These differences are summarised in table 11.1.

Table 11.1 *Differences between tests and continuous assessment*

	Continuous Assessment	Tests
How long is there?	often no time limit	a set time limit
When is it done?	over a period of time	one block of time
Where is it done?	in class, at home, in a library	in classroom or hall
How is it done?	may be able to ask questions, may discuss with others, may use books	usually in silence, usually own work, may use a dictionary
Who sets the tasks?	teacher, teacher and learner	teacher or outsider
Who 'grades' the work?	teacher, learner, peers	teacher or outsider

Classroom assessment may be carried out by the teacher or the learners (self- or peer assessment).

11.3.1   *Teacher assessment*

Orientation 11b

Without using tests, how do you (or could you) formally assess your learners? What do you assess? What methods do you use? How do you record the results? What do you share with your learners?

One of the most common formal teacher assessment procedures is the grading of written assignments, done in class or as homework. However, other activities can also be assessed: tasks on reading or listening passages, pair or group interactions. With reading and listening, everyone can be assessed at the same time, although this is not necessary; with pair or group work, assessment may be spread over several occasions because of the time involved. If the classroom assessment is part of a pass/fail assessment procedure, it is good for the learners if more work than stipulated is assessed. In that case, just the best results can be used.

Continuous teacher assessment is important for the feedback that both teacher and learners receive. While grades may be a formal requirement, they provide limited information and may mean little to a learner. Descriptors and comments are more informative (see later).

11.3.2   *Peer and self-assessment*

Peer and self-assessment are used to supplement teacher assessments and have most value as an aid to learning. As a contribution to formal measures, they will only be valid if they are consistent, and research indicates that this is only achieved over time. This is hardly surprising – even trained and professional examiners need regular standardising and moderating meetings to ensure consistency! Peer and self-assessment are therefore qualitative rather than quantitative.

As a learning device peer or self-assessment is increasingly recognised as effective. Lynch (1988) reported that the 'experience of trying out this form of evaluation [which was peer assessment in an EAP situation of oral presentations using anonymous questionnaires] makes us want to persevere with it. We believe it has a marked effect on the extent to which speakers take their audience into account' (p. 124). A questionnaire required peers to circle their response to questions such as: 'Did the speaker show clearly when they were moving to a new point? Yes / Generally / No'. There was also space to fill in what the main strengths were and to make suggestions for the future. Peer assessment of writing work has also been successful.

There can be good, practical reasons for introducing peer assessment: in large classes (see chapter 10), it is not possible for a single teacher to comment on draft writing or to assess all the tasks. If constructive peer assessment procedures are developed, these can reduce the burden on the teacher and contribute to effective study techniques for the learners. Peer and self-assessment help learners to become more self-directed.

We would distinguish between this self-assessment of a particular task and the overall self-assessment used sometimes in needs analysis. Blue (1988b) discusses the reliability of this and notes students' over- and under-estimating of their abilities.

11.4 Classroom tests

11.4.1 Purposes

ESP tests may be given as part of a PSA, to place, to check progress, or to measure proficiency. As part of a PSA, an organisation may selectively test students to determine which macro-skill areas identified in the needs analysis actually require most attention, or how much focus will be given to, for example, accuracy or vocabulary development. Relevant aspects only are tested at an appropriate level.

A placement test usually has some test of reading, perhaps cloze passages and a test of listening, perhaps guided note-taking. These can be marked very quickly and can be sufficiently reliable for grouping students and advising them what language classes to attend. A short written exercise may be given too, partly for validity and partly for use where the reading and listening sections do not clearly suggest which group a student is best suited to.

Progress tests measure mastery of classwork and a desirable outcome would be for all students to get full marks. Achievement tests measure mastery of a syllabus and take a longer and wider perspective than progress tests. All students gaining full marks is theoretically possible but unlikely since individuals have particular strengths and weaknesses.

A proficiency test aims to measure how well the students will perform in their target language tasks and so fits within ESP principles. To help students learn we break down communicative events and processes into separate micro-skills and language items – and then provide practice in them as discrete items and as a whole. Identifying and separating discrete language items is a teaching device; an ESP proficiency test will assess the whole rather than the discrete items; it will contain a series of tasks and measure performance on these.

11.4.2 Characteristics of tests

There are some characteristics common to all good tests: Carroll (1980) talks of *C.A.R.E.* (Comparability, Acceptability, Relevance and Economy) while Bachman and Palmer (1996) have *FAIR VP* (Fairness, Authenticity, Impact, Reliability, Validity and Practicality). In some ESP situations the practical aspects behind setting, administering and marking can be crucial. With large classes, paper shortages and costs, for instance, we cannot use a question paper that requires students to write on it as then it could not be re-used. Similarly, with a class of a hundred or more students the speed of reliable marking is significant, and cloze reading passages are more practical than open-ended comprehension.

Another crucial factor is backwash / washback / impact. All tests have a backwash effect, that is, the test will affect what is taught and how it is taught. Backwash can be negative, for instance a test that uses only multiple-choice questions will cause teachers and learners to spend too much time practising this type of question. Backwash can be extremely positive and we would wish to see all tests designed with positive backwash in mind; a good test will cause teachers to teach what learners need in ways which enhance the learning process. All the effort behind needs analysis and course design can be negated if there is an examination which does not match them.

11.5   Public examinations developed in the UK

We will discuss these because they demonstrate current thinking and they provide valuable examples for in-house test development.

11.5.1 EAP examinations

In the UK, students can take one of two main EAP examinations: IELTS or UETESOL (University Entrance Test in English for Speakers of Other Languages). IELTS is also available at centres all over the world and is therefore taken by the largest numbers. Both these examinations help admissions tutors decide whether an applicant can cope with the linguistic demands of a course.

A third examination, TEEP (Test in English for Educational Purposes), is no longer available through an examining board but is still administered by the Centre for Applied Language Studies (CALS) at Reading University. There are interesting features of this examination that are relevant for in-house test development and so it is included in the discussion that follows.

The three examinations share a number of common features which reflect current approaches to testing but there are also some significant and interesting differences.

Similarities

- None of the three examinations has a simple pass/fail mark system. The results are all reported using band descriptors (see later) and provide a separate band level for each of the four language skills. Results are not given as a percentage but on a scale:

  IELTS   0–9
  UETESOL   A,B,C,D
  TEEP.   1,2,3

  A short descriptor defines what level of proficiency each band corresponds to. In the case of speaking and writing, these descriptors can be used directly at the marking stage. For listening and reading, marks are likely to be correlated with the bands. For example: A = 70+%; B = 56–69%; C = 40–55%; D = 0–39%.

- The linguistic demands of academic courses can differ considerably, so each examination assesses the candidates' level of proficiency in the different skills, and suggests what would be appropriate for different types, of courses but each college or admissions tutor can set their own minimum requirements. For example, IELTS suggest that for linguistically demanding training courses, such as industrial safety and engineering, band 6.0 is probably acceptable; for linguistically demanding academic courses they suggest band 7.0 as probably acceptable (1995 IELTS Handbook). In practice, many universities accept a lower score because they provide language support and take other factors into account.

- While an overall band level may be awarded, as with IELTS, the separate band levels for each skill provide valuable information to, candidates, teachers and admissions tutors. For instance, undergraduate students of mathematics are unlikely to need the same writing proficiency as business studies students.

- All the questions in the three examinations are compulsory; there is no choice in the questions. This is important for ensuring consistency and fairness: different questions would introduce different criteria and make standardisation impossible.

- Each examination usually sets candidates tasks on two reading and two listening passages, and has two writing tasks. This is because research supports the view that greater consistency of performance is obtained by candidates carrying out multiple tasks.

- Similarities also exist within the very rigorous setting and marking procedures. Within our own courses we may not have the facilities to match the degree of rigour but the basic process is one we can emulate (see the section on in-house test development).

- The same examination is offered to candidates of all subject disciplines. For a test which will be taken by candidates with wide-ranging and unknown backgrounds, the one-test solution is the most convenient (Alderson, 1988). However, as background knowledge has an effect on test results (Alderson and Urquhart, 1985; Clapham, 1996), all examining boards select carrier content that is as neutral and accessible as possible.

Differences

One significant difference between TEEP and other examinations was that it was constructed on the basis of detailed research into the English-language needs of overseas university students as perceived by both lecturers and students (Weir, 1983). This resulted in a more integrated and thematically linked examination. For instance, one of the writing tasks was carried out from the notes candidates made during both listening and reading tasks. This activity mirrors closely the reality of academic study where lecture notes and reading feed into assignments, so it has high validity.

11.5.2   EOP examinations

A long-standing EOP examination is the ESP component to the PLAB (Professional and Linguistic Assessment Board of the UK General Medical Council) examination which doctors trained outside the UK must take before being able to practise in the UK. One component is a patient-doctor interview in which both communicative ability and medical competence are assessed. Australia has the Occupational English Test, a set of tests related to the medical professions (McNamara, 1996).

However, most EOP tests are business-related. Several UK examining boards (LCCI, Oxford, UCLES) offer business-related examinations and, like EAP tests, they are task-based proficiency tests. The design and format are similar, with all four skills tested separately. Written tasks include completing forms, writing memos, letters and reports, while understanding is tested using objective exercise types such as matching, multiple-choice and gap filling. The carrier content is drawn from business contexts and situations. One way in which they differ from EAP examinations is that they are generally offered at several levels, corresponding to scales 3–7 of the English Speaking Union's scale (p. 218). There are examinations in international business and in trade, business, tourism. Outside the UK, TOIEC (Test of English for International Communication) is widely used in Japan and other Asian countries. Like TOEFL, TOIEC is currently a multiple-choice examination: practical but not pedagogically desirable.

Reflection 11c

If you have access to examples of papers, compare and contrast them with each other and with your own in-house tests.

11.6   Reporting test results: band descriptors

In public ESP examinations in Britain, the practice of reporting results as a percentage (such as 60 per cent), a letter grade (such as B), or just as pass/fail has largely been replaced by band descriptors. B- or 60 per cent can only tell us that the result is better than C+ and worse than 80 per cent. To understand test results, users need to know what specific criteria they refer to – and that is what the band descriptors state.

The descriptors can be specific to a particular skill or give an overall assessment. For marking and for maximum information, skill-based descriptors are desirable. For simplicity of reporting, a final overall descriptor may be appropriate. Most scales operate with either five, seven or nine levels. If the aim is to cover all competencies, from beginner to near native competence, then nine bands are suitable. When the range of competencies within a group is narrower, for example in some tertiary ESP situations, then five bands can provide sufficient differentiation.

The English Speaking Union (ESU) produced a nine-scale level to compare the standards of UK examinations (the middle five levels are given in table 11.2). Some of these can be a useful starting point for those wishing to develop their own descriptors.

Table 11.2 *ESU language test descriptors*

Level	Descriptor
7	Uses the language effectively in most situations with few problems. Communication is effective and consistent, with few hesitations and uncertainties. (LCCI third level EBP exams, Cambridge Proficiency Examination)
6	Uses the language competently in a variety of situations but with noticeable problems. Communication is usually effective. When difficulties arise communication is recovered with ease. (UETESOL pass; Pitman higher intermediate)
5	Uses the language adequately in familiar situations. Rather frequent problems but usually succeeds in communicating general message. (Pitman intermediate, First Certificate English)
4	Uses a basic range of language sufficient for familiar and non-pressurising situations. Frequent problems restrict prolonged communication but message communicated with repetition or assistance.
3	Uses a limited range of language adequate for short communication and practical needs. Problems cause frequent breakdown of communication but message usually recovered with repetition and assistance. (First level of LCCI EBP exams)

Reflection 11d

Consider some of the groups you have taught. Which of the ESU levels did they generally correspond to?

For most in-house purposes, four or five bands are suitable and can cover the expected range of ability (which in EFL versus ESL situations may not extend to levels 8 and 9). Developing suitable descriptions takes time and, as always, it pays to begin from what others have invested time and expertise on. It is helpful to use tried and tested descriptions as a starting point. (There are examples in Weir, 1990, 1993); IELTS information is available from the British Council and UCLES.) The difficulties of writing your own include: the wording (which needs to be positive), obtaining progression through the bands, deciding which features to include and prioritise and deciding when a higher level in any one feature becomes significant.

For marking writing or spoken interaction there are two kinds of descriptors, holistic and (multi-trait) analytic (see Weir, 1990; Hamp-Lyons, 1991). For experienced users, holistic descriptors are quicker and reliable; they use global impression and provide an overall perspective – see table 11.3. For diagnostic purposes and initial reliability, analytic descriptors are usually recommended; these break each feature down – see table 11.4.

Table 11.3 *Holistic descriptors matched to grades*

Mark	Descriptor for writing
18–20	Fulfils requirements of question. Communicates message clearly. Organisation and paragraphing effective. Sound grammar and good choice of words but the occasional error.
15–17	Fulfils requirements of question. Communicates message competently but not always grammatically. Organisation generally clear. Reasonable range of vocabulary.
12–14	*Either* message and organisation adequate but grammar weak; or grammar competent but poor organisation interferes with clear grasp of the message.
9–11	(fail) Simple sentences convey basic message. Lacks functional control of complex sentences. Limited vocabulary.
6–8	Some aspects of the message come through. Lacks functional control of simple sentences.
1–5	Answer inadequate, almost no correct language.

If the authorities expect a percentage or letter grade result this can be correlated with a band description as illustrated in table 11.3. These holistic bands were drafted because a mark out of twenty had to be noted. In using these bands, the first stage was to assign students to a band and then to a mark within that band. The top student level was ESU 6/7 and the bands were designed so that full marks could be awarded.

The use of descriptors is vital for standardising: A new university invested a good deal of time and money in developing a standard EAP course for all first year students with common material and common tests. However, each individual teacher used to mark their own scripts according to their own perspective and expectations. When, during an in-service training workshop, a sample of scripts was graded by each teacher, some scripts were awarded quite widely differing marks. Using the same syllabus, the same course, the same material and the same test did not provide standardised and fair results. That only came through standardisation of marking, and that came through the use of band descriptors to mark (and report) results and through following the steps outlined in figure 11.6 (see p. 225 below).

Table 11.4 *Analytic descriptors for marking writing (Weir, 1990)*

A. *Relevance and adequacy of content*

0. The answer bears almost no relation to the task set. Totally inadequate answer.
1. Answer of limited relevance to the task set. Possibly major gaps in treatment of topic and/or pointless repetition.
2. For the most part answers the tasks set, though there may be some gaps or redundant information.
3. Relevant and adequate answer to the task set.

B. *Compositional organisation*

0. No apparent organisation of content.
1. Very little organisation of content. Underlying structure not sufficiently apparent.
2. Some organisational skills in evidence, but not adequately controlled.
3. Overall shape and internal pattern clear. Organisational skills adequately controlled.

C. *Cohesion*

0. Cohesion almost totally absent. Writing so fragmentary that comprehension of the intended communication is virtually impossible.
1. Unsatisfactory cohesion may cause difficulty in comprehension of most of the intended communication.
2. For the most part satisfactory cohesion though occasional deficiencies may mean that certain parts of the communication are not always effective.
3. Satisfactory use of cohesion resulting in effective communication.

D. *Adequacy of vocabulary for purpose*

0. Vocabulary inadequate even for the most basic parts of the intended communication.
1. Frequent inadequacies in vocabulary for the task. Perhaps frequent lexical inappropriacies and/or repetition.
2. Some inadequacies in vocabulary for the task. Perhaps some lexical inappropriacies and/or circumlocution.
3. Almost no inadequacies in vocabulary for the task. Only rare inappropriacies and/or circumlocution.

E. *Grammar*

0. Almost all grammatical patterns inaccurate.
1. Frequent grammatical inaccuracies.
2. Some grammatical inaccuracies.
3. Almost no grammatical inaccuracies. (*ctd.*)

F. *Mechanical accuracy I (punctuation)*

0. Ignorance of conventions of punctuation.

1. Low standard of accuracy in punctuation.

2. Some inaccuracies in punctuation.

3. Almost no inaccuracies in punctuation.

G. *Mechanical accuracy II (spelling)*

0. Almost all spelling inaccurate.

1. Low standard of accuracy in spelling.

2. Some inaccuracies in spelling.

3. Almost no inaccuracies in spelling.

The benefits of band descriptors are real information for students, greater fairness and standardisation – especially in writing and speaking – and, in the long run, time-saving. When markers are familiar with descriptors they can mark more accurately and more quickly.

11.7 In-house test development

Significant decisions are taken on the basis of test results. Students pass or fail courses, are successful or unsuccessful in job applications, have their morale and self-confidence boosted or undermined. When we set, administer and mark tests, we have a tremendous responsibility to those students. We should *Test for Best* (Weir, 1990) and apply *C.A.R.E.* That is, our test should enable students to perform as well as possible. Tests are not to trick or confuse. Moreover, we should be fair and consistent in our marking and share as much information as possible with our students.

The whole of a test does not have to be prepared from scratch. We have already suggested that course design should build on existing courses, that adapting and modifying materials can be a better route than writing something completely new. So it will come as no surprise that we also say for tests: make use of what is available, adapt and modify it.

The process we describe for developing and marking tests was designed for situations where there were several staff and a lot of students. The setting process would be similar for just one member of staff or one student. However, if all the marking is carried out by a single individual, then standardising and moderating procedures will not apply in the same way. Lynch and Davidson (1994) discuss a similar process for criterion-referenced language test development.

11.7.1 Setting

The flow diagram below summarises the steps which we describe in more detail below:

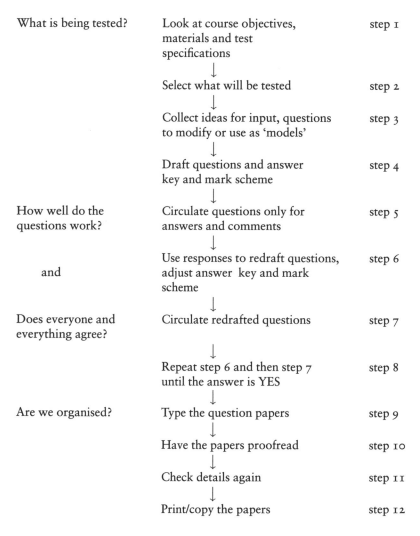

What is being tested?	Look at course objectives, materials and test specifications	step 1
	↓	
	Select what will be tested	step 2
	↓	
	Collect ideas for input, questions to modify or use as 'models'	step 3
	↓	
	Draft questions and answer key and mark scheme	step 4
How well do the questions work?	Circulate questions only for answers and comments	step 5
	↓	
and	Use responses to redraft questions, adjust answer key and mark scheme	step 6
Does everyone and everything agree?	Circulate redrafted questions	step 7
	↓	
	Repeat step 6 and then step 7 until the answer is YES	step 8
Are we organised?	Type the question papers	step 9
	↓	
	Have the papers proofread	step 10
	↓	
	Check details again	step 11
	↓	
	Print/copy the papers	step 12

Figure 11.5   A procedure for setting tests

Weir (1993) gives detailed general principles and specific guidelines for test construction (pp. 19–29) and states that 'the one inescapable guideline is that test writing should not be a solitary activity' (p. 19). We agree. As with materials, several people setting questions and passing them around for comments produces better results.

As with course design and materials development, steps 1 to 4 (in figure 11.5) are not linear or uni-directional. In practice, some key objectives will be selected for testing, some test items or input will be found and these will determine some of the other objectives. What must be checked is that all the objectives tested are course objectives and have been covered in the teaching so far. Test specifications such as the length of the test and the number of marks it carries should be clarified. When draft questions are circulated, we believe written answers should be given for all questions, including the writing – it is not enough to just 'read' the questions. We also suggest that those who comment state what they think is being tested by each item. This is important for validity. Redrafting will be necessary if any of the responses do not match the expected one, when the item does not test what was intended and when there are comments such as 'too difficult/easy', 'ambiguous', 'confusing', 'what does this mean?' The 'comment–redraft' process will continue until there is consistency.

Task 11e ●◇

A course you teach has writing and the language of comparison/contrast among the objectives you have decided to test. A colleague has drafted a test question, E11.9 (p. 262).

a) How suitable is it? Does it test the objectives? What else is tested?
b) If possible, draft an answer and compare it with other people's.

The pedagogic stages are now complete and the next stage is administrative (steps 9 to 12, figure 11.5). Working on the layout and proofing for errors are two responsibilities. The two most common problems at this stage are time and inaccuracy. In planning the timescale for test setting it is easy to forget about the organisation and production time. This can be considerable, particularly if it is not controlled by those who set the test. Proofreading is difficult; it is easy to 'see' what is expected and not what is actually there but it is unprofessional to mark candidates for accuracy and have 'mistakes' in the typed question paper. It is helpful if someone who has not been involved in preparation is one of the proofreaders.

11.7.2 Marking

The first stage in the marking process is to confirm the answer key and mark scheme for reading and listening and to standardise the marking of writing and spoken interaction. This is done at meetings with *all* markers present. A sample of scripts are selected in advance; any name identification is covered and a reference number or letter given instead. Where possible, each marker is given a copy to mark. Where photocopying is not possible, the scripts can be circulated round the markers who do not write anything on the scripts. Markers need a record sheet and a copy of the answer key and mark scheme (steps 1 and 2, figure 11.6 opposite).

Each person marks the sample scripts, fills in their record sheet, noting any occasion where they are uncertain of how to apply the scheme or award marks. If there are no problems then everyone will have given the same mark to each section of each script – this is unusual! Normally there are a few items where students have thought of other acceptable answers or there is some possibility of interpretation. Slips in marking or adding up marks also happen. What is important is that the group agrees exactly what will be accepted and then sticks to that in marking all the scripts – even if yet another possibility arises later (steps 3 and 4, figure 11.6). It usually takes longer to standardise writing, and step 4a is needed if quite different band levels or descriptor levels have been awarded. It is helpful to agree on benchmark scripts – a set of scripts to exemplify each of the bands. Scripts can then be compared with the benchmarks. (It is useful to keep the benchmark scripts because then a check can be made from one course to another that the same standard is operating.)

All the scripts are then marked from that scheme, preferably at one time in one place. Otherwise the group will need to meet briefly when all the scripts have been marked. If a marker feels the scheme penalises a student in some way, s/he can note the discrepancy. If, when the marks are totalled, the discrepancy would alter the band level, the group can consider that script again. Certainly, all borderline scripts should be reviewed – to check there are no 'slips' (steps 5 and 6, figure 11.6).

When standardising writing either have each script double-marked (two markers) without revealing the band levels or re-mark a sample of each marker's scripts (again without knowledge of the band level). This 'moderation' can reveal whether an individual marker is consistent, rather strict or rather lenient and action can be taken as necessary. In addition, all borderline cases should be reviewed and discussed.

Figure 11.6   Confirming the answer key and mark scheme

step 1	select range of sample scripts, make anonymous, give reference number, prepare marker record sheets
	↓
step 2	hold standardising meeting for ALL markers
	↓
step 3	mark sample scripts according to initial key and scheme
	↓
step 4	compare marks awarded, adjust and agree final key and mark scheme
	↓
step 4a	mark more sample scripts until marking is consistent
	↓
step 5	mark scripts applying agreed scheme
	↓
step 6	meet to check borderline and problem scripts

11.8   ESP test questions

There are no question types specific to ESP; what may be different is the frequency with which a question type is used. The writing of test items is very similar to that of writing class materials. Every item type that is used on a test should also be being used in teaching, although they would be handled differently; but not everything used for teaching is suitable for testing. The advantages and disadvantages of different question types in testing are thoroughly discussed by Weir (1990, 1993).

11.8.1   Writing

All study- and work-related writing is written for a readership, for a purpose, and about a specific matter, so one characteristic of ESP writing tests is the provision of input and specification of purpose and audience. This approach also means that examiners do not have a conflict between assessing language and content which increases relia-bility in marking. By setting two short pieces, a wider sample is taken and students have more chance to do well. Depending on level, 20–30 minutes is enough writing time plus an extra 10 minutes for reading and preparation.

Where writing and reading are tested separately, the input for the writing task is given mainly in non-verbal formats. This is particularly common in EAP examinations. EOP tests are more likely to integrate reading and writing. In many real-life situations, particularly in business, there has to be an immediate response to reading a document, such as sending a memo or a letter. The direct ESP test is then to set an integrated task and this is a feature of the advanced business examinations. In EAP situations, the immediate response to reading may just be a few notes. Using the information may come rather later. Examples E 11.1–11.3 are taken from EOP examinations; the format of E 11.3 might well be used in an EAP examination – perhaps with a different audience and document type.

Reflection 11f ●◆

a) Identify the audience and purpose given in examination writing tasks E11.1 to E11.3 (pp. 252–4). Consider how helpful each is.

b) What are the merits of the different methods of providing input?

c) The content of E6.2 (p. 249) looks suitable for your own in-house test. Which part of the input would you use and what would be the task you would set for students of about (i) band 4, (ii) band 7 (ESU bands p. 218)?

d) Choose one of the question formats in E11.1 to E11.3 (pp. 252–4) and write your own item using different content/audience/purpose.

11.8.2 Reading

EAP examinations usually use two medium-length passages or one longish one while for EOP there are usually several shorter texts. The carrier content and lexical load have to be chosen such that they are unlikely to either advantage or disadvantage particular people. There will be a range of question types assessing understanding; it should not be possible to answer the questions without text, for example because of background kowledge. Both the overall purpose of reading the text and the processes which will be used in responding to the test questions need to reflect the target performance. Unless the examination is an integrated one, the question types will be selected and designed so that the output from the reading comprehension requires minimal written production. Marking is thus more objective and quicker. As mentioned above, EOP examinations may set integrated reading/writing tasks with just a few specific comprehension questions.

Task 11g ●◆

Use Example E11.4 (pp. 255–7) for this task.

a) Try answering the questions without reading the texts. Can you get any of them correct?
b) In Q1 and 2, how have the setters reduced the possibility of guessing?
c) In which questions, if any, could you use different words to a colleague in your answer and still be right?
d) Produce an answer key and mark scheme for this examination question. What were some of the issues you had to decide in devising the mark scheme?

11.8.3 Spoken interaction

Spoken tests are actually assessing spoken interaction, that is, both speaking and listening, as they are interactive. (It is also possible to include a section of monologue when the student describes say a picture or talks about an interest.) The interaction can be between student and examiner, or two or three students can be tested together and interact with each other. This has practical advantages as it reduces the time to test a large group. Also the interaction is then between participants of equal rather than unequal status, and students can choose who they would wish to be tested with, which can boost confidence.

Unless the interaction is taped, the onus is on the examiner(s) to assess each person rapidly and accurately. A standard procedure for this is to use band descriptors. After a few minutes, a three-band-range selection is made; this is narrowed to two as the test proceeds and the final assessment is decided immediately afterwards.

In public examinations it is usual to have two or three phases: an introductory one to set students at ease and gain a first impression of their ability to handle social niceties, an interaction based on a given stimulus, and lastly some more open discussion. For in-house tests the interaction may be sufficient, although it sets students at ease to have a moment or two of chat. Students will need a prompt card with the written instructions as well as hearing them.

The stimulus can be in note form or through photographs and other non-verbal devices. As with writing, the student does not have to search for all the ideas and can concentrate on language and communication. The best interaction is one which is purposeful and where the result is unpredictable and negotiated – as in real life.

Reflection 11h

Look at the stimulus for some spoken interaction tests such as E11.5 (p. 258). If possible, carry out the interaction and record it.

a) How natural did it seem?
b) What range of functions and language were you using?

These stimuli can set up situations which measure language ability in functions such as social exchanges, asking questions, providing or exchanging information or explaining. What they do not attempt is the assessment of more complex interchanges such as meetings or the extended discourse of presentations. Where these are part of the course objectives, continuous assessment may be more appropriate than a test, and this will be greatly helped if the activity is video-recorded.

11.8.4 Listening

In addition, most examinations include listening comprehension, and choices have to be made about the output which will be marked. The arguments are the same as those for reading and writing: separate processes to be assessed separately or integrated activities as in real life? Again EAP tests are more likely to use non-verbal or short answer formats while business-related tests include form-filling, fax and memo-writing.

Task 11i

Look at the questions in E11.6 to E11.8 (from p. 259).

a) Can you answer any of the questions without listening?
b) How have the setters reduced the possibility of guessing?
c) In which questions, if any, might you use different words to a colleague in your answer and still be right?

11.9 Summary

In this chapter we have discussed how classroom assessment, particularly by peers and learners themselves, can support learning both in class and after a course. We have outlined procedures for setting and marking tests that help to ensure fairness and consistency. Among these is the use of band descriptors for marking written and spoken production. Band descriptors are also more informative than grades for reporting results.

11.10 Recommended reading

Weir (1990, 1993); Bachman and Palmer (1996); Heaton (1988); Hughes (1989) are good on test specification and construction.

Epilogue

This book has taken an essentially practical approach to ESP, balancing aspects of theory with discussion and suggestions for pedagogy. It was sometimes difficult to decide how theoretical or how practical the orientation of different chapters should be. We wanted to present the more theoretical aspects in ways that are both accessible to the ESP teacher and of interest to those who wish to understand the underlying framework or philosophy of ESP work. Similarly, we hope that the more practical suggestions will stimulate those interested in methodological issues as well as providing ideas for the teacher.

A strength of the ESP profession is that it has always seen itself as engaged in a practical activity in which the determination of learners' needs and the attempt to meet those needs are given priority. Many of the pioneers of ESP work were British teachers working in third world countries with limited resources and time, and in those situations a non-theoretical 'here we go' attitude prevailed. Something of that spirit has continued thirty or forty years on, even though ESP work is now much less of an expatriate affair and most ESP projects are run and taught by teachers from the country itself.

There have, however, been problems with this non-theoretical stance. It has perhaps hindered ESP's professionalisation as a self-standing discipline in universities, or as a discipline that stands alongside and complements skill courses in management training for non-native speakers. A continuation of that stance would fail to do justice to the increasing amount of principled discussion of topics such as text analysis, discourse community and teaching methodology that appear both in its main journal *English for Specific Purposes* and other applied linguistics journals.

ESP has, as John Swales suggested in his final editorial for *English for Specific Purposes* (From the Editors, in issue 13:3), tended to avoid ideological issues. It has not largely been affected by questions such as gender issues, controversies in Second Language Acquisition and issues of learners' rights. As Swales suggests, this comes from its maintenance of a view of itself as part of applied linguistics, and certainly at the more applied end of the increasingly wide spectrum of that discipline.

ESP has certainly tended to take an uncritical stance towards the target situations and has seen its role as restricted to helping learners to cope with those situations. Some have argued that EAP has been too uncritical and has been 'accommodationist' in accepting the practices of academic departments. Benesch (1996), for example, presents the results of what she calls a *critical* needs analysis carried out in an American university, which led to the ESP teacher running certain classes that aimed – with the support of the subject department – to modify the target situation.

These ideas are generating an interesting debate about the role of ESP. Many practitioners would accept that the role of demystifying for learners the academic or institutional discourse that they are confronted with is a key role for ESP. The question is how far we should go in questioning practices in departments and institutions. Many (for example Allison, 1996) argue that ESP teachers have to accept the realities of the situation that they are teaching in, and that any analysis of discourse and rhetoric leads inevitably to a greater critical awareness of communication patterns. We have argued in this book that ESP should have the role of questioning certain institutional rhetoric and practices, but the seemingly confrontational stance towards current discourse practices adopted by advocates of the critical awareness movement worries us. We do nonetheless look forward to the continuance of this important debate.

The discussion of cross-cultural issues has led to an awareness that the increasing use of English in international business and publication, and the privileging of the Anglo-American rhetorical style in these discourses may disadvantage those who use other rhetorical styles. Mauranen (1993) has argued that international journals should show greater tolerance of different rhetorical styles. Many consider this to be impossible, suggesting that editors and readers do not have the time to make allowances for possible confusion arising from the use of a different style. We believe that there is a need for greater tolerance on the part of journal editors if they are to reflect the range of international research in their journal; and the EAP profession has a role to play in persuading the gatekeepers, that is editors and referees, to change their practices in this regard. Here the experience of EBP is interesting; despite its relative youth as a branch of ESP it has taken this issue very seriously and the degree of awareness of cultural issues is at a high level. What we need in these areas (and in fact in all ESP) is more than just awareness of the problems – namely a willingness to take action to overcome the consequences.

One of the underlying themes of this book is that ESP has been open to influences from other disciplines, both from the academic world and from the business world. We believe that these influences are likely to grow, and that ESP practitioners will also play an increasing role in advising other academics and professionals on communication. Both of these developments will force ESP practitioners to engage with more ideological issues.

We thus expect two areas, critical approaches to research and discourse (see also Pennycook, 1994) and cross-cultural issues (Connor, 1996) to have an increasing influence on the development of ESP. We also expect much more questioning of the norms of ESP teaching and research: on the pedagogical side this will arise from small-scale classroom-based research (Allwright, 1988 and many examples in the *Brazilian ESPecialist*); on the research side there will be increasing concern about what language is culturally appropriate in different situations. The openness of ESP to activities and research in other disciplines should ensure continuing flexibility and will add new perspectives to enrich its practices.

Recommended reading

We include a number of books and articles related to 'critical' issues. Both Benesch (1996) and Pennycook (1994) have raised issues about what they would see as ESP's uncritical role. Allison (1996) presents a very interesting alternative perspective. Fairclough (1989, 1992) has been the most prominent critical linguist. The Ventola and Mauranen (1991) volume includes papers that discuss issues of contrastive rhetoric.

Extracts

Extract E1.2

Brieger, N. and J. Comfort, *Production and Operations, Business Management English*. Prentice Hall, 1992

2 Listening

Allan Carpenter has asked Alistair Bradley to join today's meeting on work measurement. Alistair is in charge of method study and work measurement at the existing Colex plant. Alan would like the operations team to hear about the studies carried out at Colex so that they can decide on the next step to take for the new plant. As you listen, complete Charts 4.3 and 4.4.

Chart 4.3   The six steps in work measurement

Step	Activity
1. Select	_ _ _ _ _ _ _ _ to be studied
2. Record	_ _ _ _ _ _ _ _ of the operation
3. Analyse	_ _ _ _ _ _ _ _ the work into smaller _ _ _ _ _ _ _
4. Measure	_ _ _ _ _ _ _ _ for each element
5. Establish a standard time	By taking a _ _ _ _ _ _ _ _ _ _ _
6. Production studies	1. Under _ _ _ _ _ _ _ _ conditions 2. Minimum length of such a study should be _ _ _ _ _ _ _ _ _ or _ _ _ _ _ _ _ _

Chart 4.4   The three problems in work measurement

1. Who _ worker?
2. What _ that we want to measure?
3. What _ should we use?

Extract of the Listening tapescript

AC: The issue for this meeting is establishing work measurement standards for the new Colex plant. Although some of the jobs that will be done at the new plant are very similar, or even the same as, jobs in the existing plant, there are differences in the layout as well as in some of the jobs themselves. So, that means that we need basic information for production planning and scheduling, costing, incentive schemes and so on. Alistair, here, has been involved in a number of studies at our plant here. I've asked him to join our meeting so that he can tell us what we should be thinking about and doing in terms of work measurement. Alistair, could you start by giving us an overview of work measurement, and then some examples of the studies you've carried out here? Then I think we would like to discuss their applicability to our new operations so we can decide on an action plan. How does that sound to you?

AB: Yes, that's fine.

AC: Okay.

AB: So, you'd like me to go over the basic principles first?

AC: Yes, I think that would be useful for all of us.

AB: Okay. Well, the simplest way to measure work is to time how long a task takes. But, as I am sure I will say to you more than once in this meeting, human work is a complex mixture of manual and mental skills, and just doesn't lend itself to a simple method of measurement – like the time to complete a task. So we face a number of problems, or let's say critical questions. Those are the contentious issues, so I'll leave them till a bit later. The easy part is the basic procedures for measuring work. These consist of a number of steps, which I have on the transparency here . . . Okay, let me just take you through them. First, select. Choose the operation to be studied. There's always a reason for studying an operation. Later I'll tell you why we chose to study the bottle racking. Second is record. Put down all the relevant details of the operation. This is the sheet that we use. I'll pass it round at the end. Third, analyse. Break down the work into smaller elements. The size of each element will depend on the work measurement technique that we have chosen. Then measure. Establish the basic time for each element. Next, establish a standard time. We arrive at that by adding together three figures:

- The basic time for the element.
- An allowance to cover necessary work outside the particular element under review.
- An allowance for rest and personal needs, depending on the nature of the task.

Extract E2.1

Herbert, A. J. *The Structure of Technical English*. Longman, 1965, pp. 31, 33, 35.

Section 6

Reading: Steam Boilers

Large quantities of steam *are used by* modern industry in the generation of power. It is therefore necessary to design boilers which will produce high-pressure steam as efficiently as possible. Modern boilers are frequently very large, and are sometimes capable of generating 300,000 lb of steam per hour. To achieve this rate of steam production, the boilers should operate at very high temperatures. In some boilers, temperatures of over 1650° C may be attained. The fuels which are burned in the furnace are selected for their high calorific value, and give the maximum amount of heat. They are often *pulverised by* crushers outside the furnace and forced in under pressure.

Modern boilers which employ solid fuels are usually **too large to** be hand-stoked, and stoking is then *carried out by* mechanical stokers, which ensure that an **adequate** quantity of fuel is conveyed into the furnace at the proper speed. The air which *is needed by* the fuel for combustion *is blown* across the firegrate *by* steam jets or fans. The amount of air which is allowed to enter is just more than **sufficient for** complete combustion of the fuel. An **insufficient** supply of air will prevent complete combustion, but any air **in excess of** the minimum merely reduces the temperature of combustion. The hot gases which *are produced by* the combustion of the fuel are circulated round banks of water-tubes. These are inclined at an angle over the furnace, and connect the upper and lower steam drums. A large proportion of the heat *is absorbed by* the water in the boiler. The remainder may be used to heat up the incoming air-supply through an air-heater. The water and steam in the boiler should circulate freely. The water and steam circuits are designed to allow the greatest possible fluid velocity to be attained, and rapid movement of the fluid *is achieved by* forced circulation. This assists rapid heating and also prevents the formation of steam pockets in the tubes.

WORD STUDY
Attain, Achieve (= reach)

The aircraft is capable of *attaining* a speed of 4000 miles per hour.
(*reaching / attaining / achieving*)

1. Pressures of up to 300 lb/in² were ⎱ *reached* ⎰ in the boiler.
2. An efficiency of only 4% or 5% was ⎬ *attained* ⎨ by the engine.
3. A high degree of accuracy can be ⎰ *achieved* ⎱ by cold-working the metal.

A greater efficiency should be *attainable / achievable* with certain modifications.

Absorb (= take in)

1. A sponge will ⎱ ⎰ water.
2. The spring must ⎥ *absorb* ⎥ most of the shock.
3. The water will ⎥ ⎥ a large proportion of the heat from the furnace.
4. Dark surfaces ⎰ ⎱ heat more than bright surfaces.

Sponges are *absorbent*. They have ⎰ great *absorptive* power.
⎱ a great power of *absorption*.

---

2. **Too Much or Too Little** (part of table)

The boiler	consumes	an *excessive / undue* amount of	fuel.
Too much air / An *excessive amount* of air	enters	the furnace.	
The *excess* air	reduces	the temperature of combustion.	
The temperature	was	*excessive. / excessively* high. / *too high.*	
		too high	*for* the boiler to withstand.
The metal	was	*too hard*	*to* machine. / *to be* machined.
The temperature in the combustion chamber	*exceeded / was greater than / was in excess of*	2000 C. degrees.	
The temperature	was	*high enough / sufficiently high*	*to* melt the metal. / *for* the metal to melt.
Enough / Sufficient / Adequate / An *adequate amount of*	heat	must be	supplied	*for* the metal to be melted.

Extract E2.2

Bates, M. and T. Dudley-Evans. *Nucleus General Science.* Longman, 1976, 1982. pp. 20 and 21.

Unit 3   Structure

Section 1   Parts and the whole

1. Look and read:

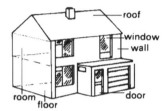

A house *consists of* walls, a roof, floors, doors and windows. (These are the *parts* of the house.)
It *contains* rooms. (The rooms are inside the house.)

Now complete this:

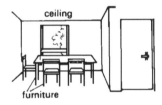

A room _____ walls, a ceiling, a floor, a _____ and _____.
A room often _____ furniture.

Answer these:

What does your classroom consist of?
What does it contain?

Complete this:

A milk bottle consists of a glass cylinder, a flat _____, a tapering _____ and a lid.
It contains _____.

Complete this:

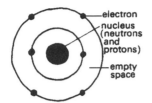

An atom of carbon consists of . . . .
It contains a _____ in the centre.
The nucleus consists of _____ and
_____ .

2. Read this:

The rooms in a house *include* a bedroom, a sitting-room *etc.* (These are some of the different kinds of room.)

Complete these:

The rooms in a school include . . .

Furniture includes . . .

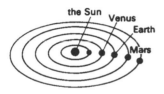

The solar system _____ the Sun and planets. Planets _____ the Earth, Mars, Venus _____ .

Look and complete:

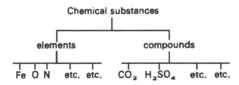

Chemical substances consist of _____ and _____ .
Elements include . . . .
Compounds include . . . .

Extracts

Extract E2.3

Skills for Learning, Foundation, University of Malaya Press, 1980.

Using contextual clues

It is not necessary to look up the meaning of every difficult word you come across in your reading. Often it is possible to deduce the meaning of an unknown word from the context. In this lesson you will get an opportunity to deduce the meaning of difficult words using contextual clues.

Activity A **Determine who 'I' and 'she' are**

| CLASS WORK |
| INDIVIDUAL WORK |
| GROUP WORK |

A story will be read to you.

Decide who 'I' and 'she' are in the story.

Activity B **Think of words to complete the sentences (1)**

| GROUP WORK |

Here are five sentences with blanks. (*only 2 given here*)

Think of as many different words or phrases as you can for each of the blanks below.

1 At children's parties ice-cream and _____ are often served.
2 I like this new gadget very much because it works better than the egg-beater, the washing machine, the _____ and the automatic dishwasher.

Activity C **Determine the meanings of the difficult words (1)**

| INDIVIDUAL WORK |
| PAIR WORK .. |
| CLASS WORK |

This is a step-by-step activity. A choice of simple, everyday words or phrases is given for the difficult word in each text.

In each case, use the context to help you decide which of the simple words or phrases has the same meaning as the difficult one. Read each text right through first to make the context more meaningful. Note down your answer.

Text A

Step 1 Our water problem is usually one of too much or too little water. Either extreme could have serious *repercussions* on the country.
a rainstorms
b effects
c drought

Step 2 Whether it be in personal *deprivation* or in our agriculture and industrial productivity, the present dry spell will certainly leave its mark on agriculture, . . .
a good luck
b values
c loss

(*continues with additional steps*)

Extract E2.4

Hutchinson, T. and A. Waters. *Interface: English for Technical Communication.* Longman, 1984, pp. 100–101, 103.

STARTER

Look at this table showing the fuel consumption of different cars. Why do cars use different amounts of fuel at different speeds? Why does consumption vary from car to car?

	DAIHATSU CHARADE	VOLKSWAGEN PASSAT	VOLVO 244 DL
mph/kph		mpg/kpl	
30/48 50/80 70/113	61/21.6 51/18.1 35/12.4	53/18.8 42/14.9 31/11	40/14.2 38/13.5 28/10

INPUT

(not all presented here)

GATHERING INFORMATION

STEP 1

Make notes about the Kenlowe fan under these headings:

a advantages
b cost
c fitting

STEP 2

What is the purpose of the coupon? Why is the information it asks for necessary?

STEP 3 (*e–l omitted*)

Re-write these sentences, using words or expressions from the INPUT to replace the ones in **bold type**. Make any necessary changes to the rest of the sentence.

a   **Do not** drive your car at a higher speed than necessary.
b   A thermostat helps to prevent energy being **used unnecessarily.**
c   Driving in town means changing gear **all the time.**
d   Bad weather **made** the aeroplane's take-off **later than expected.**

STEP 4

Read this description of a type of thermoelectric cooling fan mechanism. Draw and label a simple diagram to show how it works.

The Magnetic Clutch System
How does a thermoelectric cooling fan work? There are several different types of mechanism, but the kind used in most cars is the Magnetic Clutch System. It gets its name from the way it uses an electromagnet as a clutch to engage and disengage the fan. It operates as follows. A thermostatic switch is linked to the engine cooling system. When the engine heats up, the temperature of the coolant rises, making the switch come on. Electricity now flows to the electromagnet, and the magnet, acting as a clutch, moves the fan into a position where it can be driven by the engine. When the action of the fan has cooled the engine, the magnet is turned off, the fan moves away from the engine drive, and stops turning. The cycle is then ready to begin again.

STEP 9   Listening task

Copy this graph.

a Complete it and label it with the information on the cassette.

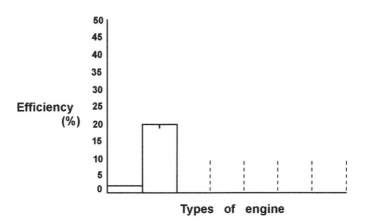

b Why are some engines more efficient than others?

TASK The thermoelectric fan is only one way in which the efficiency of a car can be improved. Designers of modern cars are trying to modify all aspects of the car (body, engine, gears and transmission, electrical system, etc.) to reduce fuel consumption.

a Make a list of all the energy-saving modifications you know about.

b Say how each one helps to save fuel.

c Write an advertisement for an energy-saving car, incorporating all the modifications you have listed. Be specific and use graphs where possible.

Extracts

Extract E3.1

Samuelson, Paul A. *Economics*. New York: McGraw Hill, 1955, pp. 63/4.

▶ THE DEMAND CURVE

The numerical data of Table 1 (*not given here*) can also be given a graphic interpretation. On the vertical scale in Fig. 1, we represent the various alternative prices of wheat, measured in dollars per bushel. On the horizontal scale, we measure the quantity of wheat (in terms of bushels) that will be bought per month.

Downward-sloping curve portrays demand:

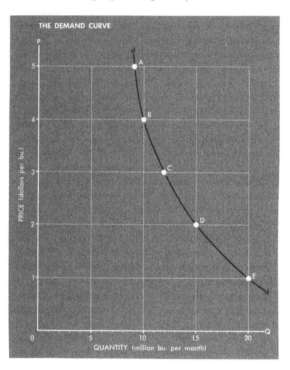

Fig. 1. Prices are measured on the vertical axis and quantities demanded on the horizontal axis. Each pair of Q, P numbers from Table 1 is plotted here as a point, and a smooth curve passed through the points gives us the demand curve. The fact that *dd* goes downward and to the right portrays the very important "law of downward-sloping demand."

Just as a city corner is located as soon as we know its street and avenue, so is a ship's position located as soon as we know its latitude and longitude. Similarly, to plot a point on this diagram, we must have two coordinate numbers: a price and a quantity. For our first point A, corresponding to $5 and 9 million bushels, we move upward 5 units and then over to the right 9 units. A circle marks the spot A. To get the next circle, at B, we go up only 4 units and over to the right 10 units. The last circle is shown by E. Through the circles we draw a smooth curve, marked *dd*.

This picturization of the demand schedule is called the "demand curve." Note how quantity and price are *inversely* related, quantity going up when price goes down. The curve slopes downward, going from northwest to southeast. This important property is given a name: the *law of downward-sloping demand*. This law is true of practically all commodities: wheat, electric razors, cotton, ethyl gasoline, cornflakes, and theater tickets.

▶ *The law of downward-sloping demand: When the price of a good is raised (at the same time that all other things are held constant), less of it will be demanded. Or, what is the same thing: If a greater quantity of a good is thrown on the market, then—other things being equal—it can be sold only at a lower price.*

Extract E3.2

Barclays Bank. Economic Surveys (Current Accounts 1983).

The direction of movement has, in general, been in line with the forecasts in our last survey, with the United States showing deteriorating trends, while Japan and, to a lesser extent European countries, have improved. For the United Kingdom and Italy the size of the movement has been reasonably close to expectations, but for a number of countries the magnitude of the swing has been greater than expected. In particular, the US deficit has widened, the French deficit has narrowed, and the Japanese surplus expanded at faster than expected rates. In contrast, the Canadian and, more importantly, the German current account performances have been disappointing, with the expected substantial improvement having failed to materialise.

Extracts

Extract E5.1

From: Chrispeels, M. J. and D. Sadava, 1977. *Plants, Food and People*, p. 26.

In the human brain, cell proliferation and cell growth occur very early in life, and are most rapid in the last few months of pregnancy and the first year after birth. Cell proliferation in the brain normally stops when the baby is six months old, and by age three the brain has already reached 80% of its adult body weight. At that time the child has only reached 20% of its adult body weight. Thus the last months as a fetus and the first years of life are crucial to the development of the brain. Protein malnutrition during this period results in a physically smaller brain as reflected by reduced head circumference. An examination of the brains of children who died from protein malnutrition during the first year of their life showed that they had 15 to 20% fewer brain cells than the normal child. These observations confirmed earlier experiments showing that rats and other animals fed protein-deficient diets in early life had physically smaller brains containing fewer cells than normal. Other experiments show that such animals are also deficient in their learning capacity. Because it is impossible to do controlled feeding experiments with children, it has been difficult to show conclusively that this is also the case in humans. Malnourished children generally score lower on intelligence and adaptive-behaviour tests than their counterparts who are adequately nourished and live in a similar environment. These studies suggest that protein malnutrition of infants may permanently restrict their mental abilities.

Extract E5.2

Adapted from an authentic memo

MEMORANDUM

RE: MINIMUM STOCK QUANTITIES

Further to my memo dated 24.06. advising you of minimum stock quantities for export to our Portuguese customers and after checking stocks the situation is as follows:

Product 1	OK
Product 2	OK
Product 3	OK
Product 4	OK
Product 5	OK
Product 6	OK
Product 7	- 1000 mts
Product 8	- 3000 mts (23rd August OK)

(continued)

Kindly ensure that these are complete before the end of August so that we can supply our customers without incurring any delays.

The next 3 months should be the busiest months of the year and the stock quantities as per my memo are absolute minimum quantities. It would take only 2 big orders to exhaust our stocks. It is therefore imperative if we want to offer a good and smooth service to Portugal that these levels are respected or exceeded at all times and that any stock-out or below the minimum level situation is acted upon very promptly.

Thank you for your collaboration.

Extract E5.3

Steeds, W. *Engineering materials, machine tools and processes*. Longmans Green & Co. Ltd., 1957, 3rd ed., p. 5.

Load-extension and **Stress-strain Curves**. If corresponding readings of load and extension in a tensile test are plotted, a load-extension diagram or curve is obtained. Alternatively the *stress* (the load ÷ original area of the specimen) may be plotted against the *strain* (the extension ÷ gauge length). The diagram shown in Fig. 4*a* is typical of annealed mild steel, while that at *b* is typical of "cold-worked" mild steel (material which has been "worked" or deformed at atmospheric temperature), most alloy steels, and many non-ferrous materials. Up to some point A, called the *limit of proportionality*, the extension or strain

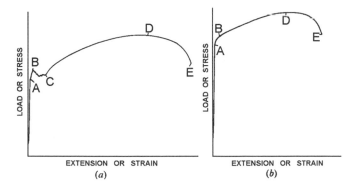

FIG. 4.

is directly proportional to the load or stress and the graph is a straight line. (In the figure the extensions up to the point A have been greatly exaggerated in order to separate the graph from the ordinate axis.) From A to B the extension increases more rapidly than in direct proportion to the load but the specimen is still elastic, so that if the load is removed the specimen will return to its original length. The stress corresponding to the point B is known as the *elastic limit*.

247

Extract E6.1

Lynch, A. *Study Listening*, CUP, 1983.

Phase 2   Recognising sentence connections

Unit 7   Reference

To make sense of what we hear, we have to understand not only what the important information in each spoken sentence is, but also how the sentences relate to each other. To do this, we have to recognise the *chains of reference* in what is said.

Look at text 1. Notice how the words that refer to the same thing have been joined up. These represent the chains of reference.

Text 1

Clearly | one of the great advantages | of ¦ underdeveloped countries ¦

such as ¦ Taiwan and Korea ¦ is that ¦ they ¦ were able to exploit

| a large supply of cheap labour |·| That | is going to be

meaningless in a future in which | labour | is used very little

in the production of goods.

Text 2

This is the original spoken version of text 1.

and of course the underdeveloped countries
one of the big advantages
once again as I mentioned before
for example Taiwan um Korea
is that they were able to exploit
the fact that they had a large supply of cheap labour
now that is going to be meaningless
in a future in which labour is not used at all for
or very used very little in the production of goods

Discussion point 1

What are the chains of reference in text 2? Draw them in.

Discussion point 2

What differences do you see between texts 1 and 2?

People normally use more words in speaking than in writing, even to say the same thing. This makes it very important to recognise the chains of reference

Extract E6.2

Flower, L. *Problem Solving: Strategies for Writing*. Orlando, Florida: Harcourt Brace, and Company, pp. 156–157.

You are writing an article on eating out for people who are following a low-carbohydrate diet, and you plan to include a paragraph on fast-food restaurants. Use the data in the following table for source material, and write a paragraph tailored to your audience. How will you chunk the data? What inferences can you draw?

Now use the table for a different purpose. You are giving a talk to a group of heart patients who must follow a low-fat, low-salt diet, and you plan to mention fast food. Write a paragraph advising them of good and poor fast-food choices. A third way you could chunk the information in this table is in terms of food value per dollar. A survey of fast-food places in Pittsburgh in April of 1984 turned up these prices: a Big Mac is $1.30; Arthur Treacher's Fish Sandwich is $1.19; Long John Silver's Fish is $1.81; an Egg McMuffin is $.99; a Taco Bell taco is $.73; and a Dairy Queen Brazier Dog is $.79. Write a discussion of fast foods in terms of the best food for your money.

NUTRITIONAL CONTENT OF POPULAR FAST FOODS

Item	Calories	Protein (grams)	Carbohydrates (grams)	Fat (grams)	Sodium (milligrams)
HAMBURGERS					
McDonald's Big Mac	541	26	39	31	962
Burger Chef Hamburger	258	11	24	13	393
FISH					
Arthur Treacher's Fish Sandwich	440	16	39	24	836
Long John Silver's Fish (2 pieces)	318	19	19	19	not available
OTHER ENTREES					
McDonald's Egg Muffin	352	18	26	20	914
Taco Bell Taco	186	15	14	8	79
Dairy Queen Brazier Dog	273	11	23	15	868
SIDE DISHES					
Burger King French Fries	214	3	28	10	5
Arthur Treacher's Cole Slaw	123	1	11	8	266
McDonald's Chocolate Shake	364	11	60	9	329
McDonald's Apple Pie	300	2	31	19	414

Source: The New York Times, September 19, 1979. Copyright © 1979 by The New York Times Company. Reprinted by permission.

Extracts

Extract E6.3

Hamp-Lyons, L. and B. Healey. *Study Writing.* CUP, 1987, pp. 76/77.

A Using the following flow diagram as your guide, write a description of the process of producing china cups. When you plan your text, consider:
1 making the text interesting with a variety of sentence types;
2 whether and when you need to use sequencers, and which ones to use;
3 choices of active or passive voice, and of tenses.

Write two paragraphs, and begin the second paragraph with 'After the rough edges are smoothed off, the cups . . .'. *(This extract does not include the flow chart for the second paragraph).*

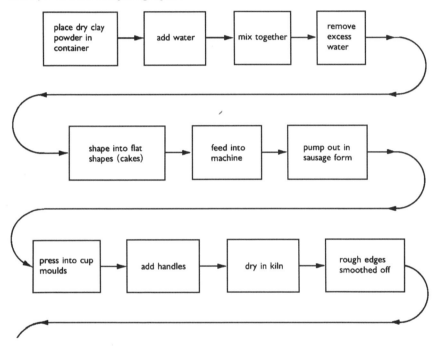

Extract E6.4

Swales, J. and C. Feak. *Academic Writing for Graduate Students.* University of Michigan Press, 1994, pp. 94/95.

[1]Table 11 shows the number of years to complete a doctoral program for both U.S. and international students at a major research university. [2]As can be seen, international students on average complete doctoral programs in less time than U.S. students in all divisions. [3]The difference in years to completion ranges from a relatively low 0.3 years in physical sciences/engineering and humanities/arts to a high of 2.8 years in individual departmental programs.

[4]The consistent difference in time to degree is not fully understood at present. [5]However, one key factor may be motivation. [6]Many international students have considerable external pressures, including sponsorship/scholarship restrictions, family obligations, and employer demands, which could influence the length of time it takes to earn a doctorate.

Here are the instructor's comments on the commentary. The instructor is a professor of comparative higher education. Mark the comments as reasonable (R) or unreasonable (U) and discuss your choices with a partner. If you find some comments reasonable, how would you edit the passage? There are no absolutely right or wrong answers here.

____ 1. In sentences 2, 3, and 4 you throw away the key finding that more rapid progress to degree *and* higher completion rates is consistently in favor of international students across all six divisions. You need to highlight this more.

____ 2. You need to stress that based on present knowledge, we can only *speculate* about the explanations. As it stands I find sentence 5 hard to interpret. Is it just your idea, or do you have any evidence for this claim?

____ 3. It is strange that you do not mention the English language factor. At least at first sight, this would seem to suggest that international students ought to be taking longer.

____ 4. Don't you think you ought to finish by suggesting ways of getting at the real causes of this striking phenomenon? Case studies? Interviews with faculty and students?

TABLE 11. Years to Doctorate for Doctoral Programs at University of Michigan, Ann Arbor, for Students Entering in 1981–83

Division	U.S. Citizens/Permanent Residents			International Students		
	N	% Ph.D.	Median Years to Ph.D.	N	% Ph.D.	Median Years to Ph.D.
Biological and health sciences	335	54	5.7	88	61	5.3
Physical sciences and engineering	469	44	5.3	430	55	5.0
Social sciences	409	35	6.0	80	59	5.3
Humanities and arts	373	33	5.3	91	53	5.0
Education	141	30	5.7	12	50	4.0
Individual departmental	16	38	6.5	4	50	3.7
Overall	1,743	41	5.3	705	56	5.0

Source: Horace H. Rackham School of Graduate Studies, University of Michigan.

Extracts

Extract E11.1

UCLES Business English Certificate 2, sample paper. 1997.

- You are taking your annual holiday at the beginning of next month and you will be out of the office for three weeks.
- Write a memo of **30–40 words** to your secretary, telling him/her:
  - when you are going on holiday and for how long
  - what should happen to your mail
  - what he/she should do in case of an emergency.
- **Write on your Answer Sheet.**

Extract E11.2

UCLES Business English Certificate 2, sample paper. 1997.

- You are the secretary in a company which makes plastic tableware. Your boss has left the letter below for you to answer.
- Write a letter of 100–200 **words** to Ms Jerome, explaining the reason for the damaged goods. Use the information in her letter and the notes from your boss.
- Do not include addresses.
- Write on your Answer Sheet.

Chris: Please write back to Ms Jerome with regrets, etc. We mustn't lose this customer! Thanks – Hugh.

QUALITY CAFETERIAS INC.
NEW ROAD
MELBOURNE

6 October 1997

The Manager
Plastic-A-Plenty Co.
Gough Industrial Estate
Melbourne

Dear Sir or Madam

PLASTIC TABLEWARE – Product nos. 0821 (forks) and 7234 (bowls)

5 years to be exact.

We have used your company as a supplier to our restaurants for several years, and until recently the quality of your products has always been good.

However, on 2 September this year, we took delivery of some plastic tableware which was of extremely poor quality. Many of the bowls were chipped and several of the forks were broken. We cannot use them in our cafeterias.

We will replace them free of charge.

I do hope that such a delivery will not be repeated, and that your supplies to us in the future will again be of high quality. If, however, we receive any further faulty plastic tableware from you, we will be obliged to find another supplier to provide us with goods which meet our own high standards. I am sure you will be able to provide us with a satisfactory explanation.

So do I! It was the faulty packing machine (now repaired).

Yours faithfully

Ann Jerome

A. Jerome
Restaurants Director

Tell her it won't happen again – she's an excellent customer, so please offer our apologies!

Extract E11.3

UCLES CEIBT Certificates in English for International Business and Trade. Specifications and sample material for the revised CEIBT. June 1998 onwards.

TASK 5

You have been asked to write a short article for Air Atlantic's staff newsletter, about the airline's business passengers. You have already noted down the topics you will cover in each paragraph, selected the relevant information to include, and highlighted the particular statistical information you wish to mention.

Now write your FOUR PARAGRAPHS, summarising the statistical information below.

Air Atlantic's Business Passengers
Topics to cover

1. *Recent trends in numbers of business passengers*
2. *Who flies business class (short-haul/long-haul flights)*
3. *Main destinations of business passengers*
4. *Numbers of aircraft with Business Class facilities*

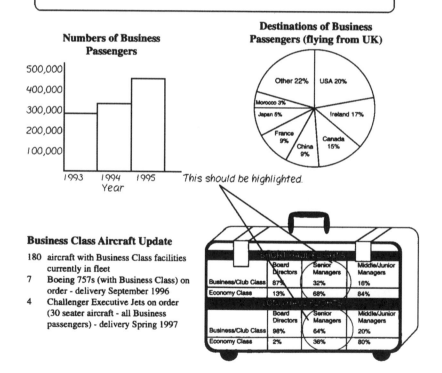

Numbers of Business Passengers

500,000
400,000
300,000
200,000
100,000

1993 1994 1995
Year

Destinations of Business Passengers (flying from UK)

Other 22% USA 20%
Morocco 3%
Japan 5% Ireland 17%
France 9% Canada 15%
China 9%

This should be highlighted.

Business Class Aircraft Update

180 aircraft with Business Class facilities currently in fleet
7 Boeing 757s (with Business Class) on order - delivery September 1996
4 Challenger Executive Jets on order (30 seater aircraft - all Business passengers) - delivery Spring 1997

SHORT-HAUL FLIGHTS

	Board Directors	Senior Managers	Middle/Junior Managers
Business/Club Class	87%	32%	16%
Economy Class	13%	68%	84%

LONG-HAUL FLIGHTS

	Board Directors	Senior Managers	Middle/Junior Managers
Business/Club Class	98%	64%	20%
Economy Class	2%	36%	80%

Extract E11.4

JMB *UETESOL*, June 1992.

Question 3A (15 marks)

Hylo Car Parks

Read the passage below and then answer the questions on pages 9 and 10 of the answer book.

1 A DESIGN ENGINEER from Plymouth plans to revolutionise multi-storey car parks.

2 Winston Harper-Douglas believes that the space between the roof of the car and the ceiling in the conventional multi-storey – at least one and a half metres – is wasted, and could be used to create extra parking capacity.

3 He calls his solution the Hylo car park. Like the conventional multi-storey, (where motorists drive inside and park their cars) it has cars stacked on many floors.

But where a traditional multi-storey might be 20 metres high and have six parking floors, a Hylo car park of the same height will have eight floors.

Extra capacity is also created because there is no longer a need for the driveways on each floor, which normally account for 30% of the entire floor area; the space saved will be used for parking.

In all, three times as many cars can be parked in an area of the same cubic capacity.

4 There is no access for motorists. Computerised lifts will bring cars up and down.

5 "Every car will be on its own pallet, and a central computer will move the cars around in a manner similar to the way letter blocks are moved in a child's hand-held word puzzle," says Harper-Douglas.

6 "All the technology is available on the market. By utilising it, I aim to take car parking into the 21st century."

7 In Harper-Douglas's vision motorists will drive their cars on to a small bogey at the car-park entrance, leave the car, key their registration number into a ticket machine, and then walk away, unaware of where their vehicles will be positioned.

8 The bogey will be shuttled through the car park by a series of computer-controlled lifts and a track guidance system, and be finally deposited in a space only marginally larger than the vehicle itself, almost like a product entering a warehouse.

9 Different sections of the car park will cater for short and long-term parkers as well as for cars of different heights and sizes.

10 On returning to the car park, the motorist will remain in the foyer, key his or her car number into the ticket machine, then wait for the computer to search for the car and request its retrieval. Harper-Douglas claims it will take a maximum of 1 minute 30 seconds for the car to be returned to the owner.

11 The Hylo car park has one great drawback – its huge cost, though Harper-Douglas claims that some of this will be offset by savings on land cost.

12 He also believes that the Hylo car park will eliminate accidents and thefts – a major problem in large multi-storey car parks at present – because motorists and other members of the public won't have access to the parking area.

13 The new car parks could appeal to property developers because offices could be built on top of them, with ample parking for the occupants.

14 "We aim to make everything as reliable as possible, says Harper-Douglas. Back-up generators, lifts and electronic scanners will ensure that should there by any problems, maintenance workers will be able to climb through the car park and fix the system.

15 Harper-Douglas has taken out a patent on the design. He says he has had serious discussions with developers for two large Hylo car parks in central London.

Section 3   Reading Skills

Question 3A (15 marks)

The passage for this question is on page 7 of the question paper.

1. From the list below select the 8 steps which refer to the way in which a Hylo car park would be used. Tick the boxes next to the letters you select.

(a) ☐   The motorist returns to the foyer.

(b) ☐   Car maintenance will be carried out if necessary.

(c) ☐   The motorist drives his or her car up through the car park.

(d) ☐   The car is returned to its owner.

(e) ☐   The motorist puts his or her keys into the ticket machine.

(f) ☐   The computer moves the car up through the car park.

(g) ☐   The car is deposited in its parking space.

(h) ☐   The motorist keys in his or her car number.

(i) ☐   The motorist drives his or her car into the lift.

(j) ☐   The computer finds the location of the car.

(k) ☐   The motorist re-enters his or her registration number in the ticket machine.

(l) ☐   The motorist drives his or her car onto a bogey.

Now place the letters you selected in the correct sequence to show the order in which they would occur in a Hylo car park.

1: _____ 2: _____ 3: _____ 4: _____ 5: _____ 6: _____ 7: _____ 8: _____

(6 marks)

2. Written below are some statements about car parks. Complete the table by putting **H** where the statement refers to **HYLO** car parks or **C** where the statement refers to **CONVENTIONAL** multi-storey car parks and by writing the paragraph number(s) in which the information occurs. If a statement does not refer to information given in the passage put **X** in BOTH boxes.

STATEMENT	Type of Car Park	Paragraph Number(s)
Theft is a problem		
They have driveways		
They are extremely expensive to build		
Car parks will be built in warehouses		
Drivers do not know where their cars are parked		
There is less than $1\frac{1}{2}$m of space between car and roof		

(6 marks)

3. The following is a brief description of a Hylo car park. Complete the summary by inserting ONE WORD or an appropriate NUMBER in each gap.

A Hylo is a design for a multi-storey car park which will provide parking for .... times more cars than a conventional car park of similar size. As the Hylo would reduce the gap between the floors, it would be possible for it to have .... extra floors for every six of a conventional car park. In the Hylo, each car would be moved around the car park on a .... , controlled by a .... and returned to its owner with a maximum delay of .... seconds. Back-up generators, lifts and electronic scanners would allow the system to be ....

(3 marks)

Extract E11.5

Weir, C. *Understanding and Developing Language Tests*. Prentice Hall, 1993,
pp. 53–54.

STUDENT'S PROMPT SHEET A

You will find below information on two cameras, A and B. Your friend has
information on two more cameras C and D. Your friend has won some money
in a competition and wants to buy a camera. Using the information you both
have, you must help him/her decide which camera to buy. Make sure you check
all the information before deciding. When you have finished discussing, you
should tell your teacher which camera you would buy, and why. Wait for the
other person to start the conversation

	Price	Weight (grams)	Size	Flash
Camera A	90	250	small	+
Camera B	80	300	medium	+

STUDENT'S PROMPT SHEET B

You have won some money in a competition and want to buy a camera. You
have £90 to spend. You will find below information on two cameras, C and D.
Your friend has information on two more cameras A and B. Using the
information you both have, you must decide which camera you would buy.
Make sure you check all the information before deciding. When you have
finished discussing you should tell your teacher which camera you would buy.
You must take the responsibility for starting the discussion and reaching a
decision. You only have ten minutes for this.

	Price	Weight (grams)	Size	Flash
Camera C	60	250	small	−
Camera D	80	550	small	+

Extract E11.6

JMB *UETESOL*, June 1990.

In this part of the test, you are going to hear the final part of a talk about *alternative medicine* once, followed by a question and answer session. As you listen you should take notes so that later you can:

BOX A

(i) Complete Table 1 on page 3.
   For the column *Condition*, use words or phrases from the list in Box A.
   For *Treatment*, give an example for each condition.
   For *Type*, write F (Folk), M (Medical), or T (Traditional).
   For the last column, write *yes*, *no*, or *sometimes*.
   Write X where no information is given.

BOX A
Any complaint
Asthma
Back pain
Baldness
Bone trouble
Cuts
Jaundice
Joints trouble
Malaria
Mental illness
Muscle pain
Sleeping problems

TABLE 1

	Condition	Treatment	Type	Is the treatment effective?
Answer 1				
Answer 2				
Answer 3				
Answer 4				

(ii) *Circle* the phrase or phrases, a–f, which best describe the doctor.

The doctor

a. spoke rudely   d. answered unhelpfully

b. spoke pleasantly   e. responded with sarcasm

c. answered clearly   f. responded with sensitivity

Extract E11.7

UCLES Business English Certificate 2, sample paper, 1997.

(Questions 13–17)

- You will hear five people talking about different topics.
- For each piece decide which topic A–H the speaker is talking about.
- Write **one** letter A–H next to the number of the piece.
- Do not use any letter more than once.
- You will hear the five pieces twice.

13. ....

14. ....

15. ....

16. ....

17. ....

A	Sales
B	Research and Development
C	Recruitment
D	Marketing
E	Productivity
F	Accounts
G	Training
H	Customer Relations

Extract 11.8

UCLES CEIBT Certificates in English for International Business and Trade. Specifications and sample material for the revised CEIBT. June 1998 onwards.

TASK 3

In Task Three you will hear a conversation about a proposed article on Ruiten's future activity. This article will feature in the annual report.

Listen to the conversation and note the main points the article will cover under the appropriate headings on the notepad.

You will hear the conversation TWICE. You will then have eight minutes to note the main points the article will cover.

Make rough notes in the space provided as you listen.

NOTEPAD
Points for Article

Personnel

- More training for new staff members
- Launch of Ruiten International Business school in 1997
- Central personnel office will only appoint key posts from 1 Jan 1997
- Local personnel offices to recruit local staff

General Outlook

-
-
-
-

Environmental Issues

-
-
-

Proposed Activity in Key Markets

-
-
-

Extracts

Extract E11.9

Draft question for in-house test.

You work in the marketing department of a company, Micov, that manufactures microwave ovens. Your market share has dropped recently, see figure a. Your market research findings into availability and after sales service are in figure b.

Write a memo for the marketing manager outlining the situation and recommending actions to improve the situation.

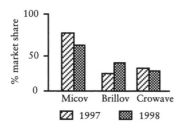

Figure a

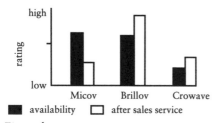

Figure b

Guidance for tasks

Chapter 1

Task 1b

1. Not an ESP class: main focus is on the language system rather than a work or study purpose. The aims of the course may be specific – concerned with aspects of grammar identified as weak – but this specificity is a rather different specificity from that of ESP. 2. An ESP course: based on a specific need, writing reports on design reports. 3. An ESP course: a specific need, the reading skill. 'Common-core' materials does not mean that this is an EGP course, rather that the focus is on the reading skill. 4. Not an ESP course: The Cambridge FCE examination is an EGP examination; there is a specific purpose but that purpose is related to General English. If learners are prepared for an ESP examination, then the course is ESP. 5. Not an ESP course, but it does have some features of an ESP course. The purpose, social English, and the range of linguistic features, is so broad that we do not feel that we can define this as an ESP course. If it was to develop a particular business relationships in particular cultural contexts then it would be ESP. 6. An ESP course of a very specific nature.

Task 1d

1. Position 2; 2. Position 4; 3. Position 3; 4. Probably Position 2; 5. Between Positions 2 and 3; 6. Position 5.

Task 1e

The real content is *identifying the key points* of the listening passage, the *language of sequence* and the *use of diagrams* to summarise the key points. The carrier content is *work measurement*.

Chapter 2

Task 2d

Clearly the answer depends on circumstances in the ESP situation. We believe that there are advantages in ESP teachers specialising, but not to the extent that they teach only one skill or in only one department or sector. Some variety and flexibility seems desirable, so we support the idea that teachers should concentrate on certain subject areas for a period of time.

EAP unit in department: Advantages = easier administration; possibility of considerable integration of the EAP work with the subject teaching. Danger = professional isolation. *Centralised unit*: opportunity to coordinate work; greater variety of teaching; professional development through joint research projects, seminars and general discussion. Perhaps the ideal is a combination of the two systems with EAP teachers based in one centre, but working in teams in key departments?

Chapter 3

Task 3b

Both students will need all the skills. Postgraduate MBA: lecture comprehension a major priority; reading comprehension fairly important; writing essays very important – the use of source material and avoiding excessive copying from those sources can be a problem so this will be a priority. PhD research student: less need of listening comprehension; priorities will be reading and writing; may well need some induction into the expectations of the department about research students and the relationship with the supervisor, so spoken interaction skills and language.

Task 3d

Different answers are possible. Our view is:

	Situation 1	Situation 2	Situation 3	Situation 4
Cooperation	Very feasible	Very feasible	Very feasible	Very feasible
Collaboration	Very feasible	Very feasible	Possible	Possible
Team-teaching	Very feasible	Possible	Possible	Unsuitable

The answers will always depend on the language unit's relationship with the subject departments.

Task 3e

The textbook extract: uses the *present simple* tense; uses very abstract language to describe the actual graph, for example 'This picturization of the demand schedule . . . Quantity, price, demand' become concepts that do things, that is move up and down. Elsewhere more concrete: the authors use '*we*' and the verb '*get*', and wheat, electric razors, cotton and so on as examples. Audience = students beginning economics, that is first year undergraduates or higher secondary school classes.

The bank review: a report, uses the *past simple* and *present perfect* tenses. The language used is that of *increase* and *decrease*. The inclusion of the names of the various countries makes the extract quite concrete, but much of the language of increase and decrease is abstract and impersonal. Audience = professionals in business and finance.

The implication for the teaching of English for economics is that we need to find exactly why students on such a course need English. Do they need to read undergraduate textbooks, articles, reports, economics journalism and so on?

Chapter 4

Reflection 4a

These are some suggestions that may be common to all situations. You will probably have some others which are specific to an organisation/country you know.

Teaching EGBP: you can develop relationships over time; you become familiar with material; you can have a regular pattern to lessons.

Teaching ESBP: you have to establish 'instant' relationships; you may use different material each time; there is no pattern to lessons/courses.

Provision for EGBP: you need regular intakes; teaching hours may concentrate in evenings – effect on use of rooms, staffing; you use class sets of books; you may have to organise the taking of public tests.

Provision for ESBP: block weeks of time; wide range of resources needed; more staff planning-time needed; groups may be smaller – effect on resources and costs.

Task 4b

For student M:

(a) Include writing skills – planning, grouping ideas, layout; developing business relationships and handling meetings; language – for describing current situations, making arrangements, expressing hopes and future outcomes; vocabulary development.

(b) Find out – about the meetings: purpose, topics, one-to-one or group, whether any difficulties regularly arise. Analyse faxes sent and received.

For student P:

(a) Meeting skills and language – agreeing purpose and process, turntaking, listening and checking, questioning, building relationships.
(b) Find out – purpose and role in meetings, whether documents are read/written in English, whether on project management or technical side. Level of spoken language.

Task 4d

Your responses will be specific to a particular country. Ours are for people coming to the UK for their course.

Course variables	Students in the UK	Business people
* group size	variable	small 1–8
* hours/day	one; six on pre-sessional courses	6–8
* materials / handouts	photocopies	printed + folder
* pace of classes	average	fast
* course length	1 semester/ 1 year	1 week
* learners' age	18–25	25–55
* physical facilities	chairs with arm-rest, lecture hall	small tables, chairs, OHP
* assessment procedures	formal exams (UK none)	none
* pre-course information	none	printed booklet
* quality and style of presentations	mixed	high
* appearance/dress of tutors	casual	smart

Task 4e

The Golden Rules of International Business

(From left to right: France, Germany, Italy, Switzerland, Sweden, Japan, Spain, Hungary, Britain.)

	F	D	I	CH	S	J	E	H	GB
Patience	5	8	3	5	2	2	5	3	5
Be on time	1	1	7	1	1	1	6	4	3
Smile	4	10	8	6	8	4	8	7	4
Introductions	2	2	1	3	5	8	1	1	6
Go drinking	10	9	10	10	9	3	10	6	9
Work late	8	7	5	7	7	5	2	10	7
Politics	6	5	4	8	6	9	4	2	8
Language	3	4	3	9	10	6	3	9	1
Dress	9	3	9	2	4	10	7	8	2
Directness	7	6	6	4	3	7	9	5	10

Like all statistics on attitudes and behaviour, the data in this table should be treated with caution. Remember that these rankings represent each nationality's view of itself – and to some extent the way each nationality would like itself to be viewed by outsiders. Nevertheless, the patterns that emerge are generally confirmed by outsiders – eg expatriates with long working experience in the cultures listed.

(Taken from *The New International Manager* by Vincent Guy and John Mattock, published by Kogan Page, 1993)

Chapter 5

Task 5b

The extract from the *biology textbook* uses a considerable amount of nominalisation. Consider the subjects of each sentence: *cell proliferation, protein malnutrition, an examination of . . ., these observations, other experiments . . .,* these are examples of nominalised forms. The text is very formal and contains no personal forms. It is about experiments and results rather than people. The reports of the experiments contain some hedging: the authors talk about it being 'difficult to show conclusively that this is also the case in humans', and in the conclusion they '*suggest* that protein malnutrition of children *may* permanently restrict their mental abilities'. The text uses a number of time markers such as *at that time* and *during this period*. It uses only one logical connector: *thus*.

The *memorandum* moves between a more formal and a more informal style; the formal style is marked by the use of impersonal expressions, such as 'advising you of minimum stock quantities, it is therefore imperative that . . .' The first person *I* is avoided, but the writer does use some personal forms '*my* memo, advising *you*, if *we* want to offer a good and smooth service'; *so that* and *therefore* are the logical connectors.

Task 5c

Readings is Category 4, *load* is Category 2, *extension* is Category 2, *plot* is Category 1, *worked* is Category 4, *rapidly* is Category 5, *proportionality* is Category 1 and *mild* is Category 1.

Task 5e

a) The semi-technical words in the biology text are: *proliferation, growth, occur, crucial, development, reflected, reduced, examination, showed, observations, confirmed, experiments, containing, deficient, capacity, controlled experiments, conclusively, score, counterparts, studies, suggest, permanently, restrict, abilities.*
The core business words in the memorandum are: *memo, advising, stock, export, customers, check, supply, incur delays, order, stock-out.*

b) Collocations biology text: *proliferation and growth occur, as reflected by, an examination of . . . shows, these observations confirmed, other experiments show . . ., deficient in their . . . capacity, show conclusively, these studies suggest.*
Business memorandum: *minimum stock quantities, checking stocks, kindly ensure that . . .* (but rather out-dated – please will/could you – more modern) *supply our customers, exhaust our stocks.*

c) Lexical phrases biology text: *are crucial to, as reflected by, an examination of . . . showed, our experiments show that . . ., it has been difficult to show that . . . these studies suggest.*
Business memorandum: *further to my memo* (though this phrase may be a little out-of-date and is best avoided), *advising you of quantities, kindly ensure that . . .* (again rather old-fashioned), *without incurring any delays, absolute minimum quantities, it is therefore imperative, these levels are respected or exceeded, is acted upon very promptly.*

Chapter 6

Task 6b

Some examples – you may have others.

advantages/disadvantages and *compare/contrast*: two lists, columns; *cause/effect*: diagram, two different shapes; *process*: flowchart; *physical structure*: diagram, sketch or photo of object; *numerical data*: graph, bar chart, table, pie chart; *location*: diagram, sketch map to show relative positions; *alternative procedures*: two parallel columns, two vertical flowcharts; *how something works*: diagram, variations on a flow chart.

Task 6d

Extract E6.1 (from Tony Lynch's *Study Listening*) shows an approach based on building up learners' control of micro-skills. Extract E1.2 (from Brieger and Comfort's *Business Management English Series*) shows a more task-oriented approach to listening.

Reflection 6e

a) uh, uh; really; that's interesting; tell me more; mmm; smile, up/down nod, lean forward, open gestures.

Task 6h

Voice: speed, loudness, variation, pausing, clarity of intonation and pronunciation; *Body Language*: appropriateness of gestures and movements, firm stance, smile; *Visuals*: introduction to, relevance of, pinpointing reason for, few words in and not reading them aloud; *Structure*: introduction sets scene, gives purpose, where going, time, how dealing with questions; logical, signposted points; powerful end; *Language*: no major misunderstandings, signposting, as appropriate and varied as reasonable; *Overall Impact*: impression of confidence, message came across, listeners included and not bored.

Task 6j

E 6.2 is an example of a *process* approach to teaching writing. It shows the writer how s/he should adapt the writing to allow for different readerships.

E 6.3 is an example of a *product* approach. Essentially students learn from a model, but have to think carefully about how to apply it. It is a good use of the model rather than the simplistic use we have criticised in the chapter.

E 6.4 is an example of a *social-constructionist* approach. The students have to think about their role as researchers and their relationship with their supervisor.

Chapter 7

Task 7a

TSA: 2, 5, 9; *LSA*: 1, 4, 6, 8; *PSA*: 3, 7, 10.

Task 7b

(a) *Current* and *future use* of English; also the standard of writing under, *your job*. (b) What participants want from the course; more on target events. (c) Yes, but keep to one piece of double-sided A4 paper.

Orientation 7c

One grouping is:

Source	Method
Documents	ESP research analysis, questions in structured interviews
Colleagues	discussion, record keeping
Learners, ex-students	questionnaires, structured interviews, assessment
People working	observation
Clients, employers	structured interviews, discussion

Task 7d

1 A double question. Respondents might need spoken or need written or need spoken and written. 2 Question and answer format do not match.

Either change the answer to yes / no; or (better) ask: How much . . .
3 Bias to question and value judgement; will the terms be understood?
Probably use several statements and a Likert scale. 4 Relevance? Could
you change the teacher or their qualification? Leave it out. 5 Will ESP
learners understand these terms? Use 1,2,3 for your first, second and
third choice: When you are talking and make a mistake do you like: a
classmate to correct you, the teacher to correct you, or the teacher to
give you a sign that there was a mistake? 6 Can you deliver? How much
can you offer? Leave it out.

Task 7e

a) one possibility: 3 low . . . high; 4 little . . . a great deal; 5 too/very
   slow . . . too/very fast; 6 poor . . . excellent;
b) these will depend on the lesson you chose. For example, a reading
   lesson could ask about text length: very short . . . very long; text
   topic: boring . . . interesting; exercise: easy . . . difficult; or waste of
   time . . . very useful.

Chapter 8

Task 8b

Case Study 1
GEC Dunchurch

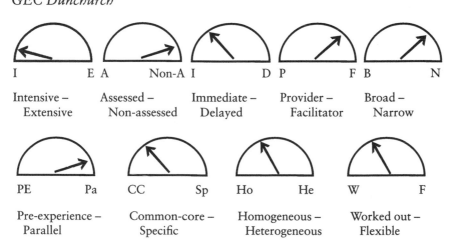

I   E A   Non-A I   D P   F B   N

Intensive –   Assessed –   Immediate –   Provider –   Broad –
Extensive   Non-assessed   Delayed   Facilitator   Narrow

PE   Pa   CC   Sp   Ho   He   W   F

Pre-experience –   Common-core –   Homogeneous –   Worked out –
Parallel   Specific   Heterogeneous   Flexible

Guidance for tasks

Case Study 2
JUST

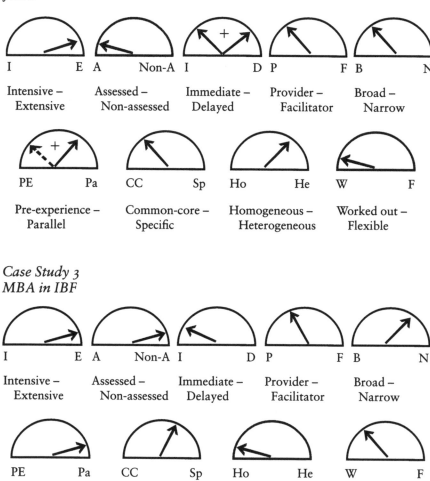

I E	A Non-A	I D	P F	B N
Intensive –	Assessed –	Immediate –	Provider –	Broad –
Extensive	Non-assessed	Delayed	Facilitator	Narrow

PE Pa	CC Sp	Ho He	W F
Pre-experience –	Common-core –	Homogeneous –	Worked out –
Parallel	Specific	Heterogeneous	Flexible

Case Study 3
MBA in IBF

I E	A Non-A	I D	P F	B N
Intensive –	Assessed –	Immediate –	Provider –	Broad –
Extensive	Non-assessed	Delayed	Facilitator	Narrow

PE Pa	CC Sp	Ho He	W F
Pre-experience –	Common-core –	Homogeneous –	Worked out –
Parallel	Specific	Heterogeneous	Flexible

Task 8c

Case study	Target events
JUST course 111	reading academic material; writing laboratory reports; listening to lectures / writing assignments
Research scientists, India	publishing in English-medium international journals
Dunchurch	giving effective presentations; handling meetings effectively
University of Birmingham MSc in IBF	writing good assignments

Task 8e

Some of the areas we covered in these courses are given below. Our grid can be extended to include a column in which suitable materials (some were mentioned in the case studies) are noted alongside the relevant feature.

Case study	Target event	Skills areas	Language		Other
			Grammar	Vocabulary	
Dunchurch	handling meetings effectively	controlling, agreeing the process, turntaking		lexical phrases	
		listening to others, asking good questions	question types		paraphrasing

Reflection 8f

Wilberg and Lewis: no activities (it is not the purpose of their book) but provide stimulus and space for a learner to add language s/he could use. They cover tenses, prepositional phrases, time phrases, vocabulary. They do not consider the moves and sociological aspects such as attitude and strength of claim. Good when you have the confidence / situation to work from learners' carrier content and framework material or to supplement material which provides practice activities (for example Panorama).

Panorama: mainly writing practice with some vocabulary input and discussion of the order of information. The guided passages progress from filling in words to completing sentences to writing guided paragraphs. The exploitation of the passages would need to encourage wider discussion and some learners would want additional activities to practise areas of weakness.

Swales and Feak: the most extensive section on data comment; do not cover tenses; provide a wide variety of activities, from analysis of information and attitude to language practice to discussion and writing part or a full data commentary. This material works well when there is plenty of time, so on long extensive or intensive courses when some reading and activity is carried out in non-teaching time.

Chapter 9

Orientation 9a

Reason: source of language; *implications*: provide plenty of varied input; provide full range; use real not invented examples.

Reason: as a learning support; *implications*: reliable; consistent; with recognisable patterns; builds/develops.

Reason: for motivation and stimulation; *implications*: challenging; new; achievable; creative; linked to learners' reality.

Reason: for reference; *implications*: self-explanatory; well laid out; complete; with explanations; with an answer key.

Task 9f

(a)

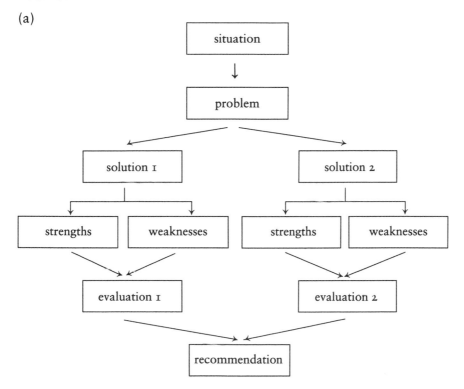

Alternatively:

	situation + problem	
Solutions	strengths	weaknesses
solution 1		
solution 2		
	recommendation	

(b) *oral presentation*: Who am I? Who are the audience? What is my (business) relationship with the audience? Where are we? Why am I giving this presentation?
written report: Who am I? Who are the readers? What is my (business) relationship with the readers? What kind of document am I writing? Why am I writing this document?

Chapter 10

Orientation 10d

Give undivided attention, record and transcribe spoken language, reformulate as appropriate; respond rather than control, go at the learner's pace, allow learner to direct; design course and materials for individual needs, shift activity or focus to suit the individual.

Chapter 11

Task 11e

(a) Suitability will depend on target group – content/level; does test comparison/contrast; also tests writing recommendations.

Reflection 11f

a) $E_{11.1}$: audience – your secretary (perhaps unrealistic as you would use your L_1?); purpose – inform. $E_{11.2}$: audience – valuable customer; purpose – apologise. $E_{11.3}$: audience – airline staff; purpose – inform. More focus might help writers decide the amount of detail to include. Also, the real article would probably include one or more of the visuals, say the bar chart and pie chart, with comments, in preference to writing a prose version of the numerical data.

Task 11g

a) We think not.
b) in Q_1 selecting is necessary before ordering; in Q_2 paragraph numbers are required, to show understanding.
c) possibly in $E_{11.4}$ no. 3 for example for last item: fixed, repaired. Possibilities very limited so answer scheme could be objective.
d) Q_1) l,h,f,g,a,k,j,d;
   Q_2)C,12; C,3; H,11; X,X; H,7; X,X;
   Q_3) three/3; two/2; bogey/pallet; computer; ninety/90; maintained/fixed.
   The mark scheme for Q_1 is tricky: there must be some marks for getting the 8 steps and some for the order. What will you do when parts of the sequence but not the whole are correct? One option is to give 7 (not 6) marks: half for each correct step and 1 for each sequence of three correct letters. Then for Q_2 give one mark for

each line with both car park type and paragraph number correct and half for each of the two X lines (5 not 6 marks). But what do you do if students write out the car park type in full, instead of giving just the initial? A decision based on circumstances must be made before marking: either allow or penalise, for example one mark for not following instructions. Q3 is half a mark for each word. But what will you do about misspelt words? At the level of the original exam correct spelling would be expected.

Task 11i

a) we think not
b) more responses than questions in E11.6 and E11.7
c) in E11.8

References

Adams, P., B. Heaton and P. Howarth. 1991. *Socio-cultural Issues in English for Academic Purposes. Review of ELT*, vol. 1 no. 2. London: Macmillan, Modern English Publications in association with The British Council.

Adams-Smith, D. 1984. Medical discourse: aspects of authors' comments. *The ESP Journal*, 3: 25–36.

Alderson, J. C. 1984. Reading in a foreign language: a reading problem or a language problem?. In J. C. Alderson and A. H. Urquhart (Eds.) *Reading in a Foreign Language*. London: Longman.

Alderson, J. C. 1988. Testing English for specific purposes: how specific can we get?. In A. Hughes (Ed.) *Testing English for University Study. ELT Documents 127*.

Alderson, J. C. 1995. *Language Testing in the 90s*. Hemel Hempstead: Prentice Hall International.

Alderson, J. C. and A. Beretta. 1992. *Evaluating Second Language Education* Cambridge: Cambridge University Press.

Alderson, J. C. and M. Scott. 1992. Insiders, outsiders and participatory evaluation. In J. C. Alderson and A. Beretta (Eds.) *Evaluating Second Language Education*. Cambridge: Cambridge University Press, pp. 25–58.

Alderson, C. and A. H. Urquhart. 1984. *Reading in a Foreign Language*. London: Longman.

Alderson, J. C. and A. H. Urquhart. 1985. This test is unfair: I'm not an economist. In P. C. Hauptman, R. Le Blanc and M. B. Wesche (Eds.) *Second Language Performance Testing*. Ottawa: University of Ottawa Press.

Allen, J. P. B. and H. Widdowson (Eds.). 1974 and later years. *English in Focus Series*. Oxford: Oxford University Press.

Allison, D. 1996. Pragmatist discourse and English for Academic Purposes. *English for Specific Purposes*, 15: 85–104.

Allwright, J. M., R. Clark and A. Marshall-Lee. 1996. Developing a critical approach to study. In M. Hewings and A. Dudley-Evans (Eds.) *Evaluation and Course Design in EAP. Review of English Language Teaching*, 6. Hemel Hempstead: Prentice Hall Macmillan in association with The British Council.

Allwright, R. L. 1988. *Observation in the Language Classroom*. London: Longman.

Allwright, R. L. 1989. *Reports no. 3 and 12 of the LLLLLC Project*. Leeds: University of Leeds.

Allwright, R. L., M-P. Woodley and J. M. Allwright. 1988. Investigating reformulation as a practical strategy for the teaching of academic writing. *Applied Linguistics*, 9: 236–56.

Bachman, L. and A. S. Palmer. 1996. *Language Testing in Practice*. Oxford: Oxford University Press.

Backhouse, R. 1993. The debate over Milton Friedman's theoretical framework: an economist's view. In W. Henderson, A. Dudley-Evans and R. Backhouse (Eds.) *Economics and Language*. London: Routledge.

Badger, I. and P. Menzies. 1993. *The Macmillan Business English Program*. Hemel Hempstead: Macmillan.

Baker, M. 1988. Sub-technical vocabulary and the ESP teacher: an analysis of some rhetorical items in medical journal articles. *Reading in a Foreign Language*, 4: 91–105.

Barbara, L., M. A. A. Celani, H. Collins and M. Scott. 1996. A survey of communication patterns in the Brazilian business context. In M. J. St. John and C. Johnson (Eds.) *Special Issue: Business English. English for Specific Purposes*.

Barber, C. L. 1962. Some measurable characteristics of modern scientific prose. In *Contributions to English Syntax and Philology*. Reprinted in J. M. Swales (Ed.) 1988. *Episodes in ESP*.

Barham, K. and D. Oates. 1991. *International Manager: Creating Successful International Companies*. London: Business Books.

Bates, M. 1978. Writing Nucleus. In R. Mackay and A. Mountford (Eds.) *English for Specific Purposes*. London: Longman.

Bates, M. and A. Dudley-Evans. 1976. *Nucleus: General Science*. London: Longman.

Bazerman, C. 1988. *Shaping Written Knowledge*. Madison, Wisc: University of Wisconsin Press.

Bazerman, C. and J. Paradis. 1991. *Textual Dynamics of the Professions*. Madison, Wisc: University of Wisconsin Press.

BBC/ELTDU. 1972. *English for Business/ The Bellcrest File*. Oxford: Oxford University Press.

Belbin, M. 1996. *Management Teams – Why They Succeed or Fail*. Oxford: Heinemann.

Belcher, D. and G. Braine. 1995. *Academic Writing in a Second Language. Essays on Research and Pedagogy*. Norwood, NJ: Ablex Publishing Corporation.

Bell, J. 1987. *Doing Your Research Project*. Milton Keynes: Open University Press.

References

Benesch, S. 1996. Needs analysis and curriculum in EAP: an example of a critical approach. *TESOL Quarterly*, 30: 723–38.

Berger, M. and M. J. St. John. 1993. Communication, content and skills in intercultural training. *Language and Intercultural Training*, 14: 4–5.

Berkenkotter, C. and T. Huckin. 1995. *Genre Knowledge in Disciplinary Communication: Cognition/Culture/Power*. Hillsdale, NJ: Lawrence Erlbaum Assoc.

Berwick, R. 1989. Needs assessment in language programming: from theory to practice. In R. K. Johnson (Ed.) *The Second Language Curriculum*. Cambridge: Cambridge University Press.

Bhatia, V. K. 1982. An investigation into formal and functional characteristics of qualifications in legislative writing and its application to English for Academic Legal Purposes. Unpublished PhD thesis, Aston University.

Bhatia, V. K. 1983. *Applied Discourse Analysis of English Legislative Writing*. A Language Studies Unit Research Report, Aston University.

Bhatia, V. K. 1987. Language of the law. *Language Teaching*, 20: 227–234.

Bhatia, V. K. 1993. *Analysing Genre*. London: Longman.

Biber, D. 1988. *Variation across Speech and Writing*. New York: Cambridge University Press.

Biber, D., S. Conrad and R. Rappen. 1994. Corpus-based approaches to issues in applied lignuistics. *Applied Linguistics* 15: 168–9.

Bizzell, P. 1982. College composition: initiation into the academic discourse community. Review of *Four worlds of writing* and *Writing in the arts and sciences*. *Curriculum Inquiry*, 12: 191–207.

Bley-Vroman, R. and L. Selinker. 1984. Research design in rhetorical/grammatical studies: a proposed optimal research strategy. *English for Specific Purposes*. Oregon State University, 82–83: 1–4 and 86: 1–6.

Bloor, M. and T. Bloor. 1993. How economists modify propositions. In W. Henderson, A. Dudley-Evans and R. Backhouse (Eds.) *Economics and Language*. London: Routledge.

Bloor, T. and M. J. St John. 1988. Project writing: the marriage of process and product. In P. Robinson *Academic Writing: Process and Product*. ELT Documents 129.

Blue, G. 1988a. Individualising academic writing tuition. In P. Robinson (Ed.) *Academic Writing: Process and Product*. ELT Documents 129.

Blue, G. 1988b. Self-assessment: the limits of learner independence. In A. Brookes and P. Grundy (Eds.). 1988. *Individualization and Autonomy in Language Learning*. ELT Documents 131.

Blue, G. 1993. *Language, Learning and Success: Studying through English*. *Developments in ELT*. London: Macmillan, Modern English Teacher and the British Council.

Bolton, J. K. 1988. Larger is sometimes better: approaches to larger classes. Paper presented at the 22nd annual TESOL Convention, Chicago, March 1988.

Bowyers, R. 1980. War stories and romances. In *Projects in Materials Design. ELT Documents Special.*

Brazil, D. 1985. *The Communicative Value of Intonation. Discourse Analysis Monographs,* no. 8. Birmingham: English Language Research, The University of Birmingham.

Brieger, N. 1997. *Teaching Business English Handbook,* York Assoc. Publ.

Brieger, N. and S. Sweeney. 1994. *The Language of Business English.* Hemel Hempstead: Prentice Hall International.

Brindley, G. P. 1989. The role of needs analysis in adult ESL programme design. In R. K. Johnson (Ed.) *The Second Language Curriculum.* Cambridge: Cambridge University Press.

Brinton, D. M., A. Snow and M. B. Wesche. 1989. *Content-Based Second Language Instruction.* New York: Newbury House Publishers.

The British Council. 1980. *Team Teaching in ESP. ELT Documents,* 106 London: ETIC.

Brookes, A. and P. Grundy. 1988. *Individualization and Autonomy in Language Learning. ELT Documents* 131. London: Modern English Publications in association with The British Council.

Brookes, A. and P. Grundy. 1990. *Writing for Study Purposes.* Cambridge: Cambridge University Press.

Brown, D. 1994. *Teaching by Principles.* Hemel Hempstead: Prentice Hall International.

Brown, J. D. 1989. Language program evaluation: a synthesis of existing possibilities. In R. K. Johnson (Ed.) *The Second Language Curriculum.* Cambridge: Cambridge University Press.

Brown, V. 1993. Decanonizing discourses: textual analysis and the history of economic thought. In W. Henderson, A. Dudley-Evans and R. Backhouse (Eds.) *Economics and Language.* London: Routledge.

Buck, G. 1992. Listening comprehension: construct validity and trait characteristics. *Language Learning,* 42: 313–57.

Candlin, C., C. J. Bruton and J. H. Leather. 1976. Doctors in casualty: applying communicative competence to components of specialist course design. *IRAL,* 14: 245–72.

Candlin, C., C. J. Bruton, J. H. Leather and E. G. Woods, 1981. Designing modular materials for communicative language learning; an example: doctor-patient communication skills. In L. Selinker, E. Tarone and V. Hanzeli (Eds.) *English for Academic and Technical Purposes: Studies in Honour of Louis Trimble.* Rowley, MA: Newbury House.

Carrell, P. 1983. Some issues in studying the role of schemata, or background knowledge, in second language comprehension. *Reading in a Foreign Language,* 1: 81–92.

Carrell, P., J. Devine and D. Eskey (Eds.), 1988. *Interactive Approaches to Second Language Reading.* Cambridge: Cambridge University Press.

References

Carter, R. and M. McCarthy. 1988. *Vocabulary and Language Teaching*. London: Harlow.

Carroll, B. J. 1980. *Testing Communicative Performance: an Interim Study*. Oxford: Pergamon.

Carroll, B. J. and P. J. Hall 1985. *Make Your Own Language Tests*. Oxford: Pergamon.

Cauldwell, R. 1996. Direct encounters with fast speech to teach listening. *System*, 24: 521–528.

Celani, M. A. A., J. L. Holmes, R. C. G. Ramos and M. R. Scott. 1988. *The Brazilian ESP Project: an Evaluation*. São Paulo: Editoria de PUC-SP.

Chambers, F. 1980. A re-evaluation of needs analysis. *ESP Journal*, 1: 25–33.

Charles, D. 1984. The use of case studies in Business English. In G. James (Ed.) *The ESP Classroom. Exeter Linguistic Studies*, 7. Exeter: University of Exeter.

Charles, M. 1994. Layered negotiations in business: interdependencies between discourse and the business relationship. Unpublished PhD thesis, The University of Birmingham.

Charles, M. 1996. Business negotiations: interdependence between discourse and the business relationship. *English for Specific Purposes*, 15: 19–36.

Chaudron, C., L. Loschky and J. Cook. 1995. Second language listening comprehension and lecture note-taking. In J. Flowerdew (Ed.) *Academic Listening: Research Perspectives*. Cambridge: Cambridge University Press.

Cheung, D. and I. Wong. 1988. The communication skills and ESP interface: the course at the Nanyang Technological Institute, Singapore. In M. Tickoo (Ed.) *ESP: State of the Art. RLC Anthology Series*, 21. SEAMEO Regional Language Centre, Singapore.

Chrispeels, M. J. and D. Sadava. 1977. *Plants, Food and People*. San Francisco: W. H. Freeman.

Chukwuma, H., T. Obah, P. Robinson and M. J. St John 1991. A comparative study of communicative skills projects: factors affecting success. Paper presented at the 1991 BALEAP Conference, Southampton University, UK.

Clapham, C. 1996. *The Development of the IELTS: a Study of the Effect of Background on Reading Comprehension*. Cambridge: Cambridge University Press.

Coleman, H. 1988. *Report no. 4 of the LLLLLC Project*. Leeds: University of Leeds.

Coleman, H. 1997. 'Teaching large classes and training for sustainability'. In A. Abbott and M. Beaumont (Eds.) *The Development of ELT: The Dunford Seminars 1978–1993*. Hemel Hempstead: Prentice Hall Macmillan in association with the British Council.

Collins Cobuild Basic Grammar, Glasgow: Collins, 1995.

Comfort, J. and D. Utley. 1995. *Effective Presentations*. Oxford: Oxford University Press.

Connor, U. 1996. *Contrastive Rhetoric: Cross-cultural Aspects of Second Language Writing.* Cambridge: Cambridge University Press.

Cotton, D. and R. Owen. 1980. *Agenda.* London: Harrap.

Coulthard, M. and M. C. Ashby. 1976. A linguistic description of doctor-patient interviews. In M. Wadsworth and D. Robinson (Eds.) *Studies in Everyday Medical Life.* London: Martin Robertson.

Crofts, J. N. 1977. Subjects and objects in ESP teaching materials. Paper presented to the Second Regional ESP Conference, held in Isfahan, November 1997, cited in J. M. Swales (1980).

Crookes, G. 1986. Towards a validated analysis of scientific text structure. *Applied Linguistics,* 7: 57–70.

Cunningsworth, A. 1995. *Choosing Your Coursebook.* Oxford: Heinemann.

Davies, F. and T. Greene. 1984. *Reading for Learning in the Sciences.* London: Oliver & Boyd.

Dillon, G. 1991. *Contending Rhetorics.* Bloomington: University of Indiana Press.

Douglas, D. 1977. *From School to University.* Khartoum, Sudan: Khartoum University Press.

Drucker, P. F. 1991. *Management Tasks, Responsibilities and Practices.* Oxford: Heinemann.

Drucker, P. F. 1993. *Managing for the Future.* Oxford: Heinemann.

Dubois, B. L. 1980. The use of slides in biomedical speeches. *English for Specific Purposes,* 1: 45–50.

Dubois, B. L. 1981. Non-technical arguments in biomedical speeches. *Perspectives in Biology and Medicine,* 24: 399–410.

Dubois, B. L. 1985. Popularization at the highest level: poster sessions at biomedical meetings. *International Journal of the Sociology of Language,* 56: 67–85.

Dubois, B. L. 1987. Something in the order of around forty to forty four: imprecise numerical expressions in biomedical slide talks. *Language in Society,* 16: 527–41.

Duckworth, M. 1995. *Grammar and Practice.* Oxford: Oxford University Press.

Dudley-Evans, A. 1984. The team-teaching of writing skills. In R. Williams, J. M. Swales and J. Kirkman (Eds.) *Common Ground: Shared Interests in ESP and Communication Studies. ELT Documents,* 117.

Dudley-Evans, A. 1987a. *Genre Analysis and ESP. ELR Journal* no. 1. Birmingham: ELR.

Dudley-Evans, A. 1987b. The use of an ESP textbook in Egyptian secondary schools. In J. M. Swales and H. Mustafa (Eds.) *English for Specific Purposes in the Arab World.* Birmingham: Language Studies Unit, Aston University.

Dudley-Evans, A. 1993. The debate over Milton Friedman's theoretical framework: an applied linguist's view. In W. Henderson, A. Dudley-Evans and R. Backhouse (Eds.) *Economics and Language.* London: Routledge.

Dudley-Evans, A. 1994. Genre analysis: an approach to text analysis for ESP. In M. Coulthard (Ed.) *Advances in Written Text Analysis*. London: Routledge.

Dudley-Evans, A. 1995. Common-core and specific approaches to the teaching of academic writing. In D. Belcher and G. Braine (Eds.) *Academic Writing in a Second Language*. Norwood, NJ: Ablex Publishing Corporation.

Dudley-Evans, A. and W. Henderson. 1990. *The Language of Economics: the Analysis of Economics Discourse*. ELT Documents no. 134. London: Modern English Publications in association with The British Council.

Dudley-Evans, A. and T. F. Johns. 1981. A team-teaching approach to lecture comprehension. In *The Teaching of Listening Comprehension. ELT Documents Special*. Oxford: Pergamon in association with The British Council.

Dudley-Evans, A. and M. J. St John. 1996. *Report on Business English: A Review of Research and Published Teaching Materials. TOEIC Research Report* no. 2. Princeton, NJ: The Chauncey Group International.

Dunn, R. and S. Griggs. 1990. Research on the learning style characteristics of selected racial and ethnic groups. *Reading, Writing and Learning Disabilities*, 6: 261–80.

Ellis, M., N. O'Driscoll and A. Pilbeam. 1987 onwards. *Longman Business English Skills Series*. London: Longman.

Ellis, M. and C. Johnson. 1994. *Teaching Business English*. Oxford: Oxford University Press.

Ewer, J. and G. Latorre. 1969. *A Course in Basic Scientific English*. London: Longman.

Ewer, J. and G. Hughes-Davies. 1971, 1972. Further notes on developing an English programme for students of science and technology. *English Language Teaching*, 26, 1 and 3. Reprinted in J. M. Swales (Ed.) *Episodes in ESP*.

Fairclough, N. 1989. *Language and Power*. London: Longman.

Fairclough, N. 1992. *Discourse and Social Change*. Cambridge: Polity Press.

Firth, A. 1995. *The Discourse of Negotiation: Studies of Language in the Workplace*. Oxford: Pergamon.

Fisher, R and W. Ury. 1981. *Getting to Yes*. New York: Houghton Mifflin and Co.

Flower, L. 1985. *Problem Solving Strategies for Writing*. 2nd ed. San Diego: Harcourt Brace Jovanovich.

Flowerdew, J. 1994. *Academic Listening: Research Perspectives*. Cambridge: Cambridge University Press.

Flowerdew, L. 1995. Designing CALL courseware for an ESP situation: a report on a case study. *English for Specific Purposes*, 14: 19–36.

Flowerdew, L. (in press) CALL Materials derived from integrating 'expert' and 'interlanguage' corpora findings. *English for Specific Purposes*.

Foley, J. 1979. Problems of understanding science and technological textbooks in English for first year students at the University of Petroleum and Minerals. Unpublished PhD thesis, University of London.

Furneaux, C., C. Locke, P. Robinson and A. Tonkyn. 1991. Talking heads and shifting bottoms: the ethnography of seminars. In P. Adams, B. Heaton and P. Howarth (Eds.) *Socio-cultural Issues in English for Academic Purposes. Review of English Language Teaching*, 1:2. London: Modern English Teacher in association with The British Council.

Gains, J. 1998. Electronic mail – a new style of communication or just a new medium? An investigation into the text features of email. *English for Specific Purposes*.

Ghadessy, M. 1979. Frequency counts, word lists and materials preparation: a new approach. *Forum*, 17: 24–7.

Gilbert, G. N. and M. Mulkay. 1984. *Opening Pandora's Box: a Sociological Analysis of Scientific Discourse*. Cambridge: Cambridge University Press.

Grabe, W. 1993. Current developments in second language reading research. In S. Silberstein (Ed.) *State of the Art. TESOL Essays*. Alexandria, Virginia: TESOL.

Graves, G. F. 1975. Communication and language. *ETIC Archives*.

Grellet, F. 1981. *Developing Reading Skills*. Cambridge: Cambridge University Press.

Grice, H. P. 1975. Logic and conversation. In P. Cole and J. L. Morgan (Eds.) *Syntax and Semantics 3: Speech and Acts*. New York: Academic Press.

Griffiths, R. 1990. Speech rate and NNS comprehension: a preliminary study in time-benefit analysis. *Language Learning*, 40: 311–336.

Guy, V. and J. Mattock. 1993. *The New International Manager*. London: The Kogan Press.

Halliday, M. 1985. *An Introduction to Functional Grammar*. London: Arnold.

Halliday, M., P. Strevens, and A. McIntosh. 1964. *The Linguistic Sciences and Language Teaching*. Oxford: Oxford University Press.

Halliday, M. and J. Martin. 1993. *Writing Science*. London: The Falmer Press.

Hamp-Lyons, L. 1991. *Assessing Second Language Writing in Academic Contexts*. Norwood, NJ: Ablex.

Handy, C. 1992. *Understanding Organizations*. Harmondsworth, UK: Penguin 3rd edition.

Harper, D. 1986. *ESP for the University. ELT Documents* 123.

Heaton, B. 1988. *Writing English Language Tests*. London: Longman.

Henderson, W. 1982. Metaphor in economics. *Economics*. Reprinted in M. Coulthard (Ed.) *Talking about Text. Discourse Analysis Monographs* no. 13, English Language Research, The University of Birmingham, 1986.

Henderson, W. and A. Hewings. 1987. *Reading Economics: How Text Helps or Hinders*. British National Bibliography Research Fund Report 28.

Henderson, W. and A. Hewings. 1990. 'A Language of Model Building? In A. Dudley-Evans and W. Henderson (Eds.) *The Language of Economics: The Analysis of Economics Discourse. ELT Documents* 134. London: Modern English Publications in association with The British Council.

References

Henderson, W. and P. Skehan. 1980. The team-teaching of introductory economics to overseas students. In *Team Teaching in ESP. ELT Documents* 106.

Henry, A. 1996. Natural chunks of language: teaching speech through speech. *English for Specific Purposes*, 15: 295–309.

Herbert, A. J. 1965. *The Structure of Technical English*. London: Longman.

Herbolich, J. B. 1979. Box kites. *English for Specific Purposes*. English Language Institute, Oregon State University no. 29. Reprinted in J. M. Swales (Ed.) *Episodes in ESP*. Hemel Hempstead: Prentice Hall International.

Hewings, A. 1990. Aspects of the language of economics textbooks. In A. Dudley-Evans and W. Henderson (Eds.) *The Language of Economics: The Analysis of Economics Discourse. ELT Documents* 134. London: Modern English Teacher in association with The British Council.

Hewings, M. and A. Dudley-Evans. 1996. *Evaluation and Course Design in EAP*. Review of ELT, vol. 6 no. 1. Hemel Hempstead: Prentice Hall Macmillan in association with The British Council.

Higgins, J. J. 1966. Hard facts (notes on teaching English to science students). *English Language Teaching*, 21: 55–60. Reprinted in J. M. Swales (Ed.) *Episodes in ESP*. Hemel Hempstead: Prentice Hall International, 1988.

Higgins, J. J. and T. F. Johns. 1984. *Computers in Language Learning*. Glasgow: Collins.

Hindmarsh, R. 1980. *Cambridge English Lexicon*. Cambridge: Cambridge University Press.

Hinds, J. 1987. Reader versus writer responsibility: a new typology. In U. Connor and R. B. Kaplan (Eds.) *Writing Across Languages: Analysis of L2 Text*. Reading, MA: Addison-Wesley.

Hoey, M. 1983. *On the Surface of Discourse*. London: Allen & Unwin.

Hofstede, G. 1983. *Culture's Consequences: International Differences in Work-Related Values*. Beverley Hills, CA: Sage.

Hofstede, G. 1980. *Cultures and Organisations: Software of the Mind*. New York: McGraw Hill.

Holden, B. 1993. Analysing corporate training needs – a three way approach. *Language and Intercultural Training*, 14: 4–6.

Hollett, V. 1991. *Business Objectives*. Oxford: Oxford University Press.

Holliday, A. 1995. Assessing language needs within an institutional context: an ethnographic approach. *English for Specific Purposes*, 14: 115–126.

Holliday, A. and T. Cooke. 1982. An ecological approach to ESP. In *Issues in ESP*. Lancaster Practical Papers in English Language Education 5. Lancaster: Lancaster University, pp. 123–43.

Hopkins, A. and A. Dudley-Evans. 1988. A genre-based investigation of the discussion sections in articles and dissertations. *English for Specific Purposes*, 7: 113–22.

Hosenfeld, C. 1977. A preliminary investigation of the reading strategies of successful and non-successful second language learners. *System*, 5: 110–23.

Houghton, D. 1980. A collaborative approach to the teaching of vocabulary for accounting students. In *Team Teaching in ESP. ELT Documents* 106. London: ETIC Publications, The British Council.

Houghton, D. and R. G. Wallace. 1980. *Students' Accounting Vocabulary*. London: Gower Press.

Howatt, A. P. R. 1984. *A History of English Language Teaching*. Oxford: Oxford University Press.

Howe, B. 1984. *Visitron: The Language of Meetings and Negotiations*. London: Longman.

Howe, P. 1990. The problem of the problem question in English for Academic Legal Purposes. *English for Academic Purposes*, 9: 215–36.

Howe, P. 1993. Planning a pre-sessional course in English for Academic Legal Purposes. In G. Blue (Ed.) *Language, Learning and Success: Studying Through English*. Developments in English Language Teaching. London: Modern English Teacher in association with The British Council.

Huckin, T. and L. Olsen. 1991. *Technical Writing and Professional Communication for Nonnative Speakers of English*. 2nd ed. New York: McGraw Hill.

Huggett, R. 1990. *Business Case Studies*. Cambridge: Cambridge University Press.

Hughes, A. 1989. *Testing for Language Teachers*. Cambridge: Cambridge University Press.

Hutchinson, T., A. Waters and M. Breen. 1979. An English Language Curriculum for Technical Students. *Practical Papers in English Language Education*, vol. 2, University of Lancaster.

Hutchinson, T. and A. Waters. 1980a. ESP at the crossroads. *English for Specific Purposes*. Oregon State University, 36: 1–6. Reprinted in J. M. Swales (Ed.) *Episodes in ESP*.

Hutchinson, T. and A. Waters. 1980b. Communication in the technical classroom: you just shove this little chappie in here like that. In *Projects in Materials Design*. ELT Documents Special. London: ETIC Publications, The British Council.

Hutchinson, T. and A. Waters. 1981. Performance and competence in ESP. *Applied Linguistics*, 2: 56–69.

Hutchinson, T. and A. Waters. 1984. *Interface*. London: Longman.

Hutchinson, T and A. Waters. 1987. *English for Specific Purposes*. Cambridge: Cambridge University Press.

Jansen, E. 1995. Joint Evaluation of short EFL courses between course-provider and client as a means to improve course quality. In P. Rea-Dickins and A. F. Lwaitama. *Evaluation for Development in English Language Teaching*. Review of English Language Teaching, Vol. 3 No. 3. London: Modern English Publications in association with The British Council.

References

Johns, A. 1990. L1 composition theories: implications for developing theories of L2 composition. In B. Kroll (Ed.) *Second Language Writing: Research Insights for the Classroom*. Cambridge: Cambridge University Press.

Johns, A. and A. Dudley-Evans. 1993. English for specific purposes: international in scope, specific in purpose. *TESOL Quarterly*, 25: 297–314.

Johns, T. F. 1981. Some problems of a world-wide profession. In J. McDonough and T. French (Eds.) *The ESP Teacher: Role, Development and Prospects. ELT Documents* 112.

Johns, T. F. 1989. Whence and whither classroom concordancing? In T. Bongaerts, P. de Haan, S. Lobbe and H. Wekker (Eds.) *Computer Applications in Language Learning*. Dordrecht, The Netherlands: Foris.

Johns, T. F. 1991. From printout to handout: grammar and vocabulary teaching in the context of data-driven learning. In T. F. Johns and P. King (Eds.). *Classroom Concordancing*. University of Birmingham: *English Language Research Journal*, 4.

Johns, T. F. and F. Davies. 1983. Text as a vehicle for information: the classroom use of written texts in teaching reading in a foreign language. *Reading in a Foreign Language*, 1: 1–19.

Johns, T. F. and A. Dudley-Evans. 1980. An experiment in team-teaching of overseas postgraduate students of transportation and plant biology. In *Team Teaching in ESP. ELT Documents* 106.

Jones, C. 1991. An integrated model for ESP syllabus design. *English for Specific Purposes*, 10: 155–72.

Jordan, M. P. 1984. *Rhetoric of Everyday English Texts*. London: Allen & Unwin.

Jordan, R. R. 1990. *Academic Writing*. Glasgow: Collins.

Jordan, R. R. 1997. *English for Academic Purposes: A Guide and Resource Book for Teachers*. Cambridge: Cambridge University Press.

Jordan, R. R. and R. Mackay. 1973. A survey of the spoken English problems of overseas postgraduates at the universities of Manchester and Newcastle. *Journal of the Institute of Education*. Newcastle University.

Kennedy, G., J. Benson and J. McMillan. 1987. *Managing Negotiations*. Hemel Hempstead: Prentice Hall Macmillan.

Kenny, B. and W. Savage. 1997. *Language and Development: Teachers in a Changing World*. London: Longman.

Khoo, R. 1994. Empowering the EBT practitioner: a project perspective. In R. Khoo (Ed.) *The Practice of LSP: Perspectives, Programmes and Projects. Anthology Series* 34. Singapore: SEAMEO Regional Language Centre.

Kinsella, K. 1995. Understanding and empowering diverse learners in the ESL classroom. In J. Reid (Ed.) *Learning Styles in the ESL/EFL Classroom* Boston: Heinle & Heinle.

Krashen, S. 1981. *Second Language Acquisition and Learning*. Oxford: Pergamon.

Kroll, B. 1990. *Second Language Writing*. Cambridge: Cambridge University Press.

Lackstrom, J. E., L. Selinker and L. Trimble. 1973. Technical rhetorical principles and grammatical choice. *TESOL Quarterly*, 7: 127–36.

Latour, B. and S. Woolgar. 1979. *Laboratory Life: the Social Construction of Scientific Facts*. Beverley Hills, CA: Sage.

Lewis, M. 1993. *The Lexical Approach*. Hove: LTP Publications.

Limaye, M. R. and D. A. Victor. 1991. Cross-cultural business communication research: state of the art and hypotheses for the 1990s. *Journal of Business Communication*, 28: 277–299.

Linde, C. 1991. What's next: the social and technological management of meetings. *Pragmatics*, 1: 297–317.

Love, A. 1991. Process and product in geology: an investigation of some discourse features of two introductory textbooks. *English for Specific Purposes*, 10: 89–109.

Love, A. 1993. Lexico-grammatical features of geology textbooks: process and product revisited. *English for Specific Purposes*, 12: 197–218.

Lynch, A. 1983. *Study Listening*. Cambridge: Cambridge University Press.

Lynch, A. 1988. Peer evaluation in practice. In A. Brookes and P. Grundy (Eds.) *Individualization and Autonomy in Language Learning. ELT Documents* 131. London: Modern English Publications in association with The British Council.

Lynch, B. and F. Davidson. 1994. Criterion-referenced language test development: linking curricula, teacher and tests. *TESOL Quarterly*, 28: 727–44.

Lyne, A. A. 1983. Word frequency counts: their particular reference to the description of languages for special purposes and a technique for enhancing their usefulness. *Nottingham Linguistic Circular*, 12: 130–40.

Mackay, R. and A. Mountford. 1978. *English for Specific Purposes*. London: Longman.

McArthur, T. 1981. *Longman Lexicon of Contemporary English*. London: Longman.

McCarthy, M. 1991. *Discourse Analysis for Language Teachers*. Cambridge: Cambridge University Press.

McCloskey, D. 1994. *Knowledge and Persuasion in Economics*. Cambridge: Cambridge University Press.

McDonough, J. and C. Shaw. 1993. *Materials and Methods in ELT*. Oxford: Blackwell.

McNamara, T. 1996. *Measuring Second Language Performance*. London: Longman.

Maher, J. 1986. English for medical purposes. *Language Teaching*, 19: 112–45.

Makina-Kaunda, L. 1995. Evaluation as a tool for course development: a case study of the language programme for engineering students at the Malawi Polytechnic. In P. Rea-Dickins and A. F. Lwaitama (Eds.) *Evaluation for*

Development in English Language Teaching. Developments in English Language Teaching. London: Modern English Teacher in association with The British Council.

Malcolm, L. 1987. What rules govern tense usage in scientific articles? *English for Specific Purposes*, 6: 31–44.

Markee, N. 1997. *Managing Curricular Innovation.* Cambridge: Cambridge University Press.

Martinez, M. S. 1994. Spanish-English cognates in the subtechnical vocabulary found in engineering magazine texts. *English for Specific Purposes*, 13: 81–92.

Mascull, B. (Ed.). 1993. Languacom materials for teaching by telephone and face to face. Ivry-sur-Seine, France: Telelangue/Languacom.

Mason, M. 1990. Dancing on air: analysis of a passage from an economics textbook. In A. Dudley-Evans and W. Henderson (Eds.) *The Language of Economics of Language: the Analysis of Economics Discourse. ELT Documents 134.* London: Modern English Teacher in association with The British Council.

Master, P. 1986. *Science, Technology and Medicine.* Englewoods Cliffs, NJ: Prentice Hall.

Master, P. 1991. Active verbs with inanimate subjects in scientific prose. *English for Specific Purposes*, 10: 15–34.

Mauranen, A. 1993. *Cultural Differences in Academic Rhetoric.* Frankfurt-am-Main: Peter Lang.

Mead, R. 1990. *Cross-Cultural Management Communication.* London: John Wiley & Sons.

Mehrabian, A. 1971. *Silent Messages.* London: Wadsworth.

Micheau, C. and K. Billmyer. 1987. Discourse strategies for foreign business students: preliminary research findings. *English for Specific Purposes*, 6: 87–98.

Miller, C. 1994. Genre as social action. In A. Freedman and P. Medway (Eds.) *Genre and the New Rhetoric.* London: Taylor & Francis.

Monsi, G., A. Mango, E. Mwangola and B. Murila. 1995. Kenyan universities communication skills project evaluation: process and product. In P. Rea-Dickins and A. F. Lwaitama (Eds.) *Evaluation for Development in English Language Teaching. Developments in English Language Teaching.* London: Modern English Teacher in association with The British Council.

Moore, C. 1996. Multimedia for self-access – do we really need multimedia for self-access? *BESIG Newsletter*, 1.

Mparutsa, C., A. Love and A. Morrison. 1991. Bringing concord to the ESP classroom. In T. F. Johns and P. K. King (Eds.) *Classroom Concordancing. English Language Research Journal 4.* The University of Birmingham.

Munby, J. 1978. *Communicative Syllabus Design.* Cambridge: Cambridge University Press.

Mustafa, Z. 1995. The effect of genre awareness on linguistic transfer. *English for Specific Purposes*, 14: 247–256.

Myers, G. 1989. *Writing Biology: Texts in the Construction of Scientific Knowledge*. Madison, Wisc: University of Wisconsin Press.

Nation, P. 1990. *Teaching and Learning Vocabulary*. New York: Newbury House.

Nattinger, J. 1988. Some current trends in vocabulary teaching. In R. Carter and M. McCarthy (Eds.) *Vocabulary and Language Teaching*. London: Longman.

Nattinger, J. and J. R. DeCarrico. 1992. *Lexical Phrases and Language Teaching*. Oxford: Oxford University Press.

Nelson, M. 1994. *The Complete Business English Course Generator*. London: Media-Time Ltd.

Nelson, M. 1995. Intuition and Business English Course Design. *BESIG Newsletter*, 3, p. 8.

Nesi, H. 1996. Self-access: the students you may never meet. *CALL Review*, March: 14–15.

Nickerson, C. 1998. Corporate culture and the use of written English. *English for Specific Purposes* 17.

Nolan, S. and W. Reed. 1992. *Business English. English Teachers' Resource Book*. London: Longman.

Nunan, D. 1988. *The Learner-Centred Curriculum*. Cambridge: Cambridge University Press.

Nunan, D. 1989. *Designing Tasks for the Communicative Classroom*. Cambridge: Cambridge University Press.

Nunan, D. 1991. *Language Teaching Methodology*. Hemel Hempstead: Prentice Hall International.

Nunes, M. B. C. 1992. Action research and reading difficulty. *English for Specific Purposes*, 11: 177–86.

Nuttall, C. 1982. *Teaching Reading Skills*. Cambridge: Cambridge University Press.

Obah, T. 1993. Teaching an examination strategy to technology-oriented university students in Nigeria: The (PWR) Plan. In G. Blue (Ed.) *Language, Learning and Success: Studying through English. Developments in English Language Teaching*. London: Modern English Publications in association with The British Council.

O'Brien, T. 1992. Writing for continuous assessment and in examination conditions: a comparison of undergraduate performance. Unpublished PhD thesis, University of Manchester.

Oxford, R. and N. Anderson. 1995. A cross-cultural view of learning styles. *Language Teaching*, 28: 201–15.

Pennycook, A. 1994. *The Cultural Politics of English as an International Language*. London: Longman.

Peters, A. M. 1983. *The Units of Language Acquisition*. Cambridge: Cambridge University Press.

Pettinari, C. 1982. The function of a governmental alternative in fourteen surgical reports. *Applied Linguistics*, 4: 55–76.

Pettinari, C. 1985. A comparison of the production of surgical reports by native and non-native speaking surgeons. In J. D. Benson and W. S. Greaves (Eds.) *Systemic Perspectives on Discourse*, vol. 2. Norwood, NJ: Ablex.

Phillips, M. K. and C. Shettlesworth. 1978. How to arm your students: a consideration of two approaches to providing materials for ESP. In *English for Specific Purposes. ELT Documents* 101. London: ETIC Publications, The British Council, pp. 23–35. Reprinted in J. M. Swales (Ed.) *Episodes in ESP*.

Pickett, D. 1986. *Business English: Falling between two stools*. Comlon 26: 16–21.

Pilbeam, A. 1979. The language audit. *Language Training*, 1:2.

Pilbeam, A. 1992. In this issue: beyond language training. *Language and Intercultural Training*, 13:3.

Projects in Materials Design. ELT Documents Special. London: ETIC Publications, The British Council.

Raimes, A. 1993. Out of the woods: emerging traditions in the teaching of writing. In S. Silberstein (Ed.) *State of the Art. TESOL Essays*. Alexandria, Virginia: TESOL Inc.

Reading and Thinking in English. 1979, 1980. Oxford: Oxford University Press.

Rea-Dickins, P. and A. F. Lwaitama. 1995. *Evaluation for Development in English Language Teaching. Review of English Language Teaching* Vol. 3 No. 3. London: Modern English Teacher in association with The British Council.

Read, H. H. and J. Watson. 1968. *Introduction to Geology*, vol. 1: *Principles* (2nd ed.) London: Macmillan.

Reeves, N. and C. Wright. 1996. *Linguistic Auditing*. Clevedon, Avon: Multilingual Matters.

Reid, J. 1995. *Learning Styles in the ESL/EFL Classroom*. Boston: Heinle & Heinle.

Richards, J. C. 1983. Listening comprehension: approach, design, procedure. *TESOL Quarterly*, 17: 219–39.

Richterich, L. and J. L. Chancerel. 1980. *Identifying the Needs of Adults Learning a Foreign Language*. Oxford: Pergamon.

Robinson, P. 1988. *Academic Writing. Process and Product. ELT Documents* 129. London: Modern English Publications in association with The British Council.

Robinson, P. 1991. *ESP Today: a Practitioner's Guide*. Hemel Hempstead: Prentice Hall International.

Rowley-Jolivet, E. 1998. *La communication scientifique orale: étude des caracteristiques linguistiques et discursives d'un genre*. Unpublished PhD Thesis. University of Bordeaux.

St John, M. J. 1987. Writing processes of Spanish scientists publishing in English. *English for Specific Purposes* 6: 113–20.

St John, M. J. 1988. Attitudinal changes to self-access in EAP. In A. Brookes and P. Grundy (Eds.) *Individualization and Autonomy in Language Learning. ELT Documents* 131. London: Modern English Publications in association with The British Council.

St John, M. J. 1989. An interview with Maggie Jo St John. *Past Present Future: an ELT Newsletter*. Rio de Janeiro, The British Council, 3: 3–4.

St John, M. J. 1992. Some criteria for text selection. *The ESPecialist*, 13: 103–116.

St John, M. J. 1995. Evaluation as an interactive component: a case study of a Nigerian communication skills project. In P. Rea-Dickins and A. F. Lwaitama (Eds.) *Evaluation for Development in English Language Teaching*. Review of ELT Vol. 3 No. 3. London: Modern English Publications in association with The British Council.

St John, M. J. 1996. Business is booming: Business English in the 90s. In M. J. St John and C. Johnson (Eds.) Special Issue on Business English. *English for Specific Purposes*, 15: 3–18.

St John, M. J. and C. Johnson. 1996. Special Issue on Business English. *English for Specific Purposes*, 15:1.

Salager-Meyer, F. 1994. Hedges and textual communicative function in Medical English written discourse. *English for Specific Purposes*, 13: 149–170.

Schein, E. 1985. *Organisational Culture and Leadership*. San Francisco: Jossey-Bass.

Scollon, R. and S. W. Scollon. 1995. *Intercultural Communication*. Oxford: Basil Blackwell.

Scott, M. 1981a. Teaching and unteaching coping strategies. *Working Papers of Brazilian ESP Project*, no. 1. São Paulo: Catholic University of São Paulo.

Scott, M. 1981b. Reading comprehension in English for Academic Purposes. *The ESPecialist*, 3.

Scott, M. 1996. *Wordsmith*. Oxford: Oxford University Press, available on the Internet (address p. 209).

Scott, M. and T. F. Johns. 1993. *MicroConcord*. Oxford: Oxford University Press.

Selinker, L. 1979. On the use of informants in discourse analysis and language for specialized purposes. *IRAL*, 17: 189–215.

Shalom, C. 1993. Established and evolving spoken research process genres: plenary lecture and poster session discussions at academic conferences. *English for Specific Purposes*, 12: 37–50.

Sheldon, L. 1987. *ELT Textbooks and Materials: Problems in Evaluation and Development. ELT Documents* 126. London: Modern English Publications in association with The British Council.

References

Shih, M. 1986. Content-based approaches to teaching academic writing. *TESOL Quarterly*, 20: 617–48.

Sims, B. R. and S. Guice. 1992. Differences between business letters from native and non-native speakers of English. *The Journal of Business Communication*, 29: 23–39.

Sinclair, J. 1991. *Corpus, concordance and collocation*. Oxford: Oxford University Press.

Sinclair, J. and M. Coulthard 1975. *Towards an Analysis of Discourse: the English Used by Teachers and Pupils*. Oxford: Oxford University Press.

Skelton, J. 1994. Analysis of the structure of original research papers: an aid to writing original papers for publication. *British Journal of General Practice*, 1994: 455–59.

Skills for Learning. 1980, 1981. Walton-on-Thames: Nelson and University of Malaya Press.

Smart, G. 1992. Exploring the social dimension of a workplace genre and the implications for teaching. *Carlton Papers in Applied Language Studies*, 9: 33–46.

Smart, G. 1993. Genre as community invention: a central bank's response to the executive's expectations as readers. In R. Spilka (Ed.) *Writing in the Workplace: New Research Perspectives*. Carbondale, Il: South Illinois University Press.

Snow, M. A. and D. Brinton. 1988. Content-based language instruction: investigating the effectiveness of the adjunct model. *TESOL Quarterly*, 22: 553–74.

Spack, R. 1988. Initiating ESL students into the academic discourse community: how far should we go? *TESOL Quarterly*, 18: 29–52.

Starfield, S. 1994. Cummins, EAP and academic literacy. *TESOL Quarterly*, 28: 176–179.

Stevens, V. 1991. Classroom concordancing: vocabulary materials derived from relevant, authentic text. *English for Specific Purposes*, 10: 35–46.

Strevens, P. 1971. Alternatives to daffodils. In *Science and Technology in a Second Language*. C.I.L.T. Report 7. London: Centre for Information on Language Teaching and Research, pp. 7–11.

Strevens, P. 1988. ESP after twenty years: a re-appraisal. In M. Tickoo (Ed.) *ESP: State of the Art*. Singapore: SEAMEO Regional Language Centre.

Stubbs, M. and A. Gerbig. 1993. Human in inhuman geography: on the computer-assisted analysis of long texts. In M. Hoey (Ed.). *Data, Description, Discourse*. London: Harper Collins.

Swales, J. M. 1980. The educational environment and its relevance to ESP programme design. In *Projects in Materials Design. ELT Documents Special*. London: ETIC Publications, The British Council.

Swales, J. M. 1981. *Aspects of Article Introductions. ESP Monograph* no. 1. Language Studies Unit, Aston University.

Swales, J. M. 1983. Vocabulary work in LSP – a case of neglect. Mimeo, Language Studies Unit, Aston University.

Swales, J. M. 1984. Thoughts on, in and outside the ESP Classroom. In G. James (Ed.) *The ESP Classroom*. Exeter Linguistic Studies 7. Exeter: University of Exeter.

Swales, J. M. 1985. ESP – The heart of the matter or the end of the affair? In R. Quirk and H. Widdowson (Eds.) *English in the World: Teaching and Learning the Language and the Literatures*. Cambridge: Cambridge University Press in association with The British Council.

Swales, J. M. 1988. *Episodes in ESP*. Hemel Hempstead: Prentice Hall International.

Swales, J. M. 1989. Service English course design and opportunity cost. In R. K. Johnson (Ed.) *The Second Language Curriculum*. Cambridge: Cambridge University Press.

Swales, J. M. 1990. *Genre Analysis: English in Academic and Research Settings*. Cambridge: Cambridge University Press.

Swales, J. M. 1994. From the editors: from John M. Swales. *English for Specific Purposes*, 13: 200–03.

Swales, J. M. and V. K. Bhatia. 1982. Special issues on Legal English. *English for Specific Purposes Newsletters*, 67 & 68: 1–12.

Swales, J. M. and C. Feak. 1994. *Academic Writing for Graduate Students*. Ann Arbor: University of Michigan Press.

Tadros, A. 1985. *Prediction in Text*. Birmingham: English Language Research, University of Birmingham.

Tarone, E., S. Dwyer, S. Gillette and V. Icke. 1981. On the use of the passive in two astrophysics journal papers. *English for Specific Purposes*, 1: 123–40. Updated for publication in *English for Specific Purposes*, 17: 1, 1998.: 113–32.

Thompson, D. 1993. Arguing for experimental facts in science: a study of research article results sections in biochemistry. *Written Communication*, 8: 106–28.

Thurstun, J. and C. N. Candlin. 1998. Concordancing and the teaching of the vocabulary of Academic English. *English for Specific Purposes*.

Tickoo, M. 1988. *ESP: State of the Art. RLC Anthology Series 21*. Singapore: SEAMEO Regional Language Centre.

Trimble, L. 1985. *English for Science and Technology: A Discourse Approach*. Cambridge: Cambridge University Press.

Trompenaar, 1993. *Riding the Waves of Culture: Understanding Cultural Diversity in Business*. London: Nicholas Brealey Publishing.

Tull, D. S. and D. I. Hawkins. 1976. *Marketing Research: Meaning, Measurement and Method*. London: Macmillan.

Turner, J. 1996. Between the discourse of language and the language of discourses: the contested space of EAP. Paper given at the Knowledge and Discourse Conference, Hong Kong, 1996.

References

Vance, S. 1981. *General Science Test Books. Parts 1 and 2.* London: Longman.

Ventola, E. and A. Mauranen. 1991. Non-native writing and native revising of scientific articles. In E. Ventola (Ed.) *Recent Systemic and Other Functional Views on Language.* Berlin: Mouton de Gruyter, pp. 457–492.

Waistell, M. 1993. *Executive Listening.* London: Longman.

Warren, T. 1997. The CALLCO grammar project. Paper given at the 13th BALEAP Conference, University of Wales, Swansea, April 1997.

Weir, C. J. 1983. The Associated Examining Board's Test in English for Academic Purposes. In A. Hughes and D. Porter (Eds.) *Current Developments in Language Testing.* London: Academic Press.

Weir, C. 1990. *Communicative Language Testing.* Hemel Hempstead: Prentice Hall International.

Weir, C. 1993. *Understanding and Developing Language Tests.* Hemel Hempstead: Prentice Hall International.

Weissberg, R. and S. Buker. 1990. *Writing Up Research: Experimental Report Writing for Students of English.* Englewoods Cliffs, NJ: Prentice Hall.

West, M. P. 1953. *A General Service List of English Words.* London: Longman.

West, R. 1994. Needs analysis in teaching. *Language Teaching,* 27: 1–19.

Widdowson, H. 1978. *Teaching Language as Communication.* Oxford: Oxford University Press.

Widdowson, H. 1983. *Learning Purpose and Language Use.* Oxford: Oxford University Press.

Wilberg, P. 1987. *One to One: A Teachers' Handbook.* Hove: Language Teaching Publications.

Wilberg, P. and M. Lewis. 1990. *Business English: an Individualised Learning Programme.* Hove: Language Teaching Publications.

Wilkins, D. A. 1976. *Notional Syllabuses: A Taxonomy and its Relevance to Foreign Language Curriculum Development.* Oxford: Oxford University Press.

Williams, R. 1978. EST – Is it on the right track? In C. J. Kennedy (Ed.) *English for Specific Purposes. Special Issue MALS (Midlands Applied Linguistics Association Journal).* Birmingham: The University of Birmingham, pp. 25–31.

Williams, R. 1982. *Panorama.* London: Longman.

Williams, R., J. M. Swales and J. Kirkman. 1984. *Common Ground: Shared Interests in ESP and Communication Studies.* Oxford: Pergamon Press in association with The British Council.

Willis, J. 1996. *A Framework for Task-Based Learning.* London: Longman.

Wingard, P. 1981. Some verb forms and functions in six medical texts. In L. Selinker, E. Tarone and V. Hanzeli (Eds.) *English for Academic and Technical Purposes: Studies in Honour of Louis Trimble.* Rowley, Mass: Newbury House.

Winter, E. 1982. *Towards a Contextual Grammar of English.* London: Allen & Unwin.

Winter, E. 1986. Clause relations as information structure: two basic text structures in English. In M. Coulthard (Ed.) *Talking About Text.* Discourse Analysis Monographs no. 13. Birmingham: English Language Research, The University of Birmingham.

Xue G. Y. and I. S. P. Nation. 1984. A university word list. *Language Learning and Communication,* 3: 215–29.

Yang, H. 1986. A new technique for identifying scientific/technical terms and describing science texts (an interim report). *Literary and Linguistic Computing,* 1: 93–103.

Yin, K. M. and I. Wong. 1990. A course in business communication for accountants. *English for Specific Purposes,* 9: 253–64.

Yli-Jokipii, H. 1994. *Requests in Professional Discourse: a Cross-Cultural Study of British, American and Finnish Business Writing.* Helsinki: Suomalainen Tiedeakatemia.

Zamel, V. 1983. The composing processes of advanced ESL students: six case studies. *TESOL Quarterly,* 17: 165–87.

Index

Index